Integrating Music Across
the Elementary Curriculum

Integrating Music Across the Elementary Curriculum

Kristin Harney

OXFORD

UNIVERSITY PRESS

OXFORD
UNIVERSITY PRESS

Oxford University Press is a department of the University of Oxford. It furthers
the University's objective of excellence in research, scholarship, and education
by publishing worldwide. Oxford is a registered trade mark of Oxford University
Press in the UK and certain other countries.

Published in the United States of America by Oxford University Press
198 Madison Avenue, New York, NY 10016, United States of America.

Library of Congress Cataloging-in-Publication Data
Names: Harney, Kristin, author.
Title: Integrating music across the elementary curriculum / Kristin Harney
Description: New York : Oxford University Press, 2020. |
Includes bibliographical references and index.
Identifiers: LCCN 2020007999 (print) | LCCN 2020008000 (ebook) |
ISBN 9780190085582 (hardback) | ISBN 9780190085599 (paperback) |
ISBN 9780190085612 (epub)
Subjects: LCSH: School music—Instruction and study—Activity programs. |
School music—Instruction and study—Outlines, syllabi, etc. |
Music—Instruction and study—Activity programs. |
Music—Instruction and study—Outlines, syllabi, etc. |
Education, Elementary—Activity programs. |
Interdisciplinary approach in education.
Classification: LCC MT10 .H294 2020 (print) | LCC MT10 (ebook) |
DDC 372.87/044—dc23
LC record available at https://lccn.loc.gov/2020007999
LC ebook record available at https://lccn.loc.gov/2020008000

To Jon, Minnie, and Frank, with thanks for their love and support.

Contents

Figures

Acknowledgments

I wish to thank all the people who supported me and made the creation of this book possible. I am especially grateful to the thousands of elementary, undergraduate, and graduate students I have had the privilege to teach over the past 27 years. Special thanks go to the late Dr. Claire W. McCoy, who inspired my journey into the interdisciplinary approach. Thank you to the practicing elementary teachers who reviewed and/or field-tested the lessons and strategies included in this text: Rachel Screnar, kindergarten; Josie Breault, second grade; Laura Hovland, second grade; Dawn Perry, second grade; John Nielson, third grade; Tina Martin, fourth grade; Kristin Sigler, fourth grade; Kristi Crawford, fifth grade; Patti Ritter, fifth grade; Sallie Arnold, K–5 music; Sara Croghan, K–5 music; Jessica Graf, K–5 music; Erin Small, K–5 music; and Joy Strizich, K–5 music. Thanks to experts in their disciplines for their insightful reviews of the manuscript: Liana Bauman, visual art; Bonnie Eichenberger, mathematics, Dr. Nicholas Lux, science; Dr. Allison Wynhoff Olsen, English language arts; and Dr. Christine Rogers Stanton, social studies. Thanks to my mom, Linda Zolnosky, who read every word of every draft. I would also like to express my gratitude to Jennifer Versaevel for her photography, Meta Newhouse and Liana Bauman for help with images, student Brianna Green for her artwork, and for all those who granted permission to reprint copyrighted and other material.

Introduction

This book is designed to support K–5 educators as they integrate music throughout the elementary curriculum. It contains detailed, practical ideas and examples, including full lesson plans and over a hundred teaching ideas and strategies for integrating music with visual arts, language arts, social studies, science, and mathematics. All the lessons in this book are designed to be fully taught by classroom teachers; the content is accessible to those who lack formal music training, yet is solidly rooted in research and best practices. While classroom teachers can teach these lessons on their own, this book may facilitate partnerships and collaboration between classroom teachers and music specialists, especially in instances when classroom teachers may not feel confident about their music skills or abilities. In any case, music integration ultimately benefits students by encouraging them to connect new understandings in powerful and authentic ways.

All the lessons and activities included in Chapters 2 through 6 have been reviewed by practicing teachers, and most have been field-tested in elementary classrooms. Suggestions from practicing teachers, such as the inclusion of templates and worksheets for students to record their musical perceptions, have been incorporated throughout.

Throughout the book, there is an emphasis on interdisciplinary lessons that demonstrate valid connections between disciplines while maintaining the integrity of each discipline involved. Chapter 1 provides an overview of the interdisciplinary approach and a teacher-tested model that allows teachers to successfully create their own interdisciplinary lessons. Chapters 2 through 6 explore connections between music and other areas of the elementary curriculum: visual arts, language arts, social studies, science, and mathematics. Each chapter begins with a section describing common links between music and the designated discipline for the chapter. Each chapter also includes a section addressing national standards with tables showing the specific standards that are included in each lesson and activity. This text utilizes the most recent National Core Arts Standards (2015) as well as the most recent standards in mathematics, science, social studies, and language arts. The chapters incorporate four, five, or six detailed, full-length lesson plans. Consistent with best practices for lesson plan design, each lesson includes an essential question. Each set of lesson plans is followed by an inventory of ideas cataloguing additional lesson topics, specific teaching strategies, and recommended activities.

The lessons in this book have been labeled as primary, intermediate, or upper elementary, rather than with specific grade levels. There are two reasons for this decision. First, all the lessons and activities are adaptable to a variety of ability levels.

Integrating Music Across the Elementary Curriculum. Kristin Harney, Oxford University Press (2020). © Oxford University Press.
DOI: 10.1093/oso/9780190085582.001.0001.

Second, teachers won't be able to discount a lesson simply because it is labeled with a different grade level than the one they teach.

You know your students best. All the lessons and ideas in this book are intended as tools for you to meet your students' needs. Some of the lessons may need to be spread over two or more class periods. Please adjust, adapt, or expand however works best for you and for your students. My hope is that you and your students will be creative, think critically, and have fun.

1

Overview of Music Integration in the Elementary Curriculum

We need every possible way to reveal and respond to our world for one simple but powerful reason: No one way can capture it all.

—Fowler (1992, p. 7)

Introduction

There are growing calls to foster self-expression, critical thinking, collaboration, and creativity in school settings, and music integration is a path for developing these skills. The task for teachers who employ the interdisciplinary approach is to make meaningful connections between disciplines without compromising the integrity of either discipline. Music and other disciplines can be equal partners in interdisciplinary lessons, with each subject enhancing the other.

In 2011, the President's Committee on the Arts and Humanities (PCAH) described American high school graduates as the "products of narrowed curricula, lacking the creative and critical thinking skills needed for success in post-secondary education and the workforce" (PCAH, 2011, p. 7). This statement alludes to the increasingly complex challenges of our time and reflects growing concerns about American students' readiness to meet them. A national education advocacy organization, Partnership for 21st Century Skills (P21), has identified four primary areas of focus to guide schools in addressing these concerns. They recommend an emphasis on critical thinking, communication, collaboration, and creativity, and acknowledge that "the arts are among society's most compelling and effective paths for developing 21st Century Skills" (P21, 2011, p. 5). More specifically, I believe that integrating *music* across the elementary curriculum is a powerful means for nurturing these essential skills, meeting the current and future needs of our society and our students. Additionally, teachers who integrate music across the elementary curriculum provide students with opportunities to explore concepts from multiple perspectives, foster active engagement with content, and encourage the understanding of music as connected with all of life.

Integrating Music Across the Elementary Curriculum. Kristin Harney, Oxford University Press (2020). © Oxford University Press.
DOI: 10.1093/oso/9780190085582.001.0001.

Defining music integration

Depending on the context, the term "interdisciplinary education" may or may not refer to cross-curricular projects, multiple intelligences, cooperative learning, co-operative teaching, theme-based teaching units, combined curriculum, creative curriculum, or curriculum integration. For consistency of language and common understanding, a discussion of definitions (see Box 1.1) follows.

Box 1.1   Definitions

- Discipline: A curricular area with a specific body of teachable knowledge
- Interdisciplinary: A curriculum approach that consciously applies methodology and language from more than one discipline to examine a central theme, issue, problem, topic, or experience

Jacobs, H. H. (1989). The growing need for interdisciplinary curriculum content. In H. H. Jacobs (Ed.), *Interdisciplinary Curriculum: Design and Implementation*. Alexandria, VA: Association for Supervision and Curriculum Development.

Common synonyms for the term "discipline" are "subject," "field," and "branch of learning." To be more exact, a discipline is a curricular area with "a specific body of teachable knowledge" (Jacobs, 1989, Definitions section, para. 1). This definition assumes a school setting; a particular set of skills, elements, and concepts; and a methodology for teaching that knowledge. If one discipline is a single area of the curriculum, a working definition for the term "interdisciplinary" might be something like "combining disciplines" or "between disciplines." A more precise definition of interdisciplinary is a "curriculum approach that consciously applies methodology and language from more than one discipline to examine a central theme, issue, problem, topic, or experience" (Jacobs, 1989, Definitions section, para. 4). This definition clarifies that interdisciplinary lessons don't occur by chance; instead, teachers make intentional choices to structure lessons that utilize particular skills, elements, or concepts from at least two disciplines. Additionally, this definition highlights the need for a common theme, purpose, or objective that is addressed from the perspective of multiple disciplines. These shared associations might be concept connections (enduring ideas), topics (themes or focuses), or processes (any of the active modes by which students learn, such as reading, writing, moving, etc.). The term "music integration" refers to a specific subcategory of arts integration and can be defined in several ways. It is loosely defined as teaching through and with music, creating relationships between music and other curricular subjects (Burnaford, 2007). This perspective refers to the expanded definition of arts integration developed by ArtsEdge, a teaching and learning resource created by the Kennedy Center. From this standpoint, music integration is an approach to teaching that, rather than being an isolated activity, is embedded into daily practice (Kennedy Center ArtsEdge, n.d.). Because the terms "integration" and "interdisciplinary" both occur regularly in related research and literature, I have used them interchangeably throughout this book.

Rationales for music integration and overcoming potential problems

There are numerous justifications for incorporating music in K–5 classrooms. Some of the primary rationales highlight music as a way to promote communication, emotional expression, a sense of community, physical responses, divergent thinking, self-discipline, and self-confidence. Music grabs students' emotions in ways that words and numbers do not, and music integration can increase students' interest and engagement in learning. Music supplies insight and meaning to other subjects, giving understandings a human dimension and helping students experience curricular content in a more personal way.

Unfortunately, music is often trivialized or used as an add-on in music integration lessons. Even in situations where teachers support the interdisciplinary approach, the lessons they teach may use music superficially. Ideally, in integrated learning, students will experience music as an essential aspect of the human experience, not as an inconsequential accessory. It is disappointing when music is integrated with another subject and the outcomes focus almost exclusively on the other discipline.

To address this issue, it is important to realize that music integration is not a substitute for a strong, sequential music education, taught by a certified specialist, as there are aspects of music education that can only be effectively taught in the context of music classes. Students must develop skills in music before they can apply musical skills to other learning situations; a strong background in music is necessary for students to connect new understandings in authentic ways.

While I firmly believe that the quality of teaching and learning within the discipline of music must not be overlooked, I also recognize that elementary classroom teachers have an immense potential influence on their students because of the amount of time they spend together. Ideally, elementary teachers utilize this influence to promote and meaningfully integrate music with other areas of the curriculum. The creation and sharing of high-quality interdisciplinary lessons is an achievable goal.

Lack of time is another potential problem related to music integration. The planning time for creating interdisciplinary lessons is almost always more than the time required to plan lessons in isolation; however, teachers generally agree that the benefits to students are well worth any extra time spent. The lesson plans, ideas, and strategies in this book will facilitate teachers' planning and implementation of lessons that integrate music across the elementary curriculum.

Some K–5 classroom teachers may feel intimidated by musical content or believe they do not have the necessary skills to adequately teach music. I often hear my undergraduate elementary education majors say things like "in my practicum observations, classroom teachers never integrate music" and "I'm a terrible musician; I could never do music with kids." It is possible, and perhaps likely, that these future teachers might self-select out of music activities and experiences, both for themselves and for their future students. One solution is for classroom teachers and music teachers to collaborate. While this approach may require extra time for cooperation and planning, "collaborative projects often evolve with a degree of richness that individual efforts cannot achieve" (McCoy, 2000, p. 39). When I taught elementary general music and collaborated with classroom teachers, it not only benefited the students but also was enjoyable and empowering for us as teachers. We became aware of connections between our content areas, drew on our own unique strengths and skills, and created lessons that would not have been possible had we taught them alone.

Musical activities will likely look different depending on whether they occur in K–5 classrooms or in elementary general music rooms; however, regardless of the situation, those activities should promote and empower students' musicianship. Music integration is not appropriate in every situation, but in lessons that involve music, students need to actively engage in music making and develop musical skills. The lessons, ideas, and strategies found in this book emphasize active participation. I want students to experience the fun, excitement, and hands-on nature of various musical activities as they employ the elements of music (melody, rhythm, form, harmony, and context) and participate in a variety of ways (singing, playing, creating, reading, writing, listening, moving, analyzing, and evaluating).

Review of the National Core Arts Standards

The National Core Arts Standards (NCAS) were released on June 4, 2014, and rolled out to the profession in October 2014. As the name suggests, these are more than just music standards—they are arts standards; music shares common process standards with dance, media arts, theatre, and visual arts. The four common arts processes are creating, performing, responding, and connecting. The musical behaviors in which students engage align with the standards and include singing, moving, playing nonpitched percussion instruments, composing, listening, and analyzing. Like many documents designed to guide curriculum, instruction, and assessment in a variety of contexts, the NCAS are a framework, not a one-size-fits-all mold. As teachers, we get to ask what our students need for a lifetime of authentic participation in music. The standards are a means to help us answer that question. The standards documents are available through the National Coalition for Core Arts Standards (NCCAS) and the National Association for Music Education (NAfME).

The national standards in many disciplines, including the NCAS, highlight the importance of interdisciplinarity, reminding us that "although educational institutions segment knowledge into separate packages called 'subjects,' deep understanding often depends upon the intersections and interactions of the disciplines" (Barrett, 2001, p. 27). Some classroom teachers might be surprised by the quantity of information included in the NCAS; unsure about how to cite them; doubtful of their abilities to meet, let alone address, the standards; and apprehensive about even undertaking the task. Feeling overwhelmed does not have to be the typical response to the standards, though. The standards are a tool, and teachers are invited to make the standards work for them, not the other way around. A simplified, intuitive way of expressing the anchor standards that serves as a springboard to the rest of the standards follows.

There are three anchor standards that relate to creating music. In student-friendly language, they can be summarized as (1) generate musical ideas, (2) organize and write them down, and (3) finish your musical work. There are three anchor standards that relate to the performance of music. They can be expressed as (4) learn about a piece, (5) practice it, and (6) perform it. The process of responding also has three anchor standards. Their simplified descriptions are (7) analyze music, (8) interpret meaning, and (9) evaluate music. Finally, two anchor standards relate to connecting. They can be portrayed as (10) connect music to self and (11) connect music to everything else. This streamlined language may enable teachers to more easily incorporate NCAS in their curriculum planning, ultimately benefiting students (Harney, 2015a).

The anchor standards are already indexed in a way that facilitates citing them. MU:Cr1 corresponds to Music, Creating, Anchor Standard 1; MU:Pr4 corresponds to Music, Performing, Anchor Standard 4; etc. Table 1.1 contains the simplified anchor standard language along with the full NCAS versions of the anchor standards.

Creating interdisciplinary lessons

The tools from this chapter can be used to analyze existing interdisciplinary lessons and to create your own. Two ideas to keep in mind when planning interdisciplinary lessons are (1) integrity for each discipline and (2) integrity between disciplines. These two ideas are drawn from the book *Sound Ways of Knowing: Music in the Interdisciplinary Curriculum*, by Janet Barrett, Claire McCoy, and Kari Veblen.

Integrity for each discipline

In an interdisciplinary lesson, when skills and understandings specific to each discipline are employed, each discipline maintains curricular integrity. One method for

Table 1.1 National Core Arts Standards (Copyright © 2015 National Coalition for Core Arts Standards / All Rights Reserved—Rights Administered by SEADAE); Simplified Arts Standards, used by permission, Montana Music Educators Association *Cadenza*.

	Creating	Performing	Responding	Connecting
Simplified anchor standard descriptions	1. Generate musical ideas 2. Organize and write them down 3. Finish your musical work	4. Learn about a piece 5. Practice it 6. Perform it	7. Analyze music 8. Interpret meaning 9. Evaluate music	10. Connect music to self 11. Connect music to everything else
NCAS anchor standards for citation	1. MU:Cr1: Generate and conceptualize artistic ideas and work 2. MU:Cr2: Organize and develop artistic ideas and work 3. MU:Cr3: Refine and complete artistic work	4. MU:Pr4: Select, analyze, and interpret artistic work for presentation 5. MU:Pr5: Develop and refine artistic techniques and work for presentation 6. MU:Pr6: Convey meaning through the presentation of artistic work	7. MU:Re7: Perceive and analyze artistic work 8. MU:Re8: Interpret intent and meaning in artistic work 9. MU:Re9: Apply criteria to evaluate artistic work	10. MU:Cn10: Synthesize and relate knowledge and personal experiences to make art 11. MU:Cn11: Relate artistic ideas and works with societal, cultural, and historical context to deepen understanding

ensuring that essential skills in each discipline are employed is to design lessons that address standards for each subject. Music experiences have integrity when students and teachers are engaged in the processes of creating, performing, responding, and connecting, addressing the NCAS. Other disciplines have integrity when the skills and understandings of those disciplines are used in valid ways and standards are met. When designing your own lessons that integrate music, ask yourself, "Does the lesson I'm designing allow students to apply basic skills in music and another discipline?" True integration respects the integrity and uniqueness of each of the disciplines being combined. Every lesson and idea in this book include standards for music and the respective connecting discipline.

Integrity between disciplines

In an interdisciplinary lesson, when the unique skills and understandings of each discipline are employed to examine a central idea, there is integrity between the disciplines. Integrity between disciplines is characterized by a sense of balance, complementary relationships, and mutual illumination. A rationale for integrating two or more content areas should describe a valid connection between them. Valid connections include concepts, topics, and processes that the disciplines have in common.

- Common concept: Common concepts are usually broad, overarching ideas. Establishing a common concept is the most straightforward way to ensure integrity between the disciplines. A list of potential connecting concepts between music and other disciplines is included at the beginning of Chapters 2, 3, 4, 5, and 6.
- Common topic: There are often school-wide or grade-level units focusing on a single topic that is relevant to the community or the time. The presence of a common topic does not always ensure a valid connection, though. For example, a unit focused on the Harlem Renaissance includes multiple valid intersections with music, while a school-wide fundraising project might not have such straightforward musical connections.
- Common process: Interdisciplinary lessons often highlight processes that music and other disciplines share. Process connections that are often reinforced in music integration include creating, reading, writing, listening, presenting, analyzing, and evaluating.

When designing your own lessons that integrate music, ask yourself, "Is there a logical reason to integrate music with another content area in the lesson I'm designing? Is there a valid connection between the disciplines and a common idea that students can explore from multiple perspectives?"

When classroom teachers integrate music in meaningful ways, students are led to connect knowledge and to recognize relationships between disciplines. Rather than keeping each content area separate, students discover connections and develop holistic understandings. It is my hope that the lessons and strategies in this book will enhance students' learning in powerful and authentic ways. I am extremely optimistic about the future of music integration in elementary classrooms.

2

Music and Visual Arts

Introduction

The arts are an essential aspect of human expression, and members of every culture and community create music and art to convey their unique perspectives. In 2015, for example, Olafur Eliasson, a Danish-Icelandic artist, created the second installation of *Ice Watch* to highlight the issue of global warming. He collected 12 blocks of melting ice that had sheared off the Greenland ice sheet, transported the giant pieces of ice to Paris, and installed them in a clock configuration at Place du Panthéon (see Figure 2.1). In 2016, Tubby Love wrote "Keep the Oil in the Ground," a song inspired by people of Sarayaku, Ecuador, who were striving to protect their land from big oil companies. These are two examples of artists using their respective mediums to promote awareness of climate change. Through the arts, students can know, experience, and express ideas that go beyond words and numbers. The arts enable students to encounter and communicate what otherwise cannot be expressed.

The arts teach divergent, flexible, creative thinking. Most of the time, problems in music and art have multiple solutions. When questions have more than one possible answer, students cannot only rely on strict rules, but must also engage in qualitative reasoning, make judgment calls, and defend their convictions. When multiple perspectives are celebrated, it naturally follows that there are a variety of acceptable and appropriate ways to interpret the world around us. In this digital age, we have access to virtually unlimited numbers of recordings and images. Analyzing and considering connections between music and art can facilitate students' development as knowledgeable lifelong consumers of the arts.

As important as it is to promote sensitive consumers who think creatively about the arts, it is also essential to provide opportunities that move students beyond merely appreciating the arts and allow them to become "doers" of the arts. Integrating music and art in elementary classrooms can promote active engagement with the skills and elements of both disciplines. Active and meaningful engagement in the arts includes activities such as playing instruments, singing, moving, improvising, composing, drawing, painting, sculpting, sketching, and designing. Opportunities for students to create diverse works of art, share their perspectives, and participate consistently over time are essential. Classrooms that embrace arts integration can be vibrant, inspirational, and transformational centers of learning. Through lessons that integrate music and visual arts, students can connect more deeply with the world around them, actively participate in multiple art forms, collaborate and forge social bonds, creatively solve complex problems, and foster personal identity.

Integrating Music Across the Elementary Curriculum. Kristin Harney, Oxford University Press (2020). © Oxford University Press.
DOI: 10.1093/oso/9780190085582.001.0001.

Figure 2.1 *Ice Watch* by Olafur Eliasson and Minik Rosing, Place du Panthéon, Paris, 2015.
Photo: Martin Argyroglo, © 2015 Olafur Eliasson.

The Chapter 2 lessons and inventory of ideas promote in-depth interaction with visual arts and music content. These engaging lessons and activities draw on musical and visual arts examples that represent a wide variety of styles, cultures, and historical periods.

Common links between music and art

Concurrently exploring paired concepts, elements, or skills in music and art enhances students' understanding in both disciplines. For example, students who understand the topic of theme and variation as represented in an Andy Warhol–type cupcake artwork (see Figure 2.2) will be better equipped to discern the variations in the string quartet "Happy Birthday Variations" by Peter Heidrich.

Similarly, students who sing the French children's song "Mon Petit Chat" and can discriminate between the melody and the accompaniment of the song will more easily grasp the concept of foreground and background in Renoir's *Woman With a Cat* (see Figure 2.3).

Additionally, many broad concepts may be explored through music and art, with each discipline addressing the theme from its own perspective. Enduring ideas that can be explored in music and visual arts include:

Balance
Change

Figure 2.2 Andy Warhol–type cupcake artwork.
© mazura1989/Shutterstock.com.

Figure 2.3 *Woman With a Cat* by Auguste Renoir, ca. 1875.
Image courtesy of the National Gallery of Art, Gift of Mr. and Mrs. Benjamin E. Levy.

Character
Communication
Conflict
Cooperation
Creativity
Direction
Diversity
Energy
Function
Identity
Insight
Interaction
Interdependence
Lens
Pattern
Preference
Power
Repetition
Responsibility
Ritual
Setting
Truth
Unity
Value

National standards

The disciplines of music and art are grounded by the same overarching standards document, the National Core Arts Standards. The two disciplines share four underlying artistic processes (Creating, Presenting/Performing, Responding, and Connecting) and 11 identical anchor standards. Each discipline has distinct, but related, Enduring Understandings and Essential Questions.

The National Core Arts Standards for Music and the National Core Arts Standards for Visual Arts call for interdisciplinary connections among the arts, with Anchor Standards 10 and 11 focused implicitly on multiple connections. Additionally, the Essential Question in music that is linked with Anchor Standard 11 asks, "How do the other arts, other disciplines, contexts, and daily life inform creating, performing, and responding to music?" (National Coalition for Core Arts Standards, 2015). Box 2.1 specifies the shared anchor standards in the National Core Arts Standards that are addressed in the Chapter 2 lessons and inventory of ideas. Box 2.2 offers a framework for structuring lessons and activities.

Box 2.1 National Core Arts Standards for Visual Arts (VA) and Music (MU) Included in Chapter 2 Lessons (L) and Inventory of Ideas (I)

VA:Cr1 and MU:Cr1 *(Creating)*	Generate and conceptualize artistic ideas and work	L2.3 L2.4 I1 I3 I7 I12
VA:Cr2 and MU:Cr2 *(Creating)*	Organize and develop artistic ideas and work	L2.2 L2.3 I2 I4 I10 I16
VA:Cr3 and MU:Cr3 *(Creating)*	Refine and complete artistic work	L2.3 L2.4 I4 I6 I12 I16
VA:Pr4 and MU:Pr4 *(Presenting* and *Performing)*	Select, analyze, and interpret artistic work for presentation	L2.1 L2.4 I6 I7 I14 I17 I18
VA:Pr5 and MU:Pr5 *(Presenting* and *Performing)*	Develop and refine artistic techniques and work for presentation	L2.3 L2.4 I3 I5 I13 I16
VA:Pr6 and MU:Pr6 *(Presenting* and *Performing)*	Convey meaning through the presentation of artistic work	L2.1 I4 I9 I13 I17 I18

VA:Re7 and MU:Re7 (Responding)	Perceive and analyze artistic work	L2.1 L2.2 I1 I6 I8 I10 I14 I18
VA:Re8 and MU:Re8 (Responding)	Interpret intent and meaning in artistic work	L2.1 I2 I5 I9 I11 I13
VA:Re9 and MU:Re9 (Responding)	Apply criteria to evaluate artistic work	L2.2 I1 I7 I10 I15 I17
VA:Cn10 and MU:Cn10 (Connecting)	Synthesize and relate knowledge and personal experiences to make art	L2.3 L2.4 I2 I5 I11 I12 I16 I19
VA:Cn11 and MU:Cn11 (Connecting)	Relate artistic ideas and works with societal, cultural, and historical context to deepen understanding	L2.2 I3 I8 I9 I15 I19

Box 2.2 Framework for Chapter 2 Lessons and Ideas

This chapter is designed to support K–5 educators as they integrate music and art. The lessons are designed to be fully taught by classroom teachers; however, the plans may also facilitate partnerships and collaboration between classroom teachers, music specialists, and art specialists. All lessons and activities have been reviewed by practicing teachers, and most have been field-tested in elementary classrooms. Chapter 2 lessons are labeled as primary, intermediate, or upper elementary, but all the plans and activities are adaptable to a variety of grade levels and are intended as tools for you to meet your students' needs. Some of the lessons may need to be spread over two or more class periods. Please adjust, adapt, or expand however works best for you and for your students.

Lesson 2.1: Arts Analysis Template

Grade Level: Intermediate and upper elementary, but may be adapted for primary students

Essential Question: How do artists and musicians analyze creative products and discern meaningful connections between specific artistic and musical works?

Objectives

- Following group practice, each student will accurately analyze a musical example and a work of art using an Arts Analysis Template.
- Students will discern and describe similarities and differences between a musical composition and a work of art.
- Students will present their research to the class, explaining and defending their interpretations of two selected works and the meaningful connections between them.

National Core Arts Standards addressed

- VA:Pr4 and MU:Pr4: Select, analyze, and interpret artistic work for presentation.
- VA:Pr6 and MU:Pr6: Convey meaning through the presentation of artistic work
- VA:Re7 and MU:Re7: Perceive and analyze artistic work
- VA:Re8 and MU:Re8: Interpret intent and meaning in artistic work

Materials

- Arts Analysis Template (see Table 2.1)
- Optional music: "Rosie the Riveter" by Jacob Loeb and Redd Evans
- Optional artwork: *Rosie the Riveter* by Norman Rockwell
- Additional music (i.e., popular music, classical music, examples from other cultures, etc.) for students to access
- Additional art (i.e., contemporary art, folk art, pop art, examples from other cultures, etc.) for students to access

Procedure

As preparation for individual work, collaboratively analyze a piece of music as a whole class, then complete the Arts Analysis Template together (see Table 2.1). Depending on your chosen musical example, provide opportunities for students to sing, move, create, and play a rhythmic accompaniment or otherwise musically perform the piece. Model a variety of techniques for drawing conclusions about the piece. These techniques might include a close reading of lyrics, reviewing primary source material such as interviews with the composer, examining the composer's written comments about the piece, exploring first-hand accounts of performances, studying the printed music, inspecting copyright information, and, most importantly, focused, repeated listening. Very young students might limit their exploration to the "why" and "how" questions and could even use drawings to record their responses.

Respond to each of the questions on the template:

Who is the creator? This question sometimes poses problems for students. In cases where the composer of a piece is not the performer, direct students to list both. Similarly, in cases where a number of people collaborated to create a piece, direct students to list them all. If the creator is unknown, students can simply list "anonymous."

What is the title and what is the piece about? When determining the subject or main idea of a piece, students can start with the title. Next, if the piece has lyrics or other text associated with it, students can examine them for clues. Beyond that, direct students to use additional print and online resources to search for answers and to use deductive reasoning based on what they hear or see.

Where was it created and does the style of the piece reflect that culture or place? When attempting to answer the first part of this question, students may need to make an educated guess. It may not be possible to identify the exact location an artwork was created. Ideally, even if students can't pinpoint a specific place, they can narrow it down to a country or region. Determining whether the style of the piece reflects the culture or place will require three things. First, students need to research and thoughtfully analyze the artwork to identify its

Table 2.1 Arts Analysis Template.

Arts Analysis Template (5Ws + 1H)

Who is the creator (artist, composer, and/or performer)?

What is the title and what is the piece about?

Where was it created and does the style of the piece reflect that culture or place?

When was it created and does the style of the piece reflect that time?

Why did you choose this example?

How does it make you feel and what techniques did the composer or artist use to evoke those feelings (text, tempo, harmony, instrumentation, dynamics, articulation, melody, structure, line, color, texture, content, etc.)?

References:

Courtesy of author; adaptation of the Facets Model, found in Sound Ways of Knowing (1997) by Barrett, McCoy, and Veblen.

style or genre. Next, they will need to research the styles and genres that typify the piece's country or region of origin. Finally, they will evaluate and describe any similarities and differences they identify.

When was it created and does the style of the piece reflect that time? When answering the first part of this question, the most straightforward response is to cite the copyright date. If that is not possible, again, direct students to make an educated guess. Perhaps they can narrow it down to a decade, a century, or even an era.

Why did you choose this example? This is the most subjective response on the Arts Analysis Template. Push students to elaborate on their rationale for choosing the piece they did. If they say, "I chose this piece because I like it," encourage them to explain why they like it. What specifically about the piece draws them in?

How does it make you feel and what techniques did the composer or artist use to evoke those feelings? To answer this question, students first need to identify the mood of the piece. Direct them to consider a variety of adjectives that might describe the overall feeling, encouraging them to move beyond "happy" and "sad." Next, through repeated listenings, identify the specific techniques that the composer used that generated that particular response. For example, if students describe the mood of a particular piece as somber, they might also identify musical techniques such as a minor key and a slow tempo. Additionally, students can analyze a piece's text, tempo (fast/slow), harmony (major/minor or brighter/darker), instrumentation (what instruments they identify), dynamics (loud/soft), articulation (choppy/smooth), melody (the tune), and structural elements (phrases, overall form, repetition, etc.) and examine their impact.

References. The last section of the Arts Analysis Template encourages students to follow accepted research practice by citing the sources referenced during analysis.

When the template is complete, use at least one category from the template as the inspiration for identifying a piece of visual art to examine.

- For example, if the song your class analyzed and performed was "Rosie the Riveter" by Jacob Loeb and Redd Evans from 1942, you could focus on answers from the "what" and "when" categories from the Arts Analysis Template. You might choose to look at Norman Rockwell's painting *Rosie the Riveter* (same title) from 1943 (same time period).
- If you chose to analyze and sing your state song, you might look for visual art that was created by a local artist.
- Another idea is to connect a piece of music and an example of visual art that share a common mood.

Use another Arts Analysis Template to record your research about the visual arts example you choose. The template can be used for visual arts examples in the same way you modeled using it for a musical example.

When both Arts Analysis Templates are completed, consider similarities and differences between the music and the art that emerged during analysis, highlighting in two different colors on the templates. These interactions may initiate further research.

- For example, in the previous "Rosie the Riveter" example, you would likely identify and discuss the role of popular culture in America in the 1940s, women in the workforce during World War II, propaganda related to the war effort, and the upbeat and positive message employed in both examples. Additionally, both works also include allusions. When the vocal quartet the Four Vagabonds recorded the song "Rosie the Riveter" in 1943, they used their voices to mimic the sounds of brass instruments during the bridge. They also used vocal sound effects during the chorus that represented the sound of a riveting machine. In Rockwell's *Rosie the Riveter*, various elements allude to Rosie's patriotism: having an American flag in the background, wearing a "V" for Victory pin, and wedging a copy of Hitler's *Mein Kampf* under her foot. Both the song and the painting are known as symbols of American feminism.

Individually or in small groups, students will now use the same process to analyze a musical example and a visual arts example. You may wish to provide parameters regarding the musical examples students may choose and regulate students' search for visual arts examples. You could also offer students a set of three to four musical examples and works of art from which to choose. To manage noise levels, you may wish to have students visit a computer lab or use classroom computers with headphones. After students compare and contrast their musical examples and their works of art, they will prepare short verbal summaries that represent the significant relationships and/or relevant differences they identified.

Assessment

- Set up a demonstration exhibit to highlight each student's work. Project the visual arts images and listen to excerpts of the corresponding musical examples students have chosen. Ask students to present their findings to the class by expressing and defending their appraisals of their two selected works and the meaningful connections between them.
- Collect two Arts Analysis Templates from each student, one for music, and one for art. Check each template for accurate information, correct labeling of similarities and differences, evidence of thorough research, and careful examination of creative works.

Lesson 2.2: Michael Torke's "Bright Blue Music"

Grade Level: Upper elementary, but may be adapted
Essential Question: How does analyzing and reflecting about the characteristics and elements of various musical and artistic works help people make aesthetic decisions?

Objectives

- Students will accurately evaluate characteristics and elements of one musical example ("Bright Blue Music") and three paintings (*Miss Catherine Tatton, Still Life of Oranges and Lemons With Blue Gloves*, and *Circumnavigation of the Sphering of the Poles*) and record the results of their research on Arts Analysis Templates.
- Students will demonstrate their ability to make an informed aesthetic decision by choosing the painting they feel best fits the music, then credibly defending their position during a class debate, utilizing critical analyses of the movement, repetition, context, and mood of the four works to support their perspective.

National Core Arts Standards addressed

- VA:Cr2 and MU:Cr2: Organize and develop artistic ideas and work
- VA:Re7 and MU:Re7: Perceive and analyze artistic work
- VA:Re9 and MU:Re9: Apply criteria to evaluate artistic work
- VA:Cn11 and MU:Cn11: Relate artistic ideas and works with societal, cultural, and historical context to deepen understanding

Materials

- Arts Analysis Template (see Table 2.1)
- Music: "Bright Blue Music" by Michael Torke
- Artwork: *Miss Catherine Tatton* by Thomas Gainsborough (Figure 2.4)
- Artwork: *Still Life of Oranges and Lemons With Blue Gloves* by Vincent van Gogh (Figure 2.5)
- Artwork: *Circumnavigation of the Sphering of the Poles* by Irene Rice Pereira (Figure 2.6)

Procedure

Pass out four Arts Analysis Templates (see Table 2.1) to each student. They will complete one template with information pertaining to Michael Torke's "Bright Blue

Music" and one template for each of the three visual arts examples. See Lesson 2.1 for more information about completing Arts Analysis Templates.

Listen to the first minute or so of Michael Torke's "Bright Blue Music" and give an overview of Michael Torke and his work. Alternately, allow students to research the composer, then present their findings to the class.

Michael Torke is a contemporary American composer who uses color words in the titles of many of his works (Chute, 2001). Besides "Bright Blue Music," which was composed in 1985, his color compositions include "Yellow Pages," "Blue Pages," "White Pages," "Ecstatic Orange," "Green," "Purple," "Ash," "Rust," and "Slate."

Synesthesia is a neurological condition that causes people to perceive things with one or more of their five senses in an unusual way. Michael Torke has a form of synesthesia called chromesthesia, a condition that allows him to "see" sounds in different colors. If he hears music in a certain key, he sees a specific color (Judd, 2012). There are many web resources regarding synesthesia, if your class wishes to investigate further.

Since Michael Torke was a young child, he has seen the key of D major as blue. He chose to title one of his pieces "Bright Blue Music," in part because it was written in the key of D major, and blue was the color he saw the whole time he was working on it.

Speculate with the class why Torke named his piece "Bright Blue Music" and not dark blue, dull blue, or some other adjective. Ask, "What about the music makes you think of the word 'bright'?" Listen to a longer excerpt to allow students to aurally evaluate the music's character and record their impressions on their Arts Analysis Templates.

Review students' answers and guide them to utilize musical elements to justify their positions. In particular, direct students to discuss the mood of the piece. Students might label the character of "Bright Blue Music" as exuberant, animated, or upbeat. Those qualities are suggested by the energetic, persistent rhythm; the use of a major key; and instruments that play with a bright, clear sound in their upper registers. Additionally, there are melodic and rhythmic motives that are repeated throughout the piece, giving a sense of continuity to the listener. Encourage students to sing one or more of the repeating melodic ideas on a neutral syllable ("la") and/or to tap or clap along with one or more of the repeating rhythmic motives.

Display or project three separate examples of visual art. The examples included here are printed in black and white, but all three can be found online in full color. Students will analyze each work of art and record their perceptions on an Arts Analysis Template, focusing on context and mood to choose one example they feel represents the best fit with Michael Torke's "Bright Blue Music."

The English painter Thomas Gainsborough created *Miss Catherine Tatton* in 1786 (see Figure 2.4). The mood of the painting might be described as thoughtful or a bit pretentious. The woman, wearing a white dress with a blue sash and a large blue hat, is the focal point, but the colors are somewhat muted, especially in the painting's

Figure 2.4 *Miss Catherine Tatton* by Thomas Gainsborough, 1786.
Image courtesy of the National Gallery of Art, Andrew W. Mellon Collection.

subdued background. There is not much implied movement in the painting, nor are there many repeated elements. While the use of the color blue might suggest a straightforward connection with "Bright Blue Music," the context and mood are quite dissimilar.

The Dutch painter Vincent van Gogh created his *Still Life of Oranges and Lemons With Blue Gloves* in 1889 (see Figure 2.5). The mood of the painting could be labeled as reflective or colloquial as the motionless scene includes everyday objects such as a wicker basket, fruit, and garden gloves. While some repeated elements can be identified, the image is static and tranquil. The blue of the gloves contrasts with the blue of the sky; however, as in the first example, the context and the mood do not align with "Bright Blue Music."

The American Artist Irene Rice Pereira created *Circumnavigation of the Sphering of the Poles* (see Figure 2.6). The mood of the work might be described as optimistic, inviting, or vibrant. The blues in the artwork are vivid and there are additional pops of brilliant color. Pereira makes use of repetition of shapes, textures, and color throughout the piece, creating a sense of movement. Finally, the context of the piece,

Figure 2.5 *Still Life of Oranges and Lemons With Blue Gloves* by Vincent van Gogh, 1889.
Image courtesy of the National Gallery of Art, Collection of Mr. and Mrs. Paul Mellon.

as a work created in the mid-20th century by an American artist, aligns with "Bright Blue Music."

Assessment

- Organize a debate in which students deliberate about the merits of each painting and its "fit" with Michael Torke's "Bright Blue Music." Encourage students to advocate for various aspects of each piece and then ultimately come to a group consensus. Reinforce that students should not simply pick the piece they like the best, but instead critically analyze and interpret music and art to make an informed aesthetic decision. Scrutinize students' responses for accurate descriptions of musical and artistic content as they explain and defend their interpretations.
- Collect four Arts Analysis Templates from each student: one for the musical example and one for each of the three paintings. Check each template for accurate information, correct labeling of similarities and differences, evidence of thorough research, and careful examination of creative works.

Figure 2.6 *Circumnavigation of the Sphering of the Poles* by Irene Rice Pereira.
Image courtesy of the National Gallery of Art, © Djelloul Marbrook, Estate of Irene Rice Pereira.

Lesson 2.3: Connecting artistic and musical techniques: Pastiche collage

Grade Level: Primary, intermediate, or upper elementary, depending on adaptations

Essential Question: How does learning about specific creative elements and following established traditions encourage people to take creative risks and generate creative ideas?

Objectives

- Students will demonstrate their understanding of a variety of creative elements (hue/tint/shade, texture, pattern, emphasis/contrast, and foreground/background) by accurately distinguishing those elements in existing works.
- Students will apply their knowledge to correctly reproduce a variety of creative elements (hue/tint/shade, texture, pattern, emphasis/contrast, and

foreground/background) in their paintings, singing, movements, and rhythmic performances.

National Core Arts Standards addressed

- VA:Cr1 and MU:Cr1: Generate and conceptualize artistic ideas and work
- VA:Cr2 and MU:Cr2: Organize and develop artistic ideas and work
- VA:Cr3 and MU:Cr3: Refine and complete artistic work
- VA:Pr5 and MU:Pr5: Develop and refine artistic techniques and work for presentation
- VA:Cn10 and MU:Cn10: Synthesize and relate knowledge and personal experiences to make art

Materials

- Art supplies
  - Large, thick sheets of paper (for painting) divided into six equal segments
  - Tempera paint in red, blue, yellow, black, and white
  - Paintbrushes
  - Paper plates
  - Paper cups
- Musical examples
  - *Toccata and Fugue in D Minor* by Johann Sebastian Bach
  - "Marche Funèbre" (Funeral March) from *Piano Sonata No. 2* by Frédéric Chopin
  - *Piano Sonata No. 16 in C Major,* K. 545, by Wolfgang Amadeus Mozart
  - "Hallelujah Chorus" from the *Messiah* by George Frederic Handel
  - *Partita for Solo Flute in A Minor*, BWV 1013, III. "Sarabande," by Johann Sebastian Bach
  - "Sacrificial Dance" from *The Rite of Spring* by Igor Stravinsky
  - *Bolero* by Maurice Ravel
  - "Slavonic Dance No. 8 in G Minor" by Antonin Dvořák
  - "Somewhere Over the Rainbow/What a Wonderful World" by Israel Kaʻanoʻi Kamakawiwoʻole
  - "Take the 'A' Train" by Billy Strayhorn, performed by Duke Ellington
- Visual art examples
  - *A Wheatfield, With Cypresses* by Vincent Van Gogh (Figure 2.7)
  - *Still Life With Milk Jug and Fruit* by Paul Cézanne (Figure 2.8)
  - *Under the Wave off Kanagawa* by Katsushika Hokusai (Figure 2.11)
  - *Persische Nachtigallen* (*Persian Nightingales*) by Paul Klee (Figure 2.12)
  - *The Apparition in the Forest* by Moritz von Schwind (Figure 2.13)
  - *Children Playing on the Beach* by Mary Cassatt (Figure 2.14)

Procedure

A pastiche in visual arts is a work of art that imitates the qualities or characteristics of another artist or work of art. A pastiche is not an exact duplicate of the work it imitates, but instead emulates the original. In elementary classrooms, student artists often create pastiches that feature specific elements and principles of art. This strategy typically involves students analyzing an element or principle of art in an existing work, then reproducing that element themselves. For example, students might explore ways that movement is expressed in Van Gogh's *A Wheatfield, With Cypresses* (see Figure 2.7) and then use lines and shapes to imply movement in their own paintings.

Given the close relationship between visual art and music, it is logical to connect students' study of artistic techniques with an exploration of ways those same elements are expressed musically. Recognizing and considering an element such as movement in multiple disciplines can reinforce students' understanding in each. In this lesson, before students replicate various visual art techniques, they first interpret the expression of those techniques in existing works of art and in existing pieces of music.

Prepare paper plate "palettes" with red, yellow, blue, black, and white Tempera paint. Pass out palettes to students, along with paintbrushes, rinsing water, and papers divided into six segments.

Figure 2.7 *Wheatfield With Cypresses* by Vincent van Gogh, 1889.
Image courtesy of the Metropolitan Museum of Art, Purchase, The Annenberg Foundation Gift, 1993.

Five of the segments on students' papers will be separate pastiches, allowing students to demonstrate five isolated artistic techniques. In the final segment, students will create paintings that represent their interpretation of a recorded piece of music. Alternately, you might choose to have your students explore each individual technique in separate, sequential lessons. The works of art and musical compositions included with this lesson highlight each of the five separate artistic techniques, but there are endless art and music examples from which to choose. All the visual art examples are shown in black and white but are available through public domain in color.

1. Hue/tint/shade
   In the first section of their pastiche collages, students will explore tinting and shading. In art, the "hue" is the original color. Hues can be adjusted to become lighter or darker. A "tint" is created when white is added to a color, a "shade" is created when black is added to a color, and "value" refers to the relative lightness and darkness. In music, brighter and darker tonal sounds are labeled in terms of harmony. Pieces written in a major key have a brighter sound, and pieces written in a minor key have a darker sound. Singing can easily highlight the contrast between major and minor keys. Choose a song that is written in a major key, like "Twinkle, Twinkle Little Star," and have students sing it. Next, find a recording of that piece performed in a minor key. Have students listen, then sing along. They will likely say that the recording sounds "wrong," because it is not the harmony they expected for that piece. If your class is interested in harmony and wishes to further explore intervals, scales, keys, and modes, there are many resources available.
   Play musical examples and ask students if they hear a "darker" or a "brighter" overall sound.

   - Minor (darker) musical examples: *Toccata and Fugue in D Minor* by Bach; "Marche Funèbre" (Funeral March) from *Piano Sonata No. 2* by Chopin
   - Major (brighter) musical examples: *Piano Sonata No. 16 in C Major*, K. 545, by Mozart; "Hallelujah Chorus" from the *Messiah* by Handel

   Show *Still Life With Milk Jug and Fruit* by Cézanne (see Figure 2.8) and ask students to identify specific hues along with their related tints and shades, noting the values of each.
   Invite students to choose a color to tint and shade in one segment of their papers.

2. Texture
   Actual texture is the way a surface feels. If you were to touch them, thickly painted oil paintings would feel different than watercolors. Similarly, one weaving might feel nubby and another scratchy. The surface of one statue

Figure 2.8 *Still Life With Milk Jug and Fruit* by Paul Cézanne, ca. 1900.
Image courtesy of the National Gallery of Art, Gift of the W. Averell Harriman Foundation in memory of Marie N. Harriman.

might be rough while another is smooth. Implied texture is a visual representation of the way something would feel. In visual art, implied textures can be expressed by using thinner or thicker lines, varying the number of lines and shapes, choosing the ways lines and shapes overlap, and shading to show depth. In music, texture generally refers to the quantity or density of interacting parts of a piece. A thin musical texture has few overlapping elements or layers (i.e., a single voice performing alone), and a thick musical texture has many overlapping elements or layers (i.e., an octet of singers performing independent parts simultaneously). Invite a single student to tap a steady beat on a drum or desk, representing a thin musical texture. That student locks in the beat, keeping it going without variation. Choose another student to tap a different rhythm over the top of the steady beat. Create a very thick overall texture by adding students, one at a time, to the performance. Musical texture can also be identified visually. Figure 2.9 shows a thinner musical texture and Figure 2.10 shows a thicker musical texture.

Figure 2.9 Thinner musical texture.
© Hyacinth/Free-Images.com.

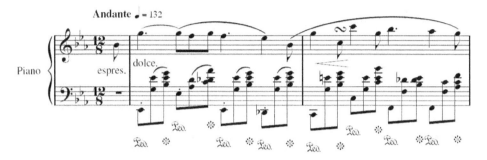

Figure 2.10 Thicker musical texture.
© RoodyAlien/Free-Images.com.

Play the following musical examples and direct students to distinguish between thin and thick musical textures.

- Thinner musical texture example: *Partita for Solo Flute in A Minor*, BWV 1013, III. "Sarabande," by Bach
- Thicker musical texture example: "Sacrificial Dance" from *The Rite of Spring* by Stravinsky

Show *Under the Wave off Kanagawa* by Hokusai (see Figure 2.11) and direct students to categorize the different textural elements by analyzing lines, shapes, and examples of shading.

In the second segment of their papers, invite students to paint, demonstrating texture.

3. Pattern
The term "pattern" refers to the repetition or reoccurrence of a design element. Patterns can be exact or varied. In visual art, patterns are created with elements such as color, line, texture, and shape. Repeating rhythmic figures and recurring melodic phrases are examples of patterns in music. Because of their repetitive nature, rhythmic and melodic patterns are usually easy for students to identify in music.

Figure 2.11 *Under the Wave off Kanagawa* by Katsushika Hokusai, ca. 1830–1832.
Image courtesy of the Metropolitan Museum of Art, Rogers Fund, 1914.

Listen to *Bolero* by Ravel and ask students to identify the repeated rhythm aurally, then perform it along with the recording. The pattern is written for snare drum, so students may "drum" on their desks with their fingers, pencils, or rhythm sticks. The rhythmic figure in Ravel's *Bolero* that is repeated continuously throughout the piece can be written as:

Show Paul Klee's *Persische Nachtigallen* (*Persian Nightingales*) (see Figure 2.12) and ask students to explain ways the Swiss artist has incorporated patterns in the work.

Ask students to paint a reoccurring design element in the third segment of their papers.

4. Emphasis/contrast
Another principle of design, emphasis, is demonstrated when an area, object, or point in a work becomes the created center of interest. In visual art, elements such as size, color, shape, texture, and placement can define a focal point. In music, composers manipulate elements such as dynamics (i.e., a loud section in the middle of a soft piece), tempo (i.e., a fast song that suddenly slows

Figure 2.12 *Persische Nachtigallen (Persian Nightingales)* by Paul Klee, 1917.
Image courtesy of the National Gallery of Art, Gift of Catherine Gamble Curran and Family, in Honor of the 50th Anniversary of the National Gallery of Art.

down), pitch (i.e., a melody that stands out because it is much higher than the accompanying instruments), and rhythm (i.e., strong accents on specific beats) to provide emphasis.

Listen to "Slavonic Dance No. 8 in G Minor" by Dvořák and encourage students to aurally identify points of emphasis in the piece and explain the musical elements involved. Direct students to collaborate in small groups to devise specific ways they can move to the music that will align with the contrasting sounds they perceive. Allow time for negotiation and rehearsal, perhaps starting and stopping the music at different points, and then invite all the groups to perform their choreographed set of dance moves with the music.

Figure 2.13 *The Apparition in the Forest* by Moritz von Schwind, 1823.
Image courtesy of the National Gallery of Art, Wolfgang Ratjen Collection, Patrons' Permanent Fund.

Show *The Apparition in the Forest* by Moritz von Schwind (see Figure 2.13) and ask students to locate the focal point and defend their point of view by describing the art elements involved.

Have students paint in the fourth segment of their papers, demonstrating their understanding of emphasis.

5. Foreground/background
   In visual art, the foreground is the part of the image that appears closest to the viewer, while the background is the portion of the scene that is farther away. An artist may also choose to differentiate foreground and background by featuring a sharply focused main subject with a blurry or more out-of-focus background. In music, the melody of a piece can be thought of as the foreground and the accompaniment as the background. In visual art and music, the background elements generally support the foreground elements.

   Listen to "Somewhere Over the Rainbow/What a Wonderful World" by Israel Kaʻanoʻi Kamakawiwoʻole and direct students to differentiate between the melody and the accompaniment. Discuss the instrumentation and ask students to determine what musical instruments or voice parts perform foreground and background roles. Discuss the expressive qualities that separate the melody from the accompaniment (smooth, flowing melody; rhythmic accompaniment; changes in dynamics). Divide the class and direct one half to sing the melody (foreground) while the other half gently taps the rhythm of the accompaniment (background), and then switch roles.

Show the painting *Children Playing on the Beach* by Mary Cassatt (see Figure 2.14) and ask students to define the foreground and the background of the picture, noting specific ways the artist has emphasized the foreground elements in the piece.

In the fifth segment of their papers, students will demonstrate foreground and background.

6. Put it all together

In the last remaining segment of students' papers, they will use the techniques they've practiced in the previous five segments to create their own work of art. As the inspiration for their work, direct students to listen to a final piece of music, Billy Strayhorn's "Take the 'A' Train," performed by Duke Ellington, and analyze what they hear. Remind students that they will not be "painting what they feel" or "painting a picture that the music suggests." Instead, they will scrutinize the musical composition and determine its primary features and component elements, based on their previous analysis of the pastiche examples.

Figure 2.14 *Children Playing on the Beach* by Mary Cassatt, 1884.
Image courtesy of the National Gallery of Art, Ailsa Mellon Bruce Collection.

Ask students to create a visual reconstruction of the musical elements they identified and paint their design in the final segment of their paper. Play the music while students work. Allow students to share their artwork and explain how it is connected to the music.

Assessment

- Informally assess students' responses during collaborative analysis of representative music and art examples, checking for in-tune singing, accurate performance of rhythms, musical independence when performing in parts, and correct identification and descriptions of creative elements.
- Collect students' pastiche collages and evaluate the precision with which students were able to express and accurately compile painted examples of hue/tint/shade, texture, pattern, emphasis/contrast, and foreground/background.

Extension

As written, Lesson 2.3 provides opportunities for students to sing, play rhythms, listen, analyze, move, and simultaneously perform melodies and accompaniments. An additional musical activity involves reversing the final step of the lesson. Instead of listening to a new piece of music and creating a visual representation of the musical elements they hear, students can examine a new piece of art, then create a musical composition or improvisation that represents the artistic elements they perceive. You might provide instruments such as bells, recorders, nonpitched percussion, or ukuleles. Alternatively, students' compositions could simply utilize voices and/or body percussion.

Lesson 2.4: French Impressionism: Claude Monet and Claude Debussy

Grade Level: Intermediate, but may be adapted
Essential Question: How do our interactions with creative works from different societal, cultural, and historical contexts impact our responses to the specific works and the ways we interpret the world?

Objectives

- Students will analyze representative musical compositions of Claude Debussy and paintings of Claude Monet and appropriately identify, describe, and evaluate the characteristic musical and artistic elements that define Impressionism, both verbally with a partner and in individual written responses.

- Students will apply their understanding of Impressionistic techniques to create a painting in the Impressionist style, then correctly explain the elements of music they chose to represent and the visual arts techniques they employed.
- Students will apply their understanding of Impressionistic techniques to create a musical improvisation in the Impressionist style, then correctly explain the elements of art they chose to represent and the musical techniques they employed.

National Core Arts Standards addressed

- VA:Cr1 and MU:Cr1: Generate and conceptualize artistic ideas and work
- VA:Cr3 and MU:Cr3: Refine and complete artistic work
- VA:Pr4 and MU:Pr4: Select, analyze, and interpret artistic work for presentation
- VA:Pr5 and MU:Pr5: Develop and refine artistic techniques and work for presentation
- VA:Cn10 and MU:Cn10: Synthesize and relate knowledge and personal experiences to make art

Materials

- Art supplies
  - White paper
  - Tempera paint in red, blue, yellow, black, and white
  - Paintbrushes
  - Paper plates
  - Paper cups
- Musical examples (Claude Debussy)
  - "Arabesque No. 1"
  - "Clair de Lune"
  - "Golliwogg's Cakewalk" from the *Children's Corner Suite*
  - "Jardins Sous la Pluie" (Gardens in the Rain) from *Estampes*
  - "Prélude à l'aprés-midi d'un faune" (Prelude to the Afternoon of a Faun)
- Musical supplies: Various pitched instruments for improvisation, such as bells, keyboards, recorders, ukuleles, etc.

(There are many excellent audio and video recordings of each of these compositions. Particularly noteworthy are audio recordings of Debussy himself playing the first four pieces on this list. The recordings can be found on an album released in 2013 by Bringins Music, titled *Claude Debussy Plays His Finest Works*.)

- Visual art examples (Claude Monet)
  - *Impression, Sunrise,* available online through the Musée Marmottan Monet website
  - *Water Lilies* (three separate examples; see Figures 2.17, 2.18 and 2.19)
  - *Cliff Walk at Pourville* (Figure 2.20)
  - *Houses of Parliament, London* (Figure 2.22)
- Historical photo examples
  - Claude Debussy (Figure 2.15)
  - Claude Monet (Figure 2.16)
  - Houses of Parliament, London (Figure 2.21)

Procedure

Introduce Impressionistic style

Ask students what the word "impression" means to them and allow time for several responses. Explain that there is a musical and artistic style called Impressionism. In that style, composers and artists try to give an impression of their subject, rather than portray their subject precisely or realistically (Pasler, 2001). Share with students that they will be discussing the work of two famous French Impressionists who both happen to be named Claude: Claude Debussy, the composer, and Claude Monet, the painter.

Give brief biographical overviews of both Claudes, or alternately, as an activity to jump-start a class discussion, assign half of your students to research Claude Debussy and half to research Claude Monet.

Claude Debussy, a French composer, lived from 1862 to 1918 (see Figure 2.15). As a young music student, he didn't like following strict composition rules. Rather than follow guidelines, he wanted to write music with a new, unique sound. He incorporated nontraditional scales, harmonies, and structures in his music. He is remembered as one of the most important composers of the Impressionistic Period (Lesure & Howat, 2001).

Claude Monet, a French painter, lived from 1840 to 1926 (see Figure 2.16). As a young student, he sometimes drew caricatures of his teachers on his work at school. As a teenager, he began painting outdoors and was especially inspired by the way light reflected off objects and water. Monet is sometimes called the Father of Impressionism. A painting Monet created in 1872 titled *Impression, Soleil Levant* (Impression, Sunrise) prompted the name of the style (Pasler, 2001).

Listen to Debussy examples and discuss

Debussy wrote many pieces for solo piano. Perform, ask a student to perform, or play recordings of three of his short compositions for piano, "Arabesque No. 1," "Clair de Lune," and "Golliwogg's Cakewalk," and an excerpt from one of his orchestral compositions, "Prélude à l'aprés-midi d'un faune." Discuss the musical elements of these pieces with students, asking them to describe their observations about high and low pitches, dynamics, and the instruments they hear. Focus their attention on

Figure 2.15 Claude Debussy.
© Nadar/Free-Images.com.

rhythmic aspects of the pieces and direct them to listen for the fluidity of the tempo as well as places where the beat is indefinite or flexible, without a strong pulse.

Ask students to use an adjective to describe the music. They may respond with terms such as "dreamy," "mysterious," or "blurred." Explain that instead of using traditional major and minor scales, Debussy often used pentatonic and whole tone scales. Additionally, his compositions emphasized unusual chord combinations, frequently lacked distinct melodies, had indeterminate tonal centers, and used instruments in ways that emphasized specific sound qualities such as muted or shimmery sounds. These musical characteristics are what gives Impressionist music a sense of mystery. Rather than conveying specific details, the music evokes a feeling or impression.

Look at Monet examples and discuss

Although Monet's paintings are shown here in black and white, they are all available through public domain online in color. Project three versions of Monet's *Water Lilies* for students (see Figures 2.17, 2.18 and 2.19). Note that in each painting, the surface of the water fills the entire canvas. Monet completed around 250 paintings

Figure 2.16 Claude Monet.
© WikiImages/Pixabay.

of the water lilies in his garden at Giverny. Paintings from the series are among Monet's most famous pieces and they are displayed in museums around the world.

Next, project *Cliff Walk at Pourville* (see Figure 2.20). Notice how the short brush strokes evoke a sense of movement in the clouds, the water, the grass, and the women's dresses.

Most of Monet's paintings are of natural objects, but he sometimes painted buildings or bridges too. Have students compare a photograph of the Houses of Parliament in London from Monet's time (see Figure 2.21) with one of Monet's own paintings of the subject (see Figure 2.22). Notice how Monet's *Houses of Parliament* almost appears to show the buildings through a thick fog.

The shapes Monet created are made with dabs of paint and many short strokes rather than strong lines. Allow students to explore and discover that the closer they are to Monet's paintings, the fuzzier they become. As they step back, the pictures begin to focus and give the impression of flowers in a pond, a cliff by the ocean, or buildings in London.

Help students to recognize connections between Debussy's and Monet's work. Just as there was not a strong sense of pulse in Debussy's music, there are not strong or

Figure 2.17   Claude Monet. *Water Lilies,* 1906.
The Art Institute of Chicago, Mr. and Mrs. Martin A. Ryerson Collection.

Figure 2.18   Claude Monet. *Water Lilies* (Agapanthus), ca. 1915–1926.
The Cleveland Museum of Art, John L. Severance Fund and an anonymous gift 1960.81.

Figure 2.19   Claude Monet. *Nympheas*, ca. 1897–1898.
The Los Angeles County Museum of Art, Mrs. Fred Hathaway Bixby Bequest (M.62.8.13).

Figure 2.20   Claude Monet. *Cliff Walk at Pourville*, 1882.
The Art Institute of Chicago, Mr. and Mrs. Lewis Larned Coburn Memorial Collection.

Figure 2.21 *Houses of Parliament*, ca. 1890.
© Library of Congress.

Figure 2.22 Claude Monet. *Houses of Parliament*, 1900–1901.
The Art Institute of Chicago, Mr. and Mrs. Martin A. Ryerson Collection.

sharp lines in Monet's paintings. Debussy incorporated contrast by varying tempos, pitches, and dynamics. One way Debussy incorporated contrast in his paintings was through the use of complementary colors. Locate an online image of Monet's painting *Impression, Sunrise* to show students. Ask them to identify the main color in the painting (blue) and the color that is utilized for contrast (orange). Project an image of the color wheel and review the definition of complementary colors, if needed. Locate the color directly across from blue on the color wheel, blue's complementary color (orange).

Guide students to listen and paint
Explain to students that they will be creating a painting in the Impressionist style and that an Impressionist composition will guide their work. Prepare paper plate "palettes" with red, yellow, blue, black, and white Tempera paint, along with paper, paintbrushes, and rinsing water for each student.

Listen to Debussy's "Jardins Sous la Pluie" (Gardens in the Rain) from *Estampes*, and brainstorm with students how they might represent the music through painting. In his piece for solo piano, Debussy gives the listener an impression of a garden on a rainy day. Ask students to interpret the sounds they hear and to consider the different types of rain that are depicted. Encourage students to imagine the effect of different types of rainstorms on a garden landscape. Debussy portrays changes in the character of the rain with a variety of musical techniques. In this piece, he emphasizes the contrast between soft and loud sounds, makes use of fluid variations in tempo throughout, and accentuates differences between high and low sounds, including broad sweeping gestures that move from high to low. As listeners, we perceive passages that are more stormy, turbulent, and dark; passages that are lighter and bright; and passages that portray a calm, gentle mood.

Direct students to incorporate and represent Impressionist characteristics of the music in their work: short brush strokes, blurry or splotchy images, and nature themes. Their images should align with what they hear. For instance, "If the music is very low and soft, perhaps use darker colors. If the music is high and fast, perhaps use brighter colors. If you hear dynamic, tempo, or register changes, you might show this by adding contrast to your painting with complementary colors."

Remind students that Debussy was conveying an impression of gardens in the rain through his music.

Take time to review brush strokes and the mixing of complementary colors and hues, if needed.

Play "Jardins Sous la Pluie" while students paint.

Guide students as they improvise in the Impressionistic style
Again, project the image of Monet's painting *Impression, Sunrise*. Direct pairs of students to improvise short musical passages using available pitched instruments. Just as students represented Impressionist characteristics from Debussy's music in the paintings they created, their musical improvisations should align with what they

see in Monet's painting. Review some of the characteristic qualities of Impressionist music and ask students to demonstrate how they might incorporate those qualities in their improvisations. For example, students can demonstrate a sense of fluidity and flexibility by playing without a strong pulse and without maintaining a consistent tempo. They can emphasize contrasts by playing high and low sounds, perhaps including broad glissandos that sweep between pitch extremes. They can portray a dreamy or blurred quality by playing clusters of notes, eliminating a sense of tonal center, or experiment with soft and loud sounds to show the difference between calmer or more chaotic atmospheres.

Assessment

- Ask students to explain Impressionism to a partner, using specific examples of musical and artistic techniques to support their generalizations. As the partner discussions conclude, pass out index cards. On their index cards, students write one to two sentences about Impressionism.
- After the paintings are complete and dry, have students sit in a circle with their paintings. Play "Jardins Sous la Pluie" again while students take turns sharing their creations and clarifying connections between the artistic choices they made in their paintings and the musical example. Similarly, ask pairs of students to share their musical improvisations with the class and justify their musical choices based on their analysis of Monet's work. Foster a positive atmosphere by encouraging students to offer commendations and compliments to their peers.

Inventory of ideas

1. Explore the concept of blend in music and art. First, listen to a song like "Here Comes the Sun" by the Beatles and discuss the aspects of vocal blend that are exhibited. Vocal blend refers to the matching of vowel sounds and accurate tuning of chords to unify the sound that is produced. Invite students to stand in block formation to facilitate listening to each other as they sing together. Challenge students to make minor adjustments to their singing to align their sound with that of their neighbor. Next, examine a watercolor like Georgia O'Keeffe's *Sunrise* and discuss the blending, or the gradual transitions between colors, that are visible. Techniques to analyze include graded wash, pigment blending, bleeding colors, and scumbling.
2. As a class, listen to and sing "You've Got a Friend in Me" from the movie *Toy Story* and James Taylor's "You've Got a Friend" to analyze and interpret their meanings. On the board, note "friend-like" qualities that are present in each piece. Both songs feature comfortable tempos, singable melodies with

memorable choruses, and straightforward lyrics that describe a friend as someone upon whom you can always count. In pairs, students will create lists of qualities that define a good friend, using their own interpretations of the songs, the lists on the board, and their own experiences. Students will then paint portraits of their partners that capture the "friend-like" qualities they possess. In the background of the portraits, have students print four or five terms from the lists they produced that apply to their partners. You could also have students write a description at the bottom of the portraits they create: "Annika is a good friend because she is . . . ," "Elizabeth is a good friend when she . . . ."

3. Print an oversized map of the United States in which each state is outlined. Cut out the states and pass out the pieces to students. Ask students to adorn their designated state with a personal characteristic and to choose a single color with which to transform their portion of the map. Listen to "Colourblind" by Darius Campbell, "We're Not That Different" by Teresa Jennings, or "Everyone Is Different" by Lanny Sherwin. Invite students to sing, perform with sign language, and/or clap to the steady beat. Identify the differences and similarities that are referenced in the songs, and then discuss the deeper meaning of unity and equality for all people. Reconstruct the United States map and relate the unity that is expressed in the song to the unity demonstrated by the various shades of colors and characteristics that make up the collage.

4. While it is common to examine and create collages in visual art, there are musical examples that students can explore as well. Charles Ives (1874–1954) used collage as a compositional technique by incorporating small fragments of music or quoting portions of melodies from a variety of different sources in his pieces such as "The Things Our Fathers Loved" (Burkholder, Sinclair, & Magee, 2013). Take the collage technique a step further using technology. Instruct students to take screenshots of many small fragments of existing photos, then create a collage by combining the images in a cohesive way. Similarly, invite students to capture small audio fragments of existing songs, then reconstruct them in a musical collage composition. Emphasize that projects using technology are for exploring the creative process, rather than generating a specific product.

5. Choose a song that is sung from an unusual perspective such as Lionel Ritchie's "Dancin' on the Ceiling" or Europe's "The Final Countdown." Project a copy of the song's lyrics. Listen to the song, and then encourage students to sing along. Ask students to make inferences from the lyrics to determine the perspective from which the song is presented (dancing upside down, in a spaceship ready to travel to Venus). Invite students to draw a scene from a unique perspective. For example, they might sketch a scene from the viewpoint of a dog, tornado, or fish; or they could portray their own impressions from an unusual location or angle such as from the top of a tree, inside a flower, or under their desk.

6. When music albums are released, there is typically newly designed cover art to accompany the collection; however, a good deal of new music is released in single format, rather than as part of an album. Choose and analyze a single piece of music, and then use the musical elements present to design and create appropriate "single cover art" to represent the song. Perform the song and display the newly designed cover.

7. Connect the element of line in visual art to the different pathways that students can use to travel through a space (walking in straight lines, gliding along curved pathways, staggering along zig-zag lines, etc.). Ask students to move, aligning their actions with a variety of musical examples you play.

8. Louis Armstrong is remembered as one of America's most innovative and influential musicians. His brilliant efforts as a trumpeter, singer, and composer contributed to the transformation of the jazz idiom. His innovations include the popularization of scat singing, dramatic effects for both trumpet and voice, and the extension of the technical potential and range of the trumpet. Perhaps most important, Armstrong is credited with the development of virtuosic solo improvising, which was a departure from the cohesive ensemble playing, the standard performance practice of the time (Anderson, 2013). Listen to one of Louis Armstrong's most well-known pieces, "What a Wonderful World," and another that highlights his jazz virtuosity, "Struttin' With Some Barbecue." Invite students to sing "What a Wonderful World" together, and encourage students to experiment with scat singing and vocal improvisation, perhaps in a call-and-response format. Delve into the work of another influential New Orleans artist, painter Ida Kohlmeyer. Like Armstrong, Kohlmeyer is known for developing a distinctive style. Her painting, *Rebus Drawing* (see Figure 2.23), demonstrates her unique expression of shapes and symbols, arranged in a relaxed grid (Arthur Roger Gallery, 2016).

9. Sing a variety of patriotic songs including "You're a Grand Old Flag," "The Star-Spangled Banner," "Yankee Doodle," "America," and "America the Beautiful." Examine visual art that is based on the American flag such as *Washington Crossing the Delaware* by Emanuel Leutze (see Figure 2.24) or *Flag* by Jasper Johns. Explore ways that composers and artists express patriotism. Ask students to describe the function of singing patriotic songs or displaying patriotic art in promoting loyalty and pride.

10. Explore pointillism in art and music. Pointillism is an artistic technique in which individual dots of color or sound are united to form a complete image or composition. *A Sunday on La Grande Jatte* by George Seurat (see Figure 2.25) is a classic representation of the pointillistic style. Project a color image of the painting and zoom in so that students can closely inspect the technique and distinguish individual dabs and dots of color. Zoom out to allow students to view the entire image that is revealed when the work is observed from a distance.

Figure 2.23 Ida Kohlmeyer. *Rebus Drawing*, 2016.
Image courtesy of the estate of Ida Kohlmeyer and Arthur Roger Gallery.

Figure 2.24 *Washington Crossing the Delaware* by Emanuel Leutze, 1851.
Image courtesy of The Metropolitan Museum of Art, Gift of John Stewart Kennedy, 1897.

Figure 2.25 George Seurat. *A Sunday on La Grande Jatte*, 1884.
The Art Institute of Chicago, Helen Birch Bartlett Memorial Collection.

Composer Anton Webern's "Five Pieces for Orchestra, Op. 10" expresses pointillism in music (Puffett, 2001). The listener hears individual points of sound, seemingly out of nowhere. Rather than the pitches coming together to form a coherent melody, they are heard as isolated and detached; however, in reality, each note is part of a carefully organized sequence that becomes more apparent upon repeated listenings. To reinforce students' understanding of pointillism, let students hear a contrasting example. Play the beginning of another of Webern's works, "Im Sommerwind," a piece that opens with a wash of sound, with each note blending into the next. Challenge students to create works of art and music that employ pointillistic techniques.

11. Specific elements of music and art are often emphasized or exaggerated. Explore exaggeration in the paintings of Bolivian artist Fernando Botero and the Bolivian folk group Los Kjarkas. Botero is well known for his puffed-up images and plump figures, and Los Kjarkas frequently employs embellished strumming techniques and vocal melodies. Ask students to describe how exaggeration in music or art affects their experience with the subjects. Challenge students to incorporate exaggeration in the music or art they create.

12. Explore artistic self-expression by comparing and contrasting various self-portraits in visual art and music. Possible visual arts examples to study include self-portraits by van Gogh (see Figure 2.26), Ducreux (see Figure 2.27), Vanderbank (see Figure 2.28), and Naerdemann (see Figure 2.29).

Figure 2.26 *Self-Portrait With a Straw Hat* by Vincent van Gogh, 1887.
Image courtesy of The Metropolitan Museum of Art, Bequest of Miss Adelaide Milton de Groot (1876–1967), 1967.

Musical examples to consider include a solo guitar "Self Portrait" by Don Ross, a solo piano "Self Portrait" by Tigran Hamasyan, a percussion "Self Portrait" by Pete Lockett, a postpunk "Self Portrait" by the band The Durutti Column, and Batman's tongue-in-cheek "Untitled Self Portrait" by Will Arnett from *The Lego Movie* soundtrack. In addition to individual self-portrait pieces, some composers, such as Bob Dylan, have titled entire albums *Self Portrait*. After analyzing existing musical and artistic self-portraits, invite students to create musical and/or visual arts self-portraits of their own.

13. Compare and contrast two versions of the song "Once Upon a Dream." Each was featured in one of the two different Disney *Sleeping Beauty* movies, and they have distinctly different characteristics. Listen to and then sing each song, write about the emotions that are expressed, and then choose specific colors to associate with those feelings and moods. On separate pieces of paper or a single sheet divided in half, create contrasting images that align with the emotions portrayed in the songs. Finally, share images with the class and justify color choices as a way to differentiate moods.

Figure 2.27 *Self-Portrait With a Harp* by Rose Adélaïde Ducreux, 1791.
Image courtesy of The Metropolitan Museum of Art, Bequest of Susan Dwight Bliss, 1966.

14. Investigate mood in existing examples of music and art. Choose a piece of music such as "Imagine" by John Lennon, "Django's Tiger" by Django Reinhardt, or "Zip-a-Dee-Doo-Dah" from the movie *Song of the South* and characterize its mood. Appraise various works of art to choose an example that exhibits the equivalent mood.

15. People sometimes feel indifferent when exact routines are repeated again and again; however, too much variety can be just as bad. Music also works well when it exhibits both unity and variety. A good example of this is the first section of Chopin's "Mazurka No. 37 in A-Flat Major" (Burkhart, 2005). The music that comprises approximately the first 30 seconds of the piece is structurally identical to the following 30 seconds. This nearly exact melodic and rhythmic repetition creates a sense of unity. Because music happens in time, melodies heard only once are easily forgotten. The repeat of the initial theme helps the listener to remember it. Chopin displays good musical design by demonstrating a balance between unity and variety. An exact repetition, without some variety, would be very dull. In this case, the repeat actually increases the sense of

Figure 2.28 *Self-Portrait* by John Vanderbank, the younger, ca. 1720.
Image courtesy of The Metropolitan Museum of Art, Purchase, Brooke Russell Astor Bequest, 2013.

Figure 2.29 *Self-Portrait* by Claudia Naerdemann.
© Claudia Naerdemann/Shutterstock.com.

drama and excitement through the use of a thicker texture, added accents, and a heightened dynamic level. While the tempo remains the same, an added intensity and animation is perceived. The repeat of the initial material appeals to listeners, precisely because it can be simultaneously heard as a reinforcement of familiar material and an intensification of the character of that material. It exemplifies the perfect balance between unity and variety. Examine the image of traditional Polish folk dresses (see Figure 2.30) and identify examples of unity and variety that are exhibited. Watch a video of Polish dancers performing a mazurka and categorize elements that exemplify unity and variety.

16. Sometimes artists and composers use unfamiliar or unusual materials in their creations. For example, artist Caroline S. Brooks's work *A Study in Butter: The Dreaming Iolanthe* was constructed of nothing but butter (see Figure 2.31), and electroacoustic composer Adrian Moore's "Study in Ink" was made up of sounds completely derived from a dry-erase marker on a whiteboard. See what other unique mediums and materials students can detect in existing works of art. Challenge them to create their own music or art from found sounds and found materials.

17. If your class is studying architecture representing specific time periods, locations, or styles, take time to also examine the music that was prevalent during that time or in that place. For example, musical selections that could complement the Duomo in Florence, Italy (see Figure 2.32), are very different than pieces that might align with Frank Gehry's Walt Disney Concert Hall in downtown Los Angeles, California (see Figure 2.33). Ask students to research and/or perform musical examples that would logically connect to each style.

18. The "Like It or Not" activity allows students to critique various works of art, generate appraisals, and express opinions. Divide students into groups. Each group

Figure 2.30 Traditional Polish folk dresses.
© Abo Photography/Shutterstock.com.

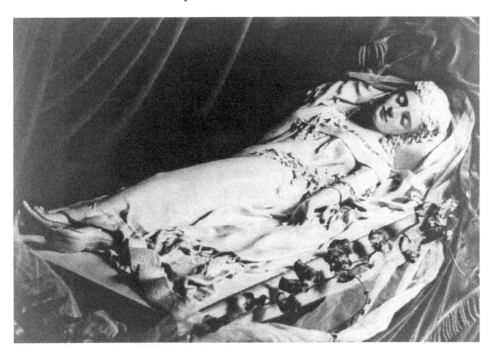

Figure 2.31 Caroline S. Brooks. *A Study in Butter: The Dreaming Iolanthe*, ca. 1878.
© The Library of Congress.

Figure 2.32 Duomo Santa Maria del Fiore in Florence, Italy, 2016.
© Picryl.

Figure 2.33 Modernist architect Frank Gehry's Walt Disney Concert Hall, Los Angeles, California, ca. 1980–2006.
© Carol M. Highsmith/The Library of Congress.

is responsible for choosing two works of visual art from the same medium (two sculptures, watercolors, screen prints, weavings, photos, oil paintings, collages, etc.). After analyzing each example, students will identify one work that the group "likes" and one that the group "doesn't like." Next, the groups will prepare five-minute presentations for the class. In the presentations, students will show each piece, noting their titles, artists, cultures, and time periods. Additionally, they will describe any important elements (line, shape, form, color, texture, perspective, etc.) and principles (pattern, movement, proportion, balance, unity, variety, etc.) in each piece. The group members will demonstrate critical analysis by describing why they preferred one artwork over the other, how they arrived at their decision, and what criteria they used. Students will locate and analyze a companion piece of music for each of their art examples. The musical examples will serve as the soundtrack to their presentations.

19. Consider three-way connections between music, art, and social studies. When your class is studying a specific period of history, a concurrent examination of the art and music that arose during that era will enrich students' understandings in all three disciplines. For example, during a unit about the Harlem Renaissance, also explore the paintings of Jacob Lawrence, an African

American painter from New York, and the music of African American singer Ella Fitzgerald, known for her renditions of "How High the Moon," "Cheek to Cheek," and "A-Tisket, A-Tasket," among many others. Allow students to create art and music that represents the period as well. Similarly, when your students study a specific culture, consider representative art and music. For example, during a unit on Hawaiian culture, examine Hawaiian music and art (Beamer & Duarte, 2009). As a music exemplar, listen to, sing, and evaluate the song "Hawaiian War Chant (Ta-Hu-Wa-Hu-Wai)"; the melody was written in the 1860s by the reigning prince of the Hawaiian Kingdom, Prince Leleiohoku. As visual arts exemplars, inspect and assess traditional Hawaiian art including wood carvings, feather leis, and petroglyphs.

3

Music and Language Arts

Introduction

At their hearts, music and language arts both emphasize human expression. Narratives, whether novels, stories, poems, songs, or symphonies, impart information and communicate emotions. Interacting with narratives in music and language arts encourages students to appreciate a wide variety of texts, critically analyze compelling themes, and develop empathy for another's point of view. By reinforcing the relationships between music and language arts, teachers encourage students to draw connections between and develop understandings in both disciplines. Integrating music and language arts enriches the learning environment, makes learning relevant, and builds a sense of classroom community.

Many lessons can be designed to reinforce student learning in music and language arts. Examples of mutually beneficial strategies and activities include increasing phonemic awareness by exploring connections between pitch discrimination and the differentiation of sounds in speech; songwriting to create new lyrics to aid memory and recall of a set of facts; playing instruments to reinforce the rhythm of chants and poems; journaling to record perceptions about music; comparing the experience of close listening to music and close reading a text; and exploring common concepts such as climax/resolution, perspective, and theme.

The creative and self-expressive aspects of music and language arts are also strongly associated. In verbal communication, students might use vocal inflection, volume, and stress to effectively convey their intent. In a musical performance, students might sing with varied dynamics, rhythmic accents, and differing registers. These connections can encourage student writers and composers to compare the way sounds come together to make words and the way pitches come together to make tunes. There are many other ways connections between music and language arts can inspire creativity. Music can serve as a writing prompt; lyrics can be examined as poetry; texts can be analyzed for structure, rhyme, and literary devices; and students can create new lyrics to align with existing songs. For example, a student or class might write new words that align with the song "Twinkle, Twinkle Little Star":

> When we're walking down the hall,
> We won't talk. No, not at all.
> We will all use walking feet
> Smile at each one that we meet.

Integrating Music Across the Elementary Curriculum. Kristin Harney, Oxford University Press (2020). © Oxford University Press.
DOI: 10.1093/oso/9780190085582.001.0001.

> When we're walking down the hall,
> We won't talk. No, not at all.

The Chapter 3 lessons and inventory of ideas promote a balanced approach to integrating language arts and music content. These lessons and strategies incorporate examples that represent a wide variety of styles, cultures, and historical periods.

Common links between music and language arts

Lessons that explore elements, skills, and broad concepts in music and language arts enhance students' understanding in both disciplines. Enduring ideas that can be explored in music and language arts include:

Action
Cause/effect
Character
Color
Conflict/resolution
Contrast
Fluency
Form/structure (beginning–middle–end; climax–resolution)
Literal and nonliteral meaning
Mood
Pattern
Perspective
Phonemic awareness/pitch discrimination
Power
Repetition
Rhythm
Setting
Sequence
Story line
Style
Subject/main idea/theme
Texture
Unity
Voice
Writing process

National standards

Both the National Core Arts Standards for Music and the Common Core State Standards (CCSS) for English Language Arts encourage interdisciplinary connections. For example, to meet Music Anchor Standard 11, students are expected to "demonstrate understanding of relationships between music and other arts, other disciplines, varied contexts, and daily life" (National Coalition for Core Arts Standards [NCCAS], 2015). Similarly, in the CCSS for English Language Arts there is an explicit focus on integrating and evaluating information from a variety of sources, including musical examples (National Governors Association Center for Best Practices, Council of Chief State School Officers, 2010a). The following boxes specify the standards that are addressed in the Chapter 3 lessons and inventory of ideas:

- Box 3.1, Common Core State Standards for English Language Arts: Reading
- Box 3.2, Common Core State Standards for English Language Arts: Writing
- Box 3.3, Common Core State Standards for English Language Arts: Speaking and Listening
- Box 3.4, Common Core State Standards for English Language Arts: Language
- Box 3.5, National Core Arts Standards for Music

Box 3.6 offers a framework for structuring Chapter 3 lessons and activities.

Box 3.1 Common Core State Standards for English Language Arts (Reading) Included in Chapter 3 Lessons (L) and Inventory of Ideas (I)

READING

Key Ideas and Details	R.1	Read closely to determine what the text says explicitly and to make logical inferences from it; cite specific textual evidence when writing or speaking to support conclusions drawn from the text	L 3.4 I 16
	R.2	Determine central ideas or themes of a text and analyze their development; summarize the key supporting details and ideas	L 3.1 L 3.5 I 5 I 18 I 20
	R.3	Analyze how and why individuals, events, or ideas develop and interact over the course of a text	L 3.3 I 3 I 4
Craft and Structure	R.4	Interpret words and phrases as they are used in a text, including determining technical, connotative, and figurative meanings, and analyze how specific word choices shape meaning or tone	L 3.4 L 3.5 I 12 I 16
	R.5	Analyze the structure of texts, including how specific sentences, paragraphs, and larger portions of the text (e.g., a section, chapter, scene, or stanza) relate to each other and the whole	L 3.1 L 3.3 L 3.4 L 3.5 I 14

READING			
	R.6	Assess how point of view or purpose shapes the content and style of a text	L3.5 I6 I13 I18
Integration of Knowledge and Ideas	R.7	Integrate and evaluate content presented in diverse media and formats, including visually and quantitatively, as well as in words	L3.4 I3 I10
	R.8	Delineate and evaluate the argument and specific claims in a text, including the validity of the reasoning as well as the relevance and sufficiency of the evidence	I2 I6
	R.9	Analyze how two or more texts address similar themes or topics in order to build knowledge or to compare the approaches the authors take	L3.1 I7
Range of Reading and Level of Text Complexity	R.10	Read and comprehend complex literary and informational texts independently and proficiently	L3.1 L3.5 I6 I18

Box 3.2 Common Core State Standards for English Language Arts (Writing) Included in Chapter 3 Lessons (L) and Inventory of Ideas (I)

WRITING			
Text Type and Purposes	W.1	Write arguments to support claims in an analysis of substantive topics or texts using valid reasoning and relevant and sufficient evidence	L3.1 L3.2 L3.4 I1 I6 I18
	W.2	Write informative/explanatory texts to examine and convey complex ideas and information clearly and accurately through the effective selection, organization, and analysis of content	L3.2 L3.3 I2 I19

WRITING

	W.3	Write narratives to develop real or imagined experiences or events using effective technique, well-chosen details, and well-structured event sequences	L3.3 L3.4 I16 I20
Production and Distribution of Writing	W.4	Produce clear and coherent writing in which the development, organization, and style are appropriate to task, purpose, and audience	L3.4 L3.5 I5 I17
	W.5	Develop and strengthen writing as needed by planning, revising, editing, rewriting, or trying a new approach	L3.3 L3.5 I16 I19
	W.6	Use technology, including the Internet, to produce and publish writing and to interact and collaborate with others	L3.2 I14 I15
Research to Build and Present Knowledge	W.7	Conduct short as well as more sustained research projects based on focused questions, demonstrating understanding of the subject under investigation	L3.2 I15 I19
	W.8	Gather relevant information from multiple print and digital sources, assess the credibility and accuracy of each source, and integrate the information while avoiding plagiarism	L3.2 I15 I18
	W.9	Draw evidence from literary or informational texts to support analysis, reflection, and research	L3.1 L3.5 I15
Range of Writing	W.10	Write routinely over extended time frames (time for research, reflection, and revision) and shorter time frames (a single sitting or a day or two) for a range of tasks, purposes, and audiences	L3.2 I2 I17 I20

Box 3.3 Common Core State Standards for English Language Arts (Speaking and Listening) Included in Chapter 3 Lessons (L) and Inventory of Ideas (I)

SPEAKING & LISTENING

Comprehension and Collaboration	SL.1	Prepare for and participate effectively in a range of conversations and collaborations with diverse partners, building on others' ideas and expressing their own clearly and persuasively	L 3.4 L 3.5 I 9 I 15
	SL.2	Integrate and evaluate information presented in diverse media and formats, including visually, quantitatively, and orally	L 3.2 L 3.3 L 3.5 I 4 I 11
	SL.3	Evaluate a speaker's point of view, reasoning, and use of evidence and rhetoric	L 3.4 I 3 I 9
Presentation of Knowledge and Ideas	SL.4	Present information, findings, and supporting evidence such that listeners can follow the line of reasoning and the organization, development, and style are appropriate to task, purpose, and audience	L 3.1 L 3.3 L 3.4 I 1 I 10 I 14
	SL.5	Make strategic use of digital media and visual displays of data to express information and enhance understanding of presentations	L 3.1 L 3.2 L 3.5 I 8 I 10
	SL.6	Adapt speech to a variety of contexts and communicative tasks, demonstrating command of formal English when indicated or appropriate	L 3.2 I 8 I 10

Box 3.4 Common Core State Standards for English Language Arts (Language) Included in Chapter 3 Lessons (L) and Inventory of Ideas (I)

LANGUAGE

Conventions of Standard English	L.1	Demonstrate command of the conventions of standard English grammar and usage when writing or speaking	L3.3 L3.4 I1 I6 I9 I15 I20
	L.2	Demonstrate command of the conventions of standard English capitalization, punctuation, and spelling when writing	L3.2 I1 I6 I16 I20
Knowledge of Language	L.3	Apply knowledge of language to understand how language functions in different contexts, to make effective choices for meaning or style, and to comprehend more fully when reading or listening	L3.1 L3.3 L3.4 L3.5 I3 I11 I14 I15 I19
Vocabulary Acquisition and Use	L.4	Determine or clarify the meaning of unknown and multiple-meaning words and phrases by using context clues, analyzing meaningful word parts, and consulting general and specialized reference materials, as appropriate	L3.3 I2 I3 I8 I12 I18
	L.5	Demonstrate understanding of figurative language, word relationships, and nuances in word meanings.	L3.1 L3.4 I2 I5 I13 I16

LANGUAGE

	L.6	Acquire and use accurately a range of general academic and domain-specific words and phrases sufficient for reading, writing, speaking, and listening at the college and career readiness level; demonstrate independence in gathering vocabulary knowledge when encountering an unknown term important to comprehension or expression	L3.2 L3.4 L3.5 I7 I10 I17

Box 3.5 National Core Arts Standards for Music Included in Chapter 3 Sample Lessons (L) and Inventory of Ideas (I)

MU:Cr1 (Create)	Generate and conceptualize artistic ideas and work	L3.3 I5 I6 I14 I18
MU:Cr2 (Create)	Organize and develop artistic ideas and work	L3.2 L3.5 I1 I13 I14 I18
MU:Cr3 (Create)	Refine and complete artistic work	L3.3 I6 I13 I14 I18
MU:Pr4 (Perform)	Select, analyze, and interpret artistic work for presentation	L3.3 L3.4 L3.5 I7 I9 I15 I20

MU:Pr5 (Perform)	Develop and refine artistic techniques and work for presentation	L3.5 I8 I10 I12
MU:Pr6 (Perform)	Convey meaning through the presentation of artistic work	L3.4 I2 I8 I16
MU:Re7 (Respond)	Perceive and analyze artistic work	L3.1 L3.2 L3.5 I2 I4 I19
MU:Re8 (Respond)	Interpret intent and meaning in artistic work	L3.1 L3.4 I9 I15 I19
MU:Re9 (Respond)	Apply criteria to evaluate artistic work	L3.5 I1 I3 I11 I19
MU:Cn10 (Connect)	Synthesize and relate knowledge and personal experiences to make art	L3.1 L3.2 L3.3 I1 I3 I5 I17 I20
MU:Cn11 (Connect)	Relate artistic ideas and works with societal, cultural, and historical context to deepen understanding	L3.3 L3.4 I11 I13

Box 3.6 Framework for Chapter 3 Lessons and Ideas

This chapter is designed to support K–5 educators as they integrate music and language arts. The lessons are designed to be fully taught by classroom teachers; however, the plans may also facilitate partnerships and collaboration between classroom teachers and music specialists. All lessons and activities have been reviewed by practicing teachers, and most have been field-tested in elementary classrooms. Chapter 3 lessons are labeled as primary, intermediate, or upper elementary, but all the plans and activities are adaptable to a variety of grade levels and are intended as tools for you to meet your students' needs. Some of the lessons may need to be spread over two or more class periods. Please adjust, adapt, or expand however works best for you and for your students.

Lesson 3.1: Comparing and contrasting three versions of Romeo and Juliet

Grade Level: Upper elementary
Essential Question: How do writers and composers approach similar themes in different artistic mediums?

Objectives

- After listening, reading, and singing, students will correctly identify and summarize the setting, plot, perspective, conflict, and mood of three versions of Romeo and Juliet.
- Students will compare and contrast three versions of the Romeo and Juliet story, collaborating to correctly classify the shared and discrete traits of the examples.
- Students will design and deliver a group presentation demonstrating their understanding of the relationships between the three works.

Common Core State Standards for English Language Arts addressed

- CCSS:R2: Key ideas and details
- CCSS:R5: Craft and structure
- CCSS:R9: Integration of knowledge and ideas
- CCSS:R10: Range of reading and level of text complexity

- CCSS:W1: Text type and purposes
- CCSS:W9: Research to build and present knowledge
- CCSS:SL4; CCSS:SL5: Presentation of knowledge and ideas
- CCSS:L3: Knowledge of language
- CCSS:L5: Vocabulary acquisition and use

National Core Arts Standards for Music addressed

- MU:Re7: Perceive and analyze artistic work
- MU:Re8: Interpret intent and meaning in artistic work
- MU:Cn10: Synthesize and relate knowledge and personal experiences to make art

Materials

- Book of your choice that retells of Romeo and Juliet in elementary-appropriate language. Some recommended adaptations:
  - *Illustrated Stories from Shakespeare*, Usborne Publishing
  - *Mr. William Shakespeare's Plays* by Marcia Williams
  - *Romeo and Juliet for Kids* by Lois Burdett
  - *Shakespeare's Stories for Young Readers* by Edith Nesbit
  - *Shakespeare Stories: Four Books in One* by Andrew Matthews
  - *The Stratford Zoo Midnight Revue Presents Romeo and Juliet* (graphic novel) by Ian Lendler
- Musical examples and printed lyrics
  - "Love Story" by Taylor Swift
  - "Rewrite the Stars" from The Greatest Showman
- Triple Venn Diagrams (Figure 3.1)

Procedure

Introduce *Romeo and Juliet* by Shakespeare and read aloud an elementary-level version (see the materials section).

Direct students to consider various aspects of the *Romeo and Juliet* story. Pass out blank index cards and ask students to label the top of their cards "Romeo and Juliet." Project a brief synopsis of the *Romeo and Juliet* script to guide students' responses. Students will keep track of their personal interpretations, using notecards to "hold their thinking." On their cards, students will:

- Define the setting
- List the sequence or create a plot chart
- Create brief character sketches of Romeo and Juliet

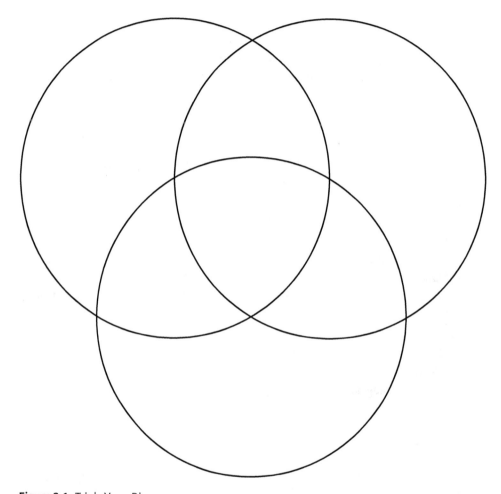

Figure 3.1 Triple Venn Diagram.
© Uncle Ulee/Shutterstock.com.

Through a class discussion, review students' responses, checking for accuracy and understanding, as well as unexpected insights that students may express. Draw students' attention to the elements of conflict in the story. Following a large-group analysis of conflict, ask students to consider how all the various aspects of the story work together to suggest an overall mood. Direct students to add to their note cards:

- Examples of external and internal conflicts
- Mood of the work

Ask pairs of students to identify songs, movies, or TV shows that they think relate to *Romeo and Juliet*. (Some examples might be Disney's *Gnomeo and Juliet, West Side Story*, Disney's *The Lion King II*, and "Romeo and Juliet" by Dire Straits.) Have students share their ideas with the whole class. Consider using short video clips to highlight a few of the examples.

Reveal to students that they will be exploring two musical works that relate to *Romeo and Juliet*: "Love Story" by Taylor Swift and "Rewrite the Stars" from the movie *The Greatest Showman*. Just as students individually analyzed elements of Shakespeare's *Romeo and Juliet,* they will analyze each piece of music.

Project the lyrics for Taylor Swift's "Love Story" and direct students to listen to the recording as they silently read along. Play the song a second time, or, alternately, locate an instrumental version and direct students to sing along. As a class, identify the tempo, harmony, narrative point of view, and language choices. Expected responses from the class analysis of musical elements of "Love Story":

- Tempo: The tempo is fairly fast, which contributes to the song's happy mood.
- Harmony: The song is written in a major key; this gives the song a bright sound; there is a key change (modulation) up a half step that adds emphasis to the section that starts with the lyrics "Marry me, Juliet" (Swift, 2008, track 3).
- Narrative point of view: The whole song is sung from Juliet's first-person narrative point of view except for the ending, which is sung from Romeo's first-person point of view.
- Language choices: Even though Juliet describes difficulties and challenges, the story has a happy ending for the characters.

Using their analysis of the musical elements and the lyrics, individuals will repeat the process they followed for Shakespeare's *Romeo and Juliet* with Taylor Swift's song, again recording their personal interpretations on index cards. Students will:

- Define the setting
- List the sequence or create a plot chart
- Create brief character sketches of Romeo and Juliet
- List examples of external and internal conflicts

- Describe the mood

Again, lead a class discussion to review students' responses regarding the music and the text, checking for accuracy, understanding, and interesting insights.

Direct small groups of students to plan and rehearse sequences of movements that align with and express the musical and literary elements they analyzed. Perform the entire song twice, giving each group one chance to sing and observe and one chance to showcase their created movements (multiple groups can perform their created movement sequences simultaneously).

Follow the same process with the song "Rewrite the Stars" from *The Greatest Showman*.

Expected responses from analysis of musical elements of "Rewrite the Stars":

- Tempo: The tempo is medium fast for most of the song. At the very end, there is a dramatic slowdown that highlights Juliet's sadness.
- Harmony: The song is written in a major key, but we often hear the relative minor chord, giving the song a sense of instability and a darker quality. We hear the highest notes of the melody every time the words "rewrite" and "keep" occur, emphasizing those ideas.
- Narrative point of view: The first verse and chorus are sung from Romeo's first-person point of view. The second verse and chorus are sung from Juliet's first-person point of view. The C section (bridge) and the following chorus are sung by Romeo and Juliet together, and the song ends with Juliet singing in the first person (Pasek & Paul, 2017 track 8).
- Language choices: The first verse and chorus from Romeo's perspective are worded positively. The second verse and chorus from Juliet's point of view are more pessimistic. The C section and the following chorus are sung by Romeo and Juliet together with lyrics that have a hopeful undertone. The final shortened verse is sung by Juliet and almost echoes the opening, but Juliet ends by maintaining that she and Romeo cannot be together.

Divide students into small groups and pass out Venn Diagram templates with three circles (see Figure 3.1) to allow students to compare and contrast three different versions of the Romeo and Juliet narrative, showing how three creators approached a similar theme. Students will work collaboratively to fill out their Venn Diagrams, using the personal interpretations they assembled on each of their three index cards.

In the areas of each circle that are farthest from the center of the graphic organizer (top left, top right, and bottom center) students will list elements that are specific to each work. Where the circles overlap, they will list shared features. The very center of the Venn Diagram will contain characteristics that all three works have in common. (If students are unfamiliar with three-circle Venn Diagrams, complete one together as a class using three items with obvious similarities and differences such as green apples, green grapes, and green beans.)

Assessment

- Written assessment: Collect individuals' index cards and groups' Venn Diagrams to evaluate students' understanding of the setting, plot, characters, themes, conflicts, and mood depicted in *Romeo and Juliet*, "Love Story," and "Rewrite the Stars."
- In-class presentations: Create large three-circle Venn Diagrams on the floor using jump ropes or hula hoops. Using information from their written diagrams, students will prepare a brief presentation for the class, comparing and contrasting one aspect of *Romeo and Juliet*, "Love Story," and "Rewrite the Stars." As each group shares their observations with the class, they will move around the life-sized Venn Diagram and share details that provide evidence for why each element they describe aligns with the specific spot they're standing in, demonstrating their understanding of relationships between the works.

Lesson 3.2: Creating a playlist and creative writing

Grade Level: Primary, intermediate, or upper elementary, depending on adaptations
Essential Question: What criteria and processes do people use to organize and recount experiences?

Objectives

- Students will reflect on their musical lives, demonstrating self-knowledge by thoughtfully connecting music with specific times, people, and events.
- Students will compile a written or graphic record of their reflection, conveying concepts precisely and understandably.
- Students will compile a playlist of music, gathering representative examples from multiple sources and integrating individual components to create a cohesive collection.
- Students will write narrative descriptions of their playlists, appropriately defending their choice of songs and describing their collection using valid reasoning, sufficient detail, and effective organization.

Common Core State Standards for English Language Arts addressed

- CCSS:W1; CCSS:W2: Text type and purposes
- CCSS:W6: Production and distribution of writing
- CCSS:W7; CCSS:W8: Research to build and present knowledge

- CCSS:W10: Range of writing
- CCSS:SL2: Comprehension and collaboration
- CCSS:SL5: Presentation of knowledge and ideas
- CCSS:L2: Conventions of standard English
- CCSS:L6: Vocabulary acquisition and use

National Core Arts Standards for Music addressed

- MU:Cr2: Organize and develop artistic ideas and work
- MU:Re7: Perceive and analyze artistic work
- MU:Cn10: Synthesize and relate knowledge and personal experiences to make art

Materials

- Musical Inventory Logs (see Table 3.1)
- Student access to a variety of musical examples

Procedure

First, encourage students to reflect on the role of music in their lives, both in the past and in the present, examining various influences impacting their musical listening and participation (Harney, 2017).

- Time: Invite students to identify musical examples that they connect with broad life stages. These examples might include their earliest musical memories, music from preschool, favorite songs as toddlers, current favorite songs, songs from any school productions, songs they can play on an instrument, music for listening, music for dancing, or songs they like to sing. Additionally, guide students to consider music that represents specific moments in time or is linked with an important or memorable life event.
- People: Encourage students to think about the musical examples that they associate with important people in their lives. Are there certain songs that will always remind them of their best friends? Their moms? Other significant individuals?
- Purpose: Are there any specific pieces or styles of music that the students typically experience while participating in certain activities (getting ready for school, cleaning up, gymnastics practice, etc.)? Do students ever choose music because they know it will make them feel a certain way (promote a specific mood)? Are there any songs with which students especially identify because of the message contained within the piece?

Next, guide students to document and visually express their musical inventories.

- One option is to pass out Musical Inventory Log Templates to guide students' reflections (see Table 3.1).
- Another idea is to leave the structure more open ended and suggest categories to encourage the creation of more personalized models. Figure 3.2 shows one student's individualized representation. Following their initial reflections, students' choices for their own models can utilize varied ways to show relationships between elements, directionality, etc. Possible categories they might include in their personalized logs include musical styles, musical involvement, chronology, or personally meaningful music.
- Students will then compile a playlist containing pieces that represent and reflect themselves.
    - Depending on the technology available to you, students might simply list titles and composers/performers, or they might curate an actual playlist using Google Play, Spotify, YouTube Playlist, mp3 files on flash drives, etc.
    - Parameters for the collection should include recommendations about length of the playlist (not to exceed a certain number of minutes or number of tracks), details about content (clearly define what is acceptable for school), and instructions about playlist titles (consider having students create titles for their playlists that incorporate their names somehow).

Finally, students will write narrative descriptions of their playlists, providing a rationale for their collections, explaining the particular relationship they feel exists among their selections, and arguing to support the inclusion of each track (Harney, 2017). Encourage them to use concrete details, specific quotes, and examples to support their conclusions. Their descriptions could include a complete list of the selections in their playlist, together with the titles, names of

Table 3.1 Musical Inventory Log Template

Time		People		Purpose	
List important music from different stages of your life		List music connected to important people in your life		List music for certain activities/moods/messages	
Age	Music	Person	Music	Purpose	Music

Courtesy of author.

Figure 3.2 Student Example, Personalized Musical Inventory Log.
Image used with permission.

composers/performers, and durations for all tracks, just as they would appear on a commercial CD.

Assessment

- Collect students' musical inventories and assess the breadth and depth of information presented, specifically noting whether information about individual songs, times, people, and events are conveyed precisely and understandably.
- Collect students' physical or digital playlists and narrative descriptions. Examine the way students defended their choice of songs and described their collections, looking for valid reasoning, sufficient detail, personal examples, and effective organization.

Lesson 3.2 variations

- Allow time for students to share songs from their playlists with the class and express the reasons those songs are important to them.
- Rather than each student creating an entire playlist, students in the class could contribute a single song to a class playlist.
- Invite primary students to reflect about a single song and allow them to share their perceptions in age-appropriate ways. These might include verbal presentations to the class, dictating responses to the teacher, or drawing pictures to reflect specific times, people, or purposes associated with their songs.
- Following students' creation of playlists, consider creating a playlist of your own to share with your students.

Lesson 3.3: Storytelling through movement: "Troika" by Sergei Prokofiev

Grade Level: Primary
Essential Question: How are music, creative movement, and storytelling related?

Objectives

- Students will analyze the structure of "Troika," design plans for creative movement that align with the structure, accurately represent their plans in coherent writing, and verbally present their ideas.
- Students will perform by moving to the music of "Troika," aurally discriminating changes in the instrumentation and correctly indicating the structure by aligning the creative movements from the plans they designed.

Common Core State Standards for English Language Arts addressed

- CCSS:R3: Key ideas and details
- CCSS:R5: Craft and structure
- CCSS:W2; CCSS:W3: Text type and purposes
- CCSS:W5: Production and distribution of writing
- CCSS:SL2: Comprehension and collaboration
- CCSS:SL4: Presentation of knowledge and ideas
- CCSS:L1: Conventions of standard English
- CCSS:L3: Knowledge of language
- CCSS:L4: Vocabulary acquisition and use

National Core Arts Standards for Music addressed

- MU:Cr1: Generate and conceptualize artistic ideas and work
- MU:Cr3: Refine and complete artistic work
- MU:Pr4: Select, analyze, and interpret artistic work for presentation
- MU:Cn10: Synthesize and relate knowledge and personal experiences to make art
- MU:Cn11: Relate artistic ideas and works with societal, cultural, and historical context to deepen understanding

Materials

- Musical example: "Troika" from *Lieutenant Kijé* by Sergei Prokofiev
- Photograph: Russian troika (Figure 3.3)

Procedure

The procedure for this lesson includes a sample script you may use with students.

Figure 3.3 Russian Troika.
© Olga Vasileva/Shutterstock.com.

1. First, set the scene.

   "Imagine it is the middle of winter and we will be taking a special trip—an afternoon sleigh ride to a park. It is very snowy outside, so we are going to have to travel to the park in a sleigh. We have a very special sleigh that needs a certain number of horses to pull it. Listen to the name of the type of sleigh and see if you can tell how many horses we will have: troika."

2. Allow for a variety of student guesses.

   "A troika is a special type of Russian sleigh that takes one, two, three horses to pull it."

3. Show image of a Russian troika (see Figure 3.3).

   "Troika" is also the name of the piece of music by Prokofiev that we're going to hear. The word "troika" uses the same prefix as lots of other words you know like tricycle, triangle, trio, trilogy, or triple-scoop ice cream that all refer to three of something, so a troika is a sleigh pulled by three horses."

4. Next, brainstorm with students about activities they might do at a park in the wintertime and generate a list on the board. Possible ideas include throwing snowballs, building a snowman, drinking hot chocolate, making a snow angel, designing a snow fort, skiing, snowboarding, sledding, playing hockey, and ice skating.

   "These are great ideas. Our list will help us decide which activities we'd like to act out during the recording."

5. Provide students with some context for what they are going to hear in Prokofiev's "Troika."

   "In the music, every time you hear one special instrument, you'll know that the sleigh is moving. Does anyone have a guess what instrument tells us the sleigh is moving?"

6. Allow for student input.

   "Yes, the sleigh bells, which are sometimes called jingle bells, are the instrument you'll hear that will tell us that we're on the move. Grab your horses' reins."

7. Mimic holding reins out in front of your body and encourage students to copy you.

   "Every time you hear the sleigh bells, you're going to show me that you hear them by holding the reins and bouncing your hands with the steady beat."

8. Mimic bouncing the reins.

   "What do you think happens when the sleigh bells stop—what will that tell us?"

9. Hold your hands still.

   "We've stopped. We're somewhere in the park where we're going to get out and play. We're going to stop and play three different times, but we need to plan our story, so we're going to listen to the music sitting down. I don't want you to act out the story yet; I want you to listen and decide what you'd like to do for each stop in the park."

10. Model the introduction of the song for students.

    "First of all, I have to find my house."

11. Stand somewhere in the classroom.

    "Next, I have to look for my barn. My barn is over there, right under the clock."

12. Look toward your "barn" and describe where it is in the classroom.

    "I have to get to the barn by the end of the piece's introduction. It's deep, deep snow, so I'm going to take huge, slow, exaggerated steps, lifting my feet way up above the snow with each step as I follow the beat of the introduction to get over to my barn."

13. Demonstrate your steps while you describe.

    "You should be able to tell I'm going through the deep snow."

14. Go back to your house and start the recording. It will take you 16 beats of deep-snow walking to get to your barn. Keep the music playing. During the next four beats (which conclude the introduction section), say:

    "There's my sleigh. I step into the sleigh with one foot, step in with the other foot, sit down, and grab the reins. When you hear the sleigh bells, show me with your hands."

15. Everyone remains seated and mimics "driving" the sleigh in time with the steady beat of the sleigh bells. As soon as you hear the sleigh bells stop, say:

    "Here's the first stop at the park. What a beautiful winter day. What does this music make you think that you might be doing?"

16. This section is fairly short. The next occurrence of the sleigh bells will likely interrupt their brainstorming.

    "Oh, my goodness, we're already going? Did you have time to build a fort? No, you'll need to pick something quick for that first stop."

17. Keep bouncing the reins until the sleigh bells stop again.

    "Here's the second stop at the park. What does this music sound like you might be doing?"

18. Once the sleigh bells start again, say:

    "That stop was a little longer, wasn't it? There's a big snowbank ahead; we're almost going to tip over—see if you can hear it."

19. If you hear the "snowbank," mimic a tipping motion with your whole body. When the sleigh bells stop again, say:

    "Here is the third stop. This will be our longest stop. So, the order of our stops is first a short stop, then a medium one, then our longest stop. Think what you might do that takes a long time."

20. When the sleigh bells start again, say:

    "Now we're on our way back to our barns. You need to get back to your barn before the coda."

21. When the sleigh bells stop for the final time, you will hear the music transition to the "deep snow" music. Mimic doing high steps on the beat back through the snow to get to your house by the end of the piece.

22. As a class, recreate the structure of "Troika." Alternately, you could have a worksheet prepared with the form already indicated. The basic structure is

Introduction	Twenty beats through deep snow
A	Sleigh ride
B	First stop
A	Sleigh ride

C	Second stop
A	Sleigh ride
D	Third stop
A	Sleigh ride
Coda	Seven beats through deep snow

23. Ask each student to write out a plot sequence and devise a narrative that describes his or her invented trip to the park, following the same overall sequence as the structure of "Troika." Alternately, students might give an oral telling or draw the main sections of their narrative. Use a variety of prompts to guide students' thinking and encourage them to consider character motivations as they develop their narratives:

    "Think about how you will describe your walk from your house to your barn. What are your horses like? What is your sleigh like? What kind of day is it? What does it feel like to ride in the sleigh? What do you see and hear? What will you do at each stop in the park? Why did you choose those activities? You ride in your sleigh many times. How is each sleigh ride similar and different? How do you feel when you get back to your barn? Describe the walk back to your house. What was the best part of your day?"

24. Next, students will discuss their invented trips to the park with a partner, making sure to clearly communicate the different activities included in their narratives. During this writer's workshop time, students will practice their stories and receive feedback from their partners (what makes sense, what appears out of order, which action is the most entertaining, etc.). Given a partner's feedback, students will revise their narratives, then rehearse their actions.

25. Finally, act out the narrative with the recording.

    "Quietly walk to your house, wherever it is in the classroom, and stand in the front doorway."

26. Wait for students to get set.

    "Now, look at your barn. You're going to walk there through the deep snow. When I start the music, you'll start walking. Make sure to listen for when the sleigh bells start so you know when to move around the space. Listen for when the sleigh bells stop so you know when to act out the activities you chose to do in each part of the park."

27. During the introduction and coda sections, students move between their "houses" and their "barns." During the A sections with the sleigh bells, students gallop around the room and bounce the reins on the beat. During the B, C, and D sections, students perform their predetermined actions. The first time you do the activity, you will likely need to call out the sections to redirect students. Consider trying the movement activity again with an added challenge.

    "We're going to try it one more time, but this time I'm not going to say anything out loud. It will be up to you to listen carefully to the music so that you know exactly which part of the story we're on. I'll be watching. Good luck!"

28. You might also ask some students to perform while others view the performances.
29. Conclude with a reflection. Ask students to sit down at the front door of their houses and discuss their final performances, asking questions such as, "What worked?" "What didn't?" "What did you notice?" "How were people's actions similar and dissimilar, and how did the musical elements contribute to that?"

Assessment

- Inspect students' narratives that describe their invented trips to the park. Check for coherent expression of ideas, details that support their points of view, and alignment with the structure of "Troika."
- Observe students' creative movement performances and assess the alignment of their movements with the structure of "Troika" and the plans they designed.
- Ask students to rate themselves on a 1 to 5 scale, with 5 being the highest, on a variety of items, including their musical analysis, planning, alignment of actions with plans, and participation.

Lesson 3.4: Literal and nonliteral meanings in "America the Beautiful"

Grade Level: Intermediate or upper elementary
Essential Question: How does examining the descriptive language in a text help us to discern composers' expressive intent and make interpretive decisions?

Objectives

- Students will accurately interpret and explain various literary devices including simile, metaphor, idiom, hyperbole, personification, onomatopoeia, alliteration, and assonance. They will work collaboratively to detect literary devices in "America the Beautiful" and apply their findings to determine meaning.
- Students will explore the historical background of "America the Beautiful" and examine ways the lyrics transformed over time. They will perform the song, singing with appropriate expressive qualities to reflect the creator's intent.
- Students will create written descriptions that integrate literal and nonliteral phrases and incorporate vivid details.
- Students will participate in small-group presentations, demonstrating appropriate behaviors as presenters and listeners, including sharing their points of

view, expressing themselves clearly, persuading listeners, listening attentively, summarizing points, and asking relevant follow-up questions.

Common Core State Standards for English Language Arts addressed

- CCSS:R1: Key ideas and details
- CCSS:R4; CCSS:R5: Craft and structure
- CCSS:R7: Integration of knowledge and ideas
- CCSS:W1; CCSS:W3: Text type and purposes
- CCSS:W4: Production and distribution of writing
- CCSS:SL1; CCSS:SL3: Comprehension and collaboration
- CCSS:SL4: Presentation of knowledge and ideas
- CCSS:L1: Conventions of standard English
- CCSS:L3: Knowledge of language
- CCSS:L5; CCSS:L6: Vocabulary acquisition and use

National Core Arts Standards for Music addressed

- MU:Pr4: Select, analyze, and interpret artistic work for presentation
- MU:Pr6: Convey meaning through the presentation of artistic work
- MU:Re8: Interpret intent and meaning in artistic work
- MU:Cn11: Relate artistic ideas and works with societal, cultural, and historical context to deepen understanding

Materials

- Musical examples
  - Audio and/or video recording of "America the Beautiful" by Katherine Lee Bates
  - Printed music showing 1919 edition of "America the Beautiful" (Figure 3.7)
  - Printed excerpts of "America the Beautiful" lyrics
- Historical photographs
  - *Gateway to the Gardens of the Gods and Stupendous Pike's Peak (14,157 ft.), Colorado, U.S.A.* (Figure 3.4)
  - *Ascending Pike's Peak in Early Summer—Train at 12,000 ft. altitude, Colorado, U.S.A.* (Figure 3.5)
  - Stereoscope: Antique optical toy (Figure 3.6)

Procedure

Share background information about Katherine Lee Bates and the creation of "America the Beautiful." Alternately, direct students to research the topic in preparation for class presentations and discussion.

In 1893, Katharine Lee Bates, a teacher from Wellesley College, traveled to Colorado Springs, Colorado, to teach a short summer class. While there, she took a train trip to visit the summit of Pikes Peak, one of the highest points in the Rocky Mountains. Figure 3.4 shows a stereoscopic photograph of Pike's Peak from 1905 and Figure 3.5 shows the trip up Pike's Peak from 1906. The images are duplicated side by side so that when they are viewed through a stereoscope (see Figure 3.6), the images appear to have a three dimensional–type depth. Stereoscopes were early attempts at virtual reality; the same basic technology is utilized today in Google Cardboard viewers for cell phones. Bates was so inspired by the expansive view and by the beauty of the landscape around her that she wrote a poem about it.

As a class, listen to "America the Beautiful." For your musical example, consider showing a video recording with the lyrics superimposed so that students can silently follow along with the lyrics while they listen. Next, invite students to sing along, focusing on accurate pitches, rhythms, and diction. If you have a piano, guitar, or other instrument available, accompany the students while they perform the piece again, challenging them to sing the entire first verse from memory. They could also try singing the piece acapella.

Review literal meaning and nonliteral (figurative) meaning. First, ask students for their working definitions of "literal" and "nonliteral." Students might define the word "literal" as "using the real meaning of words" or "saying exactly what you

Figure 3.4 *Gateway to the Gardens of the Gods and Stupendous Pike's Peak (14,157 ft.), Colorado, U.S.A.*, 1905.
© The Library of Congress.

Figure 3.5 *Ascending Pike's Peak in Early Summer—Train at 12,000 ft. Altitude, Colorado, U.S.A.*, 1906.
© The Library of Congress.

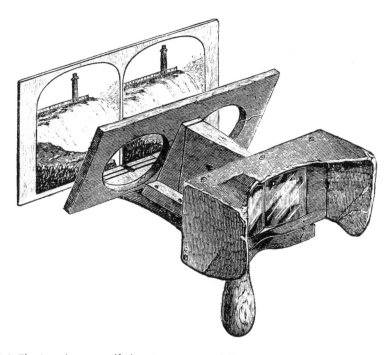

Figure 3.6 The American grandfather stereoscope, 1861.
© Popular Science Monthly, Volume 21/Wikimedia.

mean." They might define "nonliteral" as "when words have don't have their normal meaning" or "using words in different ways for a specific purpose."

Literary devices help us use language to become more effective and interesting writers. Ask students to recall the various literary devices they have studied and direct them to think of examples that represent each type. Some of the most common types you might explore with elementary students are listed, defined, and shown with examples in Table 3.2.

Next, students will analyze the lyrics of "America the Beautiful" with a language arts lens to find meaning in the song. Pass out copies of individual verses to students. Figure 3.7 shows the lyrics of "America the Beautiful" as printed in a 1919 edition of the song. In pairs, students will highlight and label instances where they identify literary devices to create a line of reasoning to explain the author's intent and meaning. Students will speculate about the literal and nonliteral meanings of their assigned verses, then report to the whole class about their portions of the lyrics. Table 3.3 shows some of the phrases students might identify.

Table 3.2 Literary Devices, Definitions, and Examples

Literary Devices	Definitions	Examples
Simile	Making a direct comparison between two things using the words "like" or "as"	She is as busy as a bee. The lake is like a mirror. This backpack is as light as a feather.
Metaphor	Making an implied comparison between two things without using the words "like" or "as"	Jacob was a monkey at the store today. She is a night owl. The test was a breeze.
Idiom	When a set of words are known as a "saying" or an "expression" and mean something different when they are together that they don't mean separately	It is raining cats and dogs. You're driving me up the wall.
Hyperbole	Exaggerating to describe something as better or worse than it really is	I've told you a million times. I'm so hungry, I could eat a horse. The ticking of the clock was deafening.
Personification	Giving human characteristics or qualities to something other than a person	The sun was smiling down. The lawnmower hugged the edge of the driveway.
Onomatopoeia	Using words that imitate the sound of an action or object	I love the sound of a single buzzing bee. The snake gave a quiet hiss. I heard the clang of the trolley bell.
Alliteration	Using two or more words in close succession that begin with the same sound	Donna designs delightful dresses. We would wash with water while we waited.
Assonance	Using two or more words in close succession that repeat the same vowel sound	Pam acted mad about the damp cat in her lap. Take away the plain glazed cakes you made.

Courtesy of author.

Bates's poem was first published in 1895 (Sherr, 2001). Read, then sing the words from the original first stanza and ask students to listen for differences between this version and the version they previously analyzed and performed.

> O beautiful for halcyon skies,
> For amber waves of grain,

For purple mountain majesties
Above the enameled plain!
America! America!
God shed His grace on thee,
Till souls wax fair as earth and air
And music-hearted sea! (Bates, 1897)

Figure 3.7 "America the Beautiful," sheet music, in *National Songs of the Allies,* 1919.
© The Library of Congress.

The words of the original first stanza are similar to the version of "America the Beautiful" we know today, but they are not exactly the same. Bates herself adjusted the text as it became more popular. Almost right away, people began singing her

Table 3.3 Examples of Literary Devices in "America the Beautiful"

Literary Device	Examples from "America the Beautiful"
Simile	
Metaphor	Waves of grain
Idiom	Sea to shining sea
Hyperbole	
Personification	O beautiful for pilgrim feet, whose stern impassion'd stress O beautiful for patriot dream, that sees beyond the years And crown thy good Purple mountain majesties
Onomatopoeia	
Alliteration	Spacious skies Mountain majesties
Assonance	Waves of grain Freedom beat Cities gleam

Courtesy of author.

poem to various tunes. The most popular choice was a tune called "Materna" by composer Samuel A. Ward. The pairing of Bates's poem and Ward's tune is the version we sing today. They were first published together in 1912.

Have students analyze the structure of the poem "America the Beautiful." Each stanza is organized in phrases that contain a consistent number of syllables across verses. The syllables fall into the pattern 86868686, also known as common meter doubled, or CMD.

8   O beautiful for spacious skies,
6   For amber waves of grain,
8   For purple mountain majesties
6   Above the fruited plain!
8   America! America!
6   God shed His grace on thee
8   And crown thy good with brotherhood
6   From sea to shining sea (Bates & Ward, 1919)

Lead a discussion about ways that historical and social context can influence a performance, asking individual students to explain their insights. Through group consensus, students will make interpretive decisions regarding expressive qualities they will employ in a performance of "America the Beautiful" to reflect the creator's intent. They may decide to manipulate musical elements such as dynamics, enunciation, tempo, and phrasing. As a whole class, students will sing "America the Beautiful," demonstrating their understanding through a technically accurate and expressive performance that aligns with their interpretation of the musical components of the song.

Next, ask students to identify a place they appreciate. Their location can be anywhere in the world and can represent any type of environment. In preparation for creating a musical verse, they will write brief descriptions of their places, integrating literal and nonliteral phrases that portray the location. Students' descriptions should show an appreciation for the surrounding environment, incorporate vivid details, provide rationales for the locations they chose, and persuade others to consider visiting the destinations. Direct students to revise and adjust their written descriptions to fit the syllabic pattern of 86868686 and the rhyme scheme that is found in "America the Beautiful."

Divide students into small groups and ask them to share about the creation of their verses. When students present, they should express themselves clearly, speak persuasively about their locations, and sing their verses for the group. When students are in the audience role, they should listen attentively, be ready to summarize points the speaker has made, and ask relevant follow-up questions. Invite each small group to nominate one of their group member's compositions for the entire class to sing to the tune of "America the Beautiful."

Assessment

- Evaluate students' written and verbal explanations and applications of literary devices, checking for accurate, precise information; proper use of the conventions of standard English; and effective participation as presenters and listeners.
- Evaluate students' planning strategies and preparation for a final performance of "America the Beautiful," as well as their final singing performance of the work, observing the suitability of the interpretive decisions they made regarding expressive qualities in reflecting the creator's intent.
- Post eight papers around the perimeter of the room, each clearly printed with one of the following literary devices: simile, metaphor, idiom, hyperbole, personification, onomatopoeia, alliteration, and assonance. For an informal snapshot of student understanding, project a phrase or sentence that displays a literary device. Ask students to determine the device exhibited, move without speaking, and stand in front of the corresponding paper to indicate their answer. Repeat with a variety of prompts.

Lesson 3.5: Blackout poetry, word choice, and Sibelius's "Finlandia"

Grade Level: Intermediate or upper elementary

Essential Question: How do composers and writers create works that effectively communicate?

Objectives

- Students will explore Jean Sibelius's motivation to compose his work "Finlandia" and identify ways Sibelius exhibited rhetorical awareness by using specific structural, rhythmic, and stylistic techniques to portray Finnish patriotism to his audience.
- Students will apply their understanding of the context surrounding the creation of "Finlandia" to thoughtfully interpret and sing an English translation.
- Students will exhibit rhetorical awareness by engaging with word play, word selection, and conciseness to create blackout poems that effectively convey a message to an audience.

Common Core State Standards for English Language Arts addressed

- CCSS:R2: Key ideas and details
- CCSS:R4; CCSS:R5; CCSSR6: Craft and structure
- CCSS:R10: Range of reading and level of text complexity
- CCSS:W4; CCSS:W5: Production and distribution of writing
- CCSS:W9: Research to build and present knowledge
- CCSS:SL1; CCSS:SL2: Comprehension and collaboration
- CCSS:S:5: Presentation of knowledge and ideas
- CCSS:L3: Knowledge of language
- CCSS:L6: Vocabulary acquisition and use

National Core Arts Standards for Music addressed

- MU:Cr2: Organize and develop artistic ideas and work
- MU:Pr4: Select, analyze, and interpret artistic work for presentation
- MU:Pr5: Develop and refine artistic techniques and work for presentation
- MU:Re7: Perceive and analyze artistic work
- MU:Re9: Apply criteria to evaluate artistic work

Materials (see references for full information)

- Art supplies

- Black markers
- Individual pages removed from books (To eliminate possible copyright issues, use books from the public domain. Suggested titles include *Little Women* by Louisa May Alcott, *Peter Pan* by J. M. Barrie, *The Wonderful Wizard of Oz* by L. Frank Baum, *The Secret Garden* by Frances Hodgson Burnett, *Oliver Twist* and *A Christmas Carol* by Charles Dickens, *Treasure Island* by Robert Louis Stevenson, *The Adventures of Huckleberry Finn* by Mark Twain, and *The Time Machine* by H. G. Wells.)
- Recorded musical examples
  - "Finlandia" by Jean Sibelius
  - Optional recorded performance of "Finlandia" by the BBC Singers, BBC Symphony, and BBC Symphony Orchestra, conducted by Sakari Oramo
- Poetry example: "Finlandia" by V. A. Koskenniemi, translated by Keith Bosley

Procedure

Share background information about Finnish history, Jean Sibelius, and his piece "Finlandia" (Dahlström & Hepokoski, 2001) or direct students to research the country, composer, and composition in preparation for class presentations and discussions.

The symphonic tone poem "Finlandia" was written by Jean Sibelius, a composer from Finland who lived from 1865 to 1957. A symphonic tone poem is a piece of music for orchestra that is written to evoke the content of a poem or story or, in some cases, to give a musical impression of a specific landscape. In the case of "Finlandia," Sibelius was inspired by a patriotic poem, "The Breaking of Ice on the Ulea River," by Finnish poet Zachria Topelius. Through his music, Sibelius wanted to communicate the energy, pride, and resolve that is represented in the poem.

When Sibelius was born, Finland was not an independent country; it was part of the Russian Empire and was known as The Grand Duchy of Finland. Figure 3.8 shows Finland before it became an independent country.

Share an overview of Finnish history that relates to Sibelius's "Finlandia" (Lavery, 2006). In 1809, following the Finnish War, Sweden granted Russia control over Finland. The Russian czar, Alexander I, promised that the religion, laws, and government of Finland would be maintained and unshaken. This agreement was in place until 1899, when Nicholas II, the czar at that time, started imposing more Russian influence over the people of Finland. He decreed that Finnish people had to use Russian money, speak the Russian language, have all their newspapers censored by Russian authorities, and adopt the Orthodox Russian Church as their official church. The Finnish people saw these actions as Russia taking their rights and destroying Finnish culture. Some Finnish writers, artists, and musicians protested the situation and promoted the importance of Finnish culture with their compositions and creations. Since the Russian government would censor and suppress any obvious

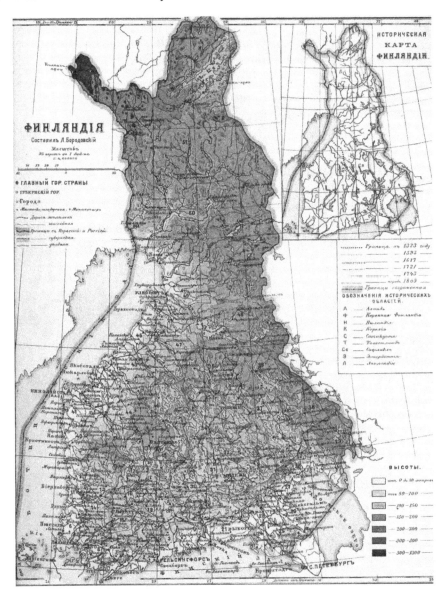

Figure 3.8 Russian map of the Grand Duchy of Finland, ca. 1900.
© Brockhaus and Efron Encyclopedic Dictionary/Wikimedia.

protests, their objections had to be covert. In late 1899, a protest concert was organized; however, the concert was publicized as a benefit called "Press Celebrations of 1899." Sibelius composed a set of pieces for the concert and gave the entire set the title "Music for the Days of the Press" so that it wouldn't raise any suspicions.

The piece lasts about eight minutes, depending on the tempo the conductor takes. There are four main ideas in the music. These musical ideas can be labeled as (1) heroism, (2) reflection, (3) rhythmic pattern, and (4) hymn. First, there is a one-minute introduction with loud, heroic chords played by the brass, bassoon, and contrabass, and a powerful timpani roll in the middle. Immediately following the introduction, a new, reflective melody is introduced by the woodwinds, which is then echoed by the strings. In the next section, which begins around 2:45, the tempo increases and the brass introduce a loud 16th-note pattern that becomes the new rhythmic motif. You can hear this rhythmic pattern punctuated throughout the third section. The end of the third section, around 5:00, is characterized by a very obvious decrescendo, which leads to the fourth musical idea, a hymn-like tune that we now know as "The Finlandia Hymn." The hymn melody is played first by the woodwinds, then the strings. The final section, approximately the last minute of the piece, is marked by a return to a previous musical idea, the loud, boisterous 16th-note rhythmic pattern. Sibelius concludes the composition with loud, full, triumphant chords played by the entire orchestra.

After the premier, people wrote words to accompany the hymn section of "Finlandia." At first, Sibelius was a bit confused by this practice. He said, "It is not intended to be sung. It is written for an orchestra. But if the world wants to sing it, it can't be helped" (Finnish Club of Helsinki, n.d., para. 17). Many people have set lyrics to the hymn tune. One of the most famous versions of the lyrics was written in 1939 by Finnish poet V. A. Koskenniemi, and these are the lyrics that Sibelius used when he created an arrangement of "Finlandia" for mixed choir in 1948. A well-known translation of Koskenniemi's poem was created by Keith Bosley and published in 1997 in the book *Skating on the Sea: Poetry from Finland*. Ask students to take turns reading Bosley's English translation:

> Finland, behold, thy daylight now is dawning,
> the threat of night has now been driven away.
> The skylark calls across the light of morning,
> the blue of heaven lets it have its way,
> and now the day the powers of night is scorning:
> thy daylight dawns, O Finland of ours!
>
> Finland, arise, and raise towards the highest
> thy head now crowned with mighty memory.
> Finland, arise, for to the world thou criest
> that thou hast thrown off thy slavery,
> beneath oppression's yoke thou never liest
> Thy morning's come, O Finland of ours! (Bosley, 1997, p. 196)

Listen to "Finlandia" with students. A performance of "Finlandia" by the BBC Singers, BBC Symphony, and BBC Symphony Orchestra, conducted by Sakari Oramo, is available on YouTube. The video draws attention to different groups of instruments as they play more prominent aspects of the music, helping to provide visual cues to the overall structure of the piece, but any orchestral recording of "Finlandia" will work. Ask students to raise their hands when they hear each new section in the music. To help students focus, you might ask them to record their impressions of the music as they listen, using a tool such as the Arts Analysis Template (see Table 2.1).

Perform the "Finlandia" hymn tune as a class. Choose one of the many translations or settings of the lyrics. Many video recordings also include lyrics as a part of the video.

Share some concluding comments about the piece with students (Dahlström & Hepakoski, 2001). Even though Finland was not a self-governing country when Sibelius wrote "Finlandia," his music supported the idea of an independent, hopeful, and strong Finnish nation. The piece became very popular and fostered national-istic pride among Finnish people. By 1901, it was already being called by the name "Finlandia." The piece is sometimes called Finland's unofficial national anthem. Finland has been an independent nation since 1917.

Introduce students to blackout poetry. Writing involves a series of choices and this portion of the lesson focuses on word selection. Inform students that they will need to choose a set of words that will best express the story they want to tell or the ideas they want to share. This is similar to the way that Sibelius employed mu-sical elements to convey his ideas about Finnish patriotism. When his piece was first performed, Sibelius was worried about it being censored. He needed to make sure to choose melodies and rhythms that would clearly convey his message to his listeners.

In blackout poetry, the poet uses an existing document, like a newspaper article, a story in a magazine, or a page from a book. To create a poem, the poet crosses out al-most all the printed text, leaving behind only the words that then become the poem. Figure 3.9 shows an example of a blackout poem. The 11 words that remain after the blackout process are the text of the poem.

Explain the steps that students will follow to create their own blackout poems. Consider creating a class blackout poem using a document camera to demonstrate each step, perhaps using a copy of the lyrics of "Finlandia" as the basis of the poem. Hand each student one page from a book. A book you have read as a class is an ideal choice. See suggested books in the public domain listed in the materials section of this lesson plan.

- Determine the maximum number of words to choose. (Students should plan to eventually settle on a fairly small number of words—no more than 10% of the total words on the page. If you want to add a step, you can have students count the total number of words on their given pages and calculate their total max-imum number of words.)
- Scan the page for words that stand out. Rather than reading the page from be-ginning to end, let your eyes move around the page. Maybe these are words that repeat, maybe there are words that follow a theme, or maybe there are words that jump out for a different reason. (Students' choice of words and themes do not need to directly relate to "Finlandia.")

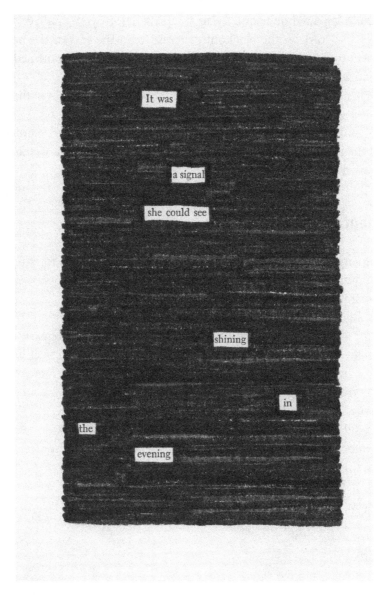

Figure 3.9 Example of blackout poetry.
Courtesy of author.

- Continue selecting words, focusing on examples that will aid in clearly conveying a message to the audience. Look up any unfamiliar words before disregarding them. Perhaps you will only choose key nouns, adjectives, and verbs as the words that will tell your story. You may want to look for connecting words like "and," "of," and "the" to help your reader understand your meaning.
- Using a pencil, lightly outline the words you plan to include in your poem.

- Try reading your poem quietly to yourself before you finalize your word choices and start on the blackout process. Read the text of the poem from top to bottom and left to right as usual, shifting from outlined word to outlined word.
- Switch to a black marker and black out all the words that are not outlined.

Listen to "Finlandia" as students work on their poems. When students have completed their poems, allow students to share with the class, clarifying decisions regarding word choice and message.

Assessment

- During large-group discussion, analysis, and singing, check for students' understanding of the structural, rhythmic, and stylistic elements of "Finlandia" demonstrated in their verbal descriptions and performances.
- Assess students' written blackout poems and verbal accounts of their work, checking for effective use of word choice and a message that is clearly conveyed.
- Informally assess students with a "roll the dice" activity. Project a set of six prompts. In table groups, each student takes turn rolling the dice and responding to the corresponding prompt:
  1. If I needed to explain today's lesson to a friend, I would say . . .
  2. I could apply what I learned today in another situation by . . .
  3. Composers and writers create works that effectively communicate by . . .
  4. I'm still confused about . . .
  5. The best thing about today's lesson was . . .
  6. One connection between music and writing is . . .

Extensions

- Explore the connection between negative space in music and poetry. In music, moments of silence impact listeners by giving an aural sense of negative space. Similarly, blackened spaces in poems heighten the impact of the remaining words and provide a visual sense of negative space.
- Explore censorship in greater detail. Show redactions, such as government records or official court documents, and discuss reasons people might black out text.
- Try a different type of word choice poetry utilizing pre-existing text. After selecting the words for the poem, instead of blacking out the remaining text, create artwork in the negative space or design a way to visually connect the words. This method allows the poet to make use of words in ways beyond a traditional left-to-right and top-to-bottom arrangement (see Figure 3.10 and Figure 3.11).

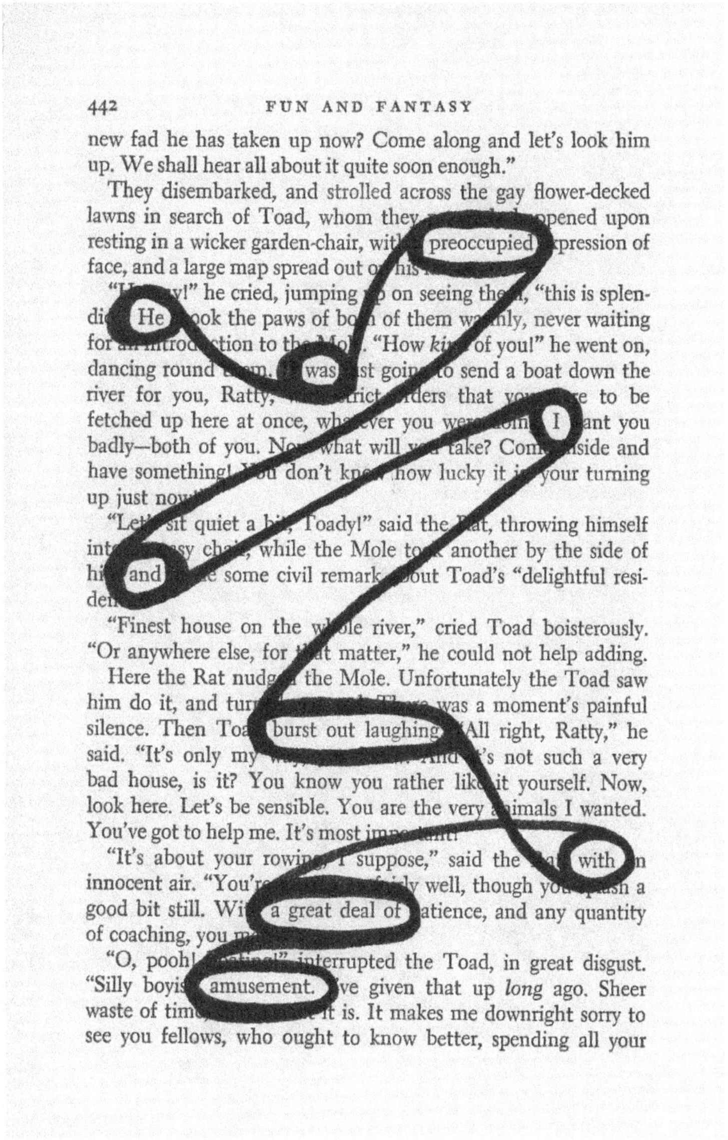

Figure 3.10 Example of alternate-style blackout poetry.
Courtesy of author.

Inventory of ideas

The following collection of ideas contains additional lesson topics, specific teaching strategies, and recommended activities.

1. Explore the idea of precision in music and writing. Listen to a recording of Tchaikovsky's popular festival piece, "1812 Overture." Toward the end of the piece, Tchaikovsky wrote in 16 cannon blasts at precise points in the score.

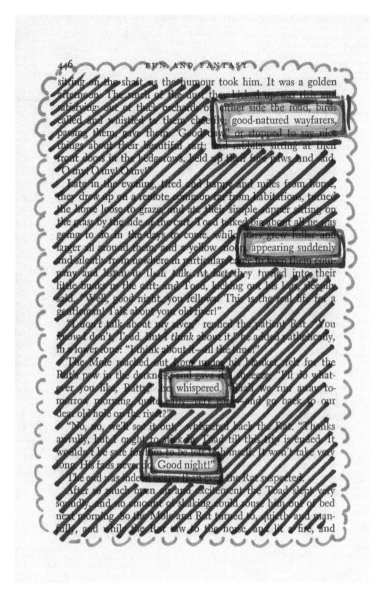

Figure 3.11 Example of alternate-style blackout poetry, 2019.
Image courtesy of Liana Bauman.

While it is now possible to place the cannons exactly in line with the rhythm of the music by using audio recordings, editing, and technological assistance, this was not an option when Tchaikovsky composed the piece in 1880. Even today, if "1812 Overture" is performed outdoors with live cannons or fireworks, precision is almost impossible. Invite students to write a letter to Tchaikovsky, describing the effect of imprecise cannons and suggesting possible adjustments to his composition.

2. The following strategies suggest additional ways that music can serve as a prompt for writing:

- Listen to and sing the song "Imagine" by John Lennon, and then pick your favorite line from the text. Use that line as the basis for a new poem or narrative. Match the emotional quality or style of the new text to the overall character of the song, as evidenced by its instrumentation, dynamics, phrasing, slow tempo, and repetition.

- Review the proper format for personal letters, and then listen to a song such as the The Chicks' "Travelin' Soldier," the American Civil War song "When Johnny Comes Marching Home," John Kander's "A Letter From Sullivan Ballou," or John Michael Montgomery's "Letters From Home." Invite students to write a letter to a current member of the armed forces. Partner with one of the many organizations that coordinate letter-writing campaigns to distribute the letters.

- Watch a performance of *The Nutcracker* ballet and write an alternate ending.

- In the song "Coal Miner's Daughter," Loretta Lynn sings about her childhood, providing specific details that allow the listener to imagine what she experienced. Ask students to write about events from when they were younger, using word choice and key details to vividly portray their experiences.

- Sing the "Star-Spangled Banner" and use context clues, reference materials, and class discussion to determine and clarify the meaning of the lyrics. Seek out a venue where your class might perform the "Star-Spangled Banner" for a specific event.

- Locate a short animated film without any dialogue. Listen to the film score without projecting the video images. Divide students into small groups and ask them to infer the setting, characters, and storyline, based solely on the soundtrack they heard. Direct students to produce a narrative that aligns with the score, then share their story with the whole class, reading over the background music. Finally, present the animated film with sounds and images. Discuss the creator's intended setting, characters, and storyline.

- Listen to and sing the song "L.O.V.E." by Nat King Cole, and then use the experience to guide students' creation of their own acrostic poems and/or lyrics. Challenge students to create melodies, rhythms, and/or accompaniments for their poems and lyrics.

3. Start with a poem, such as "Afternoon on a Hill" by Edna St. Vincent Millay. In this case, you might choose to explore rhyme, personification, setting, mood, or poetic form.

> I will be the gladdest thing
> Under the sun!
> I will touch a hundred flowers
> And not pick one.

I will look at cliffs and clouds
 With quiet eyes,
Watch the wind bow down the grass,
 And the grass rise.
And when lights begin to show
 Up from the town,
I will mark which must be mine,
 And then start down! (Millay, 1917, p. 41)

Divide students into small groups and play short excerpts from a variety of musical examples. Allow students to judge each piece in small groups, choosing which example is the best fit for the poem and justifying the criteria on which they based their decision. Alternately, you could start with a musical example and ask students to rationalize with which character from a book the piece might be associated.

4. Compare storytelling in music and literature and explore one of Mozart's best known operas, *The Magic Flute*. Read a condensed version of the story such as *The Magic Flute: The Story of Mozart's Opera* by Margaret Greaves. Ask students to retell or act out the story, demonstrating an understanding of the complex storyline by correctly describing the events and characters. Listen to highlights of the opera. Alternately, show a video such as the British Broadcasting Corporation's animated version, *The Magic Flute,* created in association with the Welsh National Opera. Following a discussion of the musical elements of the opera, ask students to describe ways that the music is important for fully understanding the story, and ways that the storyline is essential for fully appreciating the music.

5. Augment a close reading assignment by adding a close listening component, making it relevant to students' lives. Model the process with a song such as Louis Armstrong's "What a Wonderful World," Joni Mitchell's "Both Sides Now," or John Denver's "Rocky Mountain High." Ask students to choose songs to analyze on their own. For the close reading portion of the lesson, instruct students to carefully read the lyrics to determine the theme. Provide them with a notetaking method for recording passages where the theme of the text is indicated by specific literary elements. For the close listening portion, direct students to carefully listen to an instrumental-only version of the song and to again consider theme. Students will record their perceptions, noting how specific musical elements (tempo, melody, harmony, instrumentation, etc.) contribute to their understanding of the overall theme. Read and listen multiple times to clarify and reinforce understanding. Close the lesson by performing each song, recombining the lyrics and the music.

6. Investigate ways people use their voices to demonstrate their opinions or feelings about specific issues. Some ways that people are empowered to speak out include protesting, writing letters to government representatives, giving

speeches, and writing editorials. Evaluate the song "Roar" by Katy Perry as an effective mode for sharing her opinions, exploring the overall message of the song shaped by the lyrics, melody, rhythm, and style. Sing "Roar" together as a class, then encourage individual students to create song lyrics that express their personal point of view on a specific topic. Allow time for students to share their compositions with the class.

7. Compare and contrast songs that all explore a common theme, for example, "Here Comes the Sun" by the Beatles, "Here Comes the Sun" by Jacob Collier, "You Are My Sunshine" by Jimmie Davis, and "You Are the Sunshine of My Life" by Stevie Wonder.

8. Explore the connection between rhythm in music and rhythm in reading. Play a recording such as the finale of "William Tell Overture." Ask students to pat, march, conduct, or otherwise move to the beat. Connect the feeling of performing to a musical steady beat to the steady beat required in chant-like group reading. Reading examples might include short excerpts of Dr. Seuss books, Mother Goose rhymes, or other chants, raps, cheers, or poems.

9. Use a song such as "Home on the Range," "Take Me Out to the Ballgame," or "Rock Around the Clock" as a springboard for the creation of interview questions. Students will practice listening and research skills by interviewing a person about an event or topic suggested by a class performance of the song.

10. Use singing to reinforce reading skills in music and language arts. Specific skills that relate to both music and language arts include perceiving differences in symbols, reading or tracking from left to right, utilizing inflection, and strategies that impact fluency such as natural phrasing and reading at an appropriate speed. Singing familiar songs together as a group while "reading" the lyrics builds early readers' self-confidence and motivation. Additionally, songs often follow predictable or prescribed patterns and are usually a manageable length for teacher modeling or think-alouds.

11. Paul Lansky is an American composer especially known for his work with electronic music. His fascination with the human voice and with the sounds and content of speech can be heard in a collection of his pieces on the album *More Than Idle Chatter*. All the works on the album were written for computer-synthesized tape and were created by layering synthesized voices and fragments of speech. The specific way the words and fragments have been arranged, combined, and manipulated gives these pieces their particular sound and offers listeners a new way of hearing speech as music. Listen to a few excerpts from the album and discuss the intersection of speech and music with students. How do we define music? Do lyrics always tell a story?

12. Use the lyrics of a song such as "The Battle of New Orleans" by Jimmy Driftwood or "The Fox" by Nickel Creek as a text for identifying nouns, verbs, or other parts of speech. Before analyzing the song, listen to it and sing it to familiarize students with the lyrics and provide them full context for the words in use.

13. Choose a song that is unfamiliar to students and ask them to interpret the lyrics as poetry. Print the lyrics of the song and direct students to make voice recordings of the "poem." As a class, listen to the various recorded examples and explore the diverse ways the poem was interpreted. Discuss the impact that different spoken versions had. Share with students that the poem is actually a song and listen to a recording. Again, review how the performance affects the listener's interpretation, especially focusing on meaning that the melody, rhythm, and stylistic elements add. Ask students to reflect about their initial spoken interpretations of the text and to consider whether or not they would adapt their spoken interpretation after hearing the song.

14. As a community-building activity at the beginning of the year, listen to the song "I've Got a Dream" from Disney's *Tangled*. Invite individual students to write about their hopes and dreams for the year, their futures, and the future of the world. Next, engage students in a cycle of peer editing, followed by the creation of final drafts of the writing assignment. Direct students to analyze the rhythmic structure of "I've Got a Dream" in small groups (you could also use a teacher-created template). Next, ask them to create a verse that includes the dreams of each person in the group and aligns with the rhythmic structure of the song. Finally, invite small groups to perform their verses for the class.

15. Discuss the ways ideas are transmitted and changed over time by comparing and contrasting original songs and cover songs (Harney, 2015b). Historically, the term "cover song" referred to a new recording, created to compete with the original version. During the 1950s, white bands would often "cover" the songs of black singers. The currently accepted definition of a cover song is a new performance of a copyrighted song, by someone other than the original composer or performer. "A Groovy Kind of Love" is one example. Listen to a variety of covers of "A Groovy Kind of Love," including Phil Collins's 1998 version, the Mindbenders's 1965 version, and a version released earlier in 1965, written by Toni Wine and Carole Bayer Sager and performed by the musical duo Diane and Annita. Next, locate Clementi's "Sonatina in G Major, Op. 36 No. 5," written around the turn of the 19th century. When you listen to Clementi's composition, you can hear how closely it is related to "A Groovy Kind of Love," even though the style is completely different. Form small groups and ask students to analyze an original song of their choice along with a cover of that song. After analyzing the musical elements of each piece individually, students will compare the two, answering questions such as:

    What are obvious similarities and differences?
    What are more subtle similarities and differences?
    What did the cover artist change and why were those changes made?
    Which version is better known? Why do you think this is?
    What are other interesting connections that are unique to your two recordings?

16. Locate and sing a song with symbolism such as "Grandfather's Clock" by Johnny Cash. Analyze the music and text for examples of symbolism, and then write a four-line poem that includes symbolism but avoids the words "like" and "as."

17. In 1899, the *Washington Post* organized an essay contest for students (Bierley, 1984). At the celebration and awards ceremony on June 16, 1899, John Philip Sousa, composer, conductor, and leader of the Marine Band, performed the march he wrote for the occasion, "The Washington Post March" (see Figure 3.12). Essay contest winners received gold medals for their work. Create guidelines for a friendly essay contest in your classroom and have students

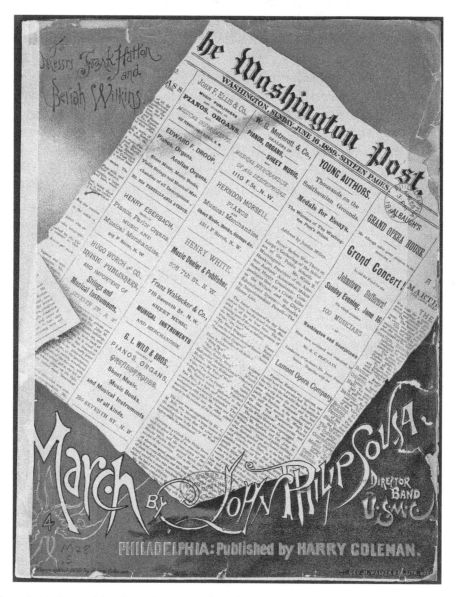

Figure 3.12 Cover of the piano sheet music for John Philip Sousa's "Washington Post," 1889.
© The Library of Congress.

submit written entries. At the awards ceremony, celebrate by listening to a recording of "The Washington Post March" and marching around the classroom with the steady beat of the music.

18. Conduct a literary and musical analysis of various advertising jingles. What is the impact of music on consumers' actions and intentions? Connect your findings to persuasive writing and ask students to write the text for a short commercial advertising a product of their choice.

19. Generate a written review of a recorded piece of music, using either a descriptive or an evaluative style. Descriptive reviews might include reflections about images that came to mind, feelings that were elicited, key words or phrases that resonated, or the overall message of the piece. Evaluative reviews might include appraisals of specific musical elements and opinions about the quality of the performance.

20. Listen to "Mr Trololo," sung by Russian Eduard Anatolyevich Khil, a recording that went viral in 2009. Since there are no actual lyrics in the song, direct students to interpret the meaning and write a response. "What might Mr. Trololo be saying and why?" This song could also make a fun clean-up song for students to sing at the very end of the school day, as the full title of the song is translated as "I am very glad because I'm finally returning back home." Google created a Doodle celebrating what would have been the singer's 83rd birthday, on September 3, 2017.

4

Music and Social Studies

Introduction

Music should be studied alongside the time period and culture in which it was created. Through the study of history, students can examine the fundamental ideas and feelings of a time period and then discern ways those ideas and feelings influenced or inspired the music of that time. Likewise, students can examine music that was created at a certain point in history and consider how those pieces influenced people living at the time. Music not only reflects the time during which it was created but also influences the way listeners think or behave.

The study of multicultural music prepares students to become global citizens and reflects the diversity of our schools, communities, and world. Accessible travel, developments in media and technology, and changes in classroom make-up are creating greater opportunities for interaction between various cultural groups. When students from different cultures explore each other's music, they gain musical understandings and learn about one another as people. Diversity, rather than homogeneity, characterizes our world and should characterize our curricular content as well.

Integrating music and social studies may promote student interest and engagement, encouraging vivid experiences with beliefs, values, and traditions. Incorporating music can be an effective way to initially hook and then continue to hold students' attention in social studies lessons. This might be attributed to music's capacity for capturing students' emotions in ways that written or spoken words cannot (Reimer, 2003). For example, Jimmy Cox's "Nobody Knows You When You're Down and Out," recorded by Bessie Smith in 1929, offers a different perspective about the "universal" wealth and prosperity of the 1920s in America. The song provides students with a window into a single individual's perception of the era and helps them to connect personally with the content.

Music also gives students a richer representation of the past, reflecting the more cultural, personal, and expressive side of history, as well as portraying the hopes, dreams, and accomplishments of people from within a specific culture, community, or time. For example, Leadbelly's "Pick a Bale of Cotton" portrays conditions on slave plantations through the descriptive lyrics and the musical elements that denote the high productivity that was demanded of workers. Another example, "Asikatali," a traditional South African Zulu freedom song, includes lyrics that can be translated as "We are the children of Africa and it's for freedom that we're fighting now . . . they took our lands, they took our homes," and "We will stand up united" (Songs for Teaching, n.d.), providing students with insights about the thoughts and actions of youth living through apartheid.

Integrating Music Across the Elementary Curriculum. Kristin Harney, Oxford University Press (2020). © Oxford University Press.
DOI: 10.1093/oso/9780190085582.001.0001.

Lessons that integrate music and social studies have the potential to enrich students' understanding in both disciplines. Students who explore the historical and cultural background of a specific piece of music are better equipped to perform, listen to, and reflect about that piece. For example, a student who understands the circumstances surrounding the creation of the song "This Land Is Your Land" by Woodie Guthrie is better prepared to give a sensitive performance of the piece; a student who recognizes the intention behind Staff Sgt. Barry Sadler's "Ballad of the Green Berets," a popular song from the Vietnam War era that portrays the military in a positive light, will listen with heightened awareness; and a student who can empathize with the situation described in Dame Ethel Smyth's "March of the Women," a song written in 1911 for the Women's Social and Political Union, will have a greater understanding of the Women's Suffrage Movement in American history.

The Chapter 4 lessons and the lesson ideas included in the Chapter 4 inventory of ideas draw on a variety of musical material, including folk songs, ballads, popular music, works from the classical repertoire, and pieces representative of multiple cultures. Students will not only experience and examine musical examples but also apply and connect their understandings to specific social studies concepts, including describing the political, economic, and social constructs of cultural groups from varying times and places; drawing conclusions about the causes and consequences of events and developments; and examining the way people transmit beliefs and values (National Council for the Social Studies [NCSS], 2010). Music can provide a safe avenue for exploring an almost unlimited array of social studies topics including immigration, citizenship, taxation, surveillance, civil rights, racism, income inequality, poverty, homelessness, sexual orientation, gender identity, gender equality, natural disasters, global warming, overpopulation, disease, terrorism, bullying, and animal rights. It is not possible to address all these worthwhile topics in this chapter, although many of the ideas are incorporated in the Chapter 4 lessons and inventory of ideas (see especially Inventory Idea 5). The integration of music and social studies also leads students to connect with the people of various cultures and times—their lives, their actions, and their reasons for making music. Chapter 4 provides K–5 teachers with compelling lessons and activities that encourage substantial interaction with social studies and music content and have the potential to enrich students' musical, historical, and cultural understandings in profound and lasting ways.

Common links between music and social studies

Natural links and connections between music and social studies go beyond casual experiences, presentations of factual information, or disconnected encounters. Enduring ideas that can be explored in music and social studies include:

Cause and effect
Change

Choice
Context
Cooperation
Diversity
Identity
Interaction
Interdependence
Perspective
Power
Relationships
Resources
Similarities and differences
Structure
Tension and release

National standards

The Chapter 4 lessons and inventory of ideas are aligned with the National Core Arts Standards for Music, the National Curriculum Standards for Social Studies (NCSSS), and the College, Career, and Civic Life Framework for Social Studies State Standards (C3). Two distinct sets of standards for social studies (NCSSS and C3) are included because of the different purposes they serve. The NCSSS themes are meant to be broad and content based. The C3 Framework Standards, on the other hand, are meant to support state-level standards revision and are pedagogically and skill driven (National Council for the Social Studies [NCSS], 2013).

Interdisciplinary connections between social studies and music are implicit in the National Core Arts Standards for Music. For example, to meet music Anchor Standard 11, students are expected to "relate artistic ideas and works with societal, cultural, and historical context to deepen understanding" (National Coalition for Core Arts Standards, 2015). Similarly, the 2010 NCSSS and C3 Framework Standards naturally connect with music. For example, to address the first NCSSS theme, Culture, it is expected that "through experience, observation, and reflection, students will identify elements of culture as well as similarities and differences among cultural groups across time and place" (NCSS, 2010). The following boxes specify the standards that are addressed in the Chapter 4 lessons and inventory of ideas:

- Box 4.1, National Curriculum Standards for Social Studies (NCSSS)
- Box 4.2, College, Career, and Civic Life Framework for Social Studies State Standards (C3)
- Box 4.3, National Core Arts Standards for Music

Box 4.4 offers a framework for structuring Chapter 4 lessons and activities.

Box 4.1 National Curriculum Standards for Social Studies Themes Included in Chapter 4 Lessons (L) and Inventory of Ideas (I)

1. Culture	Social studies programs should include experiences that provide for the study of culture and cultural diversity.	L4.2
		L4.3
		I1
		I4
		I5
		I9
		I11
		I13
		I15
		I16
		I17
2. Time, Continuity, and Change	Social studies programs should include experiences that provide for the study of the past and its legacy.	L4.3
		L4.4
		I7
		I8
		I11
		I13
		I16
3. People, Places, and Environments	Social studies programs should include experiences that provide for the study of people, places, and environments.	L4.1
		L4.3
		I1
		I2
		I3
		I7
		I10
		I15
		I17
		I19
4. Individual Development and Identity	Social studies programs should include experiences that provide for the study of individual development and identity.	L4.1
		L4.3
		I1
		I5
		I13
		I15
		I16

5. Individuals, Groups, and Institutions	Social studies programs should include experiences that provide for the study of interactions among individuals, groups, and institutions.	L4.2 L4.3 I2 I5 I9 I17
6. Power, Authority, and Governance	Social studies programs should include experiences that provide for the study of how people create, interact with, and change structures of power, authority, and governance.	L4.2 L4.4 I2 I4 I12 I18
7. Production, Distribution, and Consumption	Social studies programs should include experiences that provide for the study of how people organize for the production, distribution, and consumption of goods and services.	L4.1 L4.3 I1 I3 I4 I6 I14 I19
8. Science, Technology, and Society	Social studies programs should include experiences that provide for the study of relationships among science, technology, and society.	I1 I3 I6 I7 I10 I12 I14 I19
9. Global Connections	Social studies programs should include experiences that provide for the study of global connections and interdependence.	L4.4 I4 I5 I7 I9 I14 I15 I19
10. Civic Ideals and Practices	Social studies programs should include experiences that provide for the study of the ideals, principles, and practices of citizenship in a democratic republic.	L4.1 L4.4 I5 I8 I13 I17 I18

National Council for the Social Studies (NCSS), *National Curriculum Standards for Social Studies: A Framework for Teaching, Learning, and Assessment* (Silver Spring, MD: NCSS, 2010).

Box 4.2 College, Career, and Civic Life Framework for Social Studies State Standards (C3) Included in Chapter 4 Lessons (L) and Inventory of Ideas (I)

Dimension 1: Questions and Inquiries	Constructing Compelling Questions; Constructing Supporting Questions; Determining Helpful Sources	L 4.2
		L 4.3
		I 1
		I 3
		I 7
		I 10
		I 15
Dimension 2: Civics	Civic and Political Institutions; Participation and Deliberation; Processes, Rules, and Laws	L 4.2
		I 3
		I 6
		I 11
		I 13
		I 17
		I 18
Dimension 2: Economics	Economic Decision Making; Exchange and Markets; The National Economy; The Global Economy	L 4.3
		I 5
		I 6
		I 9
		I 12
		I 14
		I 18
Dimension 2: Geography	Geographic Representations; Human–Environment Interaction; Human Population: Spatial Patterns and Movements; Global Interconnections	L 4.1
		I 1
		I 3
		I 12
		I 17
		I 19
Dimension 2: History	Change, Continuity, and Context; Perspectives; Historical Sources and Evidence; Causation and Argumentation	L 4.2
		L 4.4
		I 2
		I 4
		I 8
		I 15
		I 16

Dimension 3: Sources and Evidence	Gathering and Evaluating Sources; Developing Claims and Using Evidence	L4.1
		L4.4
		I2
		I8
		I10
		I14
		I18
Dimension 4: Conclusions and Action	Communicating Conclusions; Critiquing Conclusions; Taking Informed Action	L4.1
		L4.3
		I5
		I7
		I9
		I19

National Council for the Social Studies (NCSS), The College, Career, and Civic Life (C3) Framework for Social Studies State Standards: Guidance for Enhancing the Rigor of K-12 Civics, Economics, Geography, and History (Silver Spring, MD: NCSS, 2013).

Box 4.3 National Core Arts Standards for Music Included in Chapter 4 Lessons (L) and Inventory of Ideas (I)

MU:Cr1 (Create)	Generate and conceptualize artistic ideas and work	L4.2
		I7
		I10
		I12
		I15
		I18
MU:Cr2 (Create)	Organize and develop artistic ideas and work	L4.3
		I7
		I10
		I12
		I16
MU:Cr3 (Create)	Refine and complete artistic work	L4.3
		I7
		I12
		I16
		I18

MU:Pr4 (Perform)	Select, analyze, and interpret artistic work for presentation	L4.1 L4.4 I3 I5 I8 I13 I19
MU:Pr5 (Perform)	Develop and refine artistic techniques and work for presentation	L4.1 I2 I8 I12 I19
MU:Pr6 (Perform)	Convey meaning through the presentation of artistic work	L4.2 L4.3 I1 I5 I7 I12 I16
MU:Re7 (Respond)	Perceive and analyze artistic work	L4.1 L4.4 I3 I6 I11 I15
MU:Re8 (Respond)	Interpret intent and meaning in artistic work	L4.2 L4.4 I5 I10 I14
MU:Re9 (Respond)	Apply criteria to evaluate artistic work	L4.2 L4.4 I2 I4 I6 I9 I17

MU:Cn10 (Connect)	Synthesize and relate knowledge and personal experiences to make art	L4.1
		L4.3
		I1
		I3
		I8
		I10
		I12
		I13
		I14
		I19
MU:Cn11 (Connect)	Relate artistic ideas and works with societal, cultural, and historical context to deepen understanding	L4.2
		L4.4
		I2
		I4
		I6
		I9
		I11
		I16
		I17

Box 4.4 Framework for Chapter 4 Lessons and Ideas

This chapter is designed to support K–5 educators as they integrate music and social studies. The lessons are designed to be fully taught by classroom teachers; however, the plans may also facilitate partnerships and collaboration between classroom teachers and music specialists. All lessons and activities have been reviewed by practicing teachers, and most have been field-tested in elementary classrooms. Chapter 4 lessons are labeled as primary, intermediate, or upper elementary, but all the plans and activities are adaptable to a variety of grade levels and are intended as tools for you to meet your students' needs. Some of the lessons may need to be spread over two or more class periods. Please adjust, adapt, or expand however works best for you and for your students.

Lesson 4.1: Everyone is important in a classroom community

Grade Level: Primary
Essential Questions: What is a community and how is each member of a community important? Why is each part of a cumulative song important?

Objectives

- Students will engage with concepts related to communities by expressing their agreement or disagreement with a variety of statements, appropriately defining and summarizing concepts, using inclusive language, and showing self-knowledge by determining ways individuals can help various communities.
- Students will perform "The Rattlin' Bog," accurately following the sequence, maintaining a steady clapped beat, and singing with correct pitches.
- Students will accurately explain the step-by-step additive process used in "The Rattlin' Bog" to a partner and interpret connections between the organization of their classroom community and the organization of the song, providing details to support their conclusions.

National Curriculum Standards for Social Studies addressed

- NCSSS 3: Social studies programs should include experiences that provide for the study of people, places, and environments.
- NCSSS 4: Social studies programs should include experiences that provide for the study of individual development and identity.
- NCSSS 7: Social studies programs should include experiences that provide for the study of how people organize for the production, distribution, and consumption of goods and services.
- NCSSS 10: Social studies programs should include experiences that provide for the study of the ideals, principles, and practices of citizenship in a democratic republic.

C3 Framework for Social Studies State Standards addressed

- C3 Dimension 2: Geography
- C3 Dimension 3: Evaluating sources and using evidence
- C4 Dimension 4: Communicating conclusions and taking informed action

National Core Arts Standards for Music addressed

- MU:Pr4: Select, analyze, and interpret artistic work for presentation

- MU:Pr5: Develop and refine artistic techniques and work for presentation
- MU:Re7: Perceive and analyze artistic work
- MU:Re9: Apply criteria to evaluate artistic work
- MU:Cn10: Synthesize and relate knowledge and personal experiences to make art

Materials

- Recorded musical example: "The Rattlin' Bog" (The Bog in the Valley) performed by the Irish Rovers
- Picture book focused on community such as:
  - *All Are Welcome* by Alexandra Penfold and Suzanne Kaufman
  - *Be Kind* by Pat Zietlow Miller, illustrated by Jen Hill
  - *Ordinary Mary's Extraordinary Deed* by Emily Pearson, illustrated by Fumi Kosaka
  - *Strictly No Elephants* by Lisa Mantchev, illustrated by Taeen Yoo
  - *The Big Umbrella* by Amy June Bates and Juniper Bates
  - *The Golden Rule* by Ilene Cooper and John Green, illustrated by Gabi Swiatkowska
- Table showing cumulative structure of "The Rattlin' Bog" (Table 4.1)

Procedure

Begin by asking your students to define the term "community" in their own words. Record their responses on the board. Guide the discussion to arrive at the traditional

Table 4.1 Lyric Structure of *The Rattlin' Bog*

Verse 1	Verse 2	Verse 3	Verse 4	Verse 5	Verse 6	Verse 7
Valley	Valley	Valley	Valley	Valley	Valley	Valley
1. Bog	Bog	Bog	Bog	Bog	Bog	Bog
Tree	2. Tree	Tree	Tree	Tree	Tree	Tree
	Limb	3. Limb	Limb	Limb	Limb	Limb
		Branch	4. Branch	Branch	Branch	Branch
			Twig	5. Twig	Twig	Twig
				Leaf	6. Leaf	Leaf
					Bug	7. Bug
						Hair

Courtesy of author.

definition: A community is a place where people live, work, and play. Another way of thinking about community is to define it as a group of people who feel connected to each other because of shared characteristics, interests, or goals. Ask students, "Is our class a community?"

Engage students in a discussion of the characteristics of a classroom community and ask them to identify things that everyone in their classroom community has in common. Student answers might include (1) all in the same grade, (2) all have the same teacher, (3) all learning the same things, (4) all have the same lunch time, (5) all live nearby, etc. Expand the discussion to include additional communities to which the classroom belongs, from small to large: school, neighborhood, town, county, state, country, continent, world, solar system, galaxy, universe.

Read and discuss a picture book with the class. The following books reinforce a positive classroom community by highlighting people who show respect, model empathy, or work together for a common purpose: *All Are Welcome* by Alexandra Penfold and Suzanne Kaufman; *Be Kind* by Pat Zietlow Miller, illustrated by Jen Hill; *Ordinary Mary's Extraordinary Deed* by Emily Pearson, illustrated by Fumi Kosaka; *Strictly No Elephants* by Lisa Mantchev, illustrated by Taeen Yoo; *The Big Umbrella* by Amy June Bates and Juniper Bates; and *The Golden Rule* by Ilene Cooper and John Green, illustrated by Gabi Swiatkowska.

Drawing on the book they just read and their own experiences, ask students to brainstorm ways that they can contribute to their classroom community. Encourage them to think about ways they can help others and ways they can share or conserve resources. Finally, help students to perceive all the different roles and voices in their community and the importance of each individual member.

Analyze and perform a cumulative song, "The Rattlin' Bog." Cumulative songs typically have a simple verse–chorus structure, with each verse becoming progressively longer than the next through a step-by-step additive process. "The Rattlin' Bog," an Irish folk song, is an excellent example of a cumulative song. Explain to students that a bog is a type of wetland where a thick layer of vegetation covers the water and that bogs are common in Ireland. "Rattlin'" is a term that means excellent or grand.

Listen to "The Rattlin' Bog," sometimes labeled as "The Bog in the Valley." There are many versions of "The Rattlin' Bog"; the lyrics listed in this lesson align with the Irish Rovers' 50th anniversary performance. "The Rattlin' Bog" starts with a chorus, the part of the song that returns over and over again.

Chorus:

> Ho ro the rattlin' bog, the bog down in the valley-o.
> Ho ro the rattlin' bog, the bog down in the valley-o. (Roud, n.d.)

It then moves to the first verse before returning to the chorus:

Verse 1:

> Now in this bog there was a tree, a rare tree, a rattlin' tree,
> Tree in the bog, in the bog down in the valley-o. (Roud, n.d.)

Table 4.1 displays the lyric structure of "The Rattlin' Bog" so students may easily follow along. For very young children, you could substitute images for the text. In each verse, the first item mentioned is labeled with the verse's number. For example, in verse 1, the first item is a bog. In verse 4, the first item is a branch. To sing each verse, start at the item labeled with the verse's number, progress down to the next item in the column, and then quickly reverse direction, singing each item in succession until you reach the top of the column for that verse. To better understand the directions, compare the complete lyrics for verse 4 with the column for verse 4 in Table 4.1.

Verse 4 lyrics:

> And on this branch there was a twig, a rare twig, a rattlin' twig,
> Twig on the branch, and the branch on the limb,
> And the limb on the tree, and the tree in the bog,
> And the bog down in the valley-o. (Roud, n.d.)

Guide students to clap along on the steady beat during the returning chorus sections while they listen and follow the lyrics. Play the song again, and direct students to continue to clap on the choruses, and to sing along as they are able. If students are up for a challenge, they can try to keep up with a recording of "The Rattlin' Bog" as performed by the Irish Descendants, a version that gets progressively faster as it goes (the order of items is slightly different).

Discuss the song "The Rattlin' Bog" as a symbol for community. In a classroom community, every individual is important, and without each person, the community isn't complete. Similarly, in a cumulative song, each verse is dependent on the last and is critically important to the meaning and structure of the song. In "The Rattlin' Bog," each new item always eventually gets tied back to the big picture, the bog in the valley. In a classroom community, each individual fits into the greater classroom environment as well. Consider expanding the discussion to larger communities. Even very young students can recognize the different contributions various people make within their local community.

Assessment

- During informal discussion, ask students to summarize or paraphrase important concepts related to communities. Listen for accurate definitions, knowledge of characteristics and resources, and inclusive language. Share a variety of statements, some that describe a community, and some that do not. Direct students to stand up if they believe a statement describes a community or sit down if they believe it does not.
- During students' group performance of "The Rattlin' Bog," listen to hear if they accurately follow the sequence, maintain a steady clapped beat, and sing with correct pitches.

- Ask students to explain the step-by-step additive process used in "The Rattlin' Bog" to a partner. Listen for clear, accurate descriptions of the process involved. Additionally, ask them to compare the organization of their classroom community to the organization of the song.

Extensions

- Guide students to apply their understanding of their classroom community to design a community service project. Depending on grade level, they might design and implement a project to clean up a specific location, contribute money to a specific cause, volunteer their time in another classroom, create materials to share with another group of students, etc. Consider using the book *Black Ants and Buddhists,* which focuses on civic learning for primary-grade students, to jump-start the conversation.
- Encourage students to connect the idea of "community" to various social issues such as bullying and treating people with equity. Examine the relationship between social responsibility and community membership. For example, students might establish that acting as a positive member of a classroom community and bullying behaviors do not align, while sharing classroom resources with a table partner does.

Lesson 4.2: Crossroads blues part 1, history of the times

Note to teachers: This lesson contains material that may be disturbing to some students. Adjust, shorten, or otherwise adapt the material to fit your students' needs. To avoid any appearance of promoting personal biases, all descriptive passages and definitions for this lesson were taken from reliable sources including academic books, encyclopedias, scholarly journals, and the Public Broadcasting System. All texts used with permission.

Grade Level: Intermediate or upper elementary

Essential Question: How are issues of power and authority highlighted in blues songs?

Objectives

- In a small group matching activity and as a class, students will explore the history of the Southern United States (Emancipation through Reconstruction) and the adoption of Jim Crow laws to spark a discussion about the potential purposes of rules and laws. Students will hypothesize about ways rules and laws can be evaluated and/or changed, identifying important values and principles of American democracy.

- Students will collaboratively analyze the lyrics of a blues song, connecting themes from the text to historical, social, political, and/or economic content. Students will present their conclusions to the class, incorporating specific examples from social studies and music content and demonstrating empathy by considering the songwriter's perspective.

National Curriculum Standards for Social Studies addressed

- NCSSS 1: Culture: Social studies programs should include experiences that provide for the study of culture and cultural diversity.
- NCSSS 3: People, Places, and Environments: Social studies programs should include experiences that provide for the study of people, places, and environments.
- NCSSS 5: Individuals, Groups, and Institutions: Social studies programs should include experiences that provide for the study of interactions among individuals, groups, and institutions.
- NCSSS 6: Power, Authority, and Governance: Social studies programs should include experiences that provide for the study of how people create and change structures of power, authority, and governance.

C3 Framework for Social Studies State Standards addressed

- C3 Dimension 1: Developing questions and planning inquiries
- C3 Dimension 2: Civics
- C3 Dimension 2: History

National Core Arts Standards for Music addressed

- MU:Pr6: Convey meaning through the presentation of artistic work
- MU:Re8: Interpret intent and meaning in artistic work
- MU:Cn10: Synthesize and relate knowledge and personal experiences to make art

Materials

- Printed accounts of Jim Crow and printed images for matching activity
  - Emancipation: Roberts and Alvord edition of Emancipation Proclamation (Figure 4.1)
  - Reconstruction: Allegorical artwork portraying Reconstruction (Figure 4.2)
  - Jim Crow: Segregated waiting room image (Figure 4.3)

- Sharecropping: Image of sharecroppers (Figure 4.4)
- The 13th, 14th, and 15th Amendments: Image showing 15th Amendment (Figure 4.5)
- Ida B. Wells: Image showing Ida B. Wells and her children (Figure 4.6)
- Tulsa race riot, 1921: Photo taken after the Tulsa race riot (Figure 4.7)
- Recorded musical examples and printed lyrics
  - "Scottsboro Boys" by Leadbelly
  - "Jim Crow Blues" by Cow Cow Davenport
  - "Jim Crow Train" by Josh White
- Index cards with prompts for closing table exercise

Background

Many times, elementary students study slavery but jump from Emancipation straight to the 1960s civil rights movement. Guide students as they study a variety of specific events from the interim. Introduce students to the personal and economic conditions of many African Americans living in the South at the turn of the 20th century as they explore Emancipation; Reconstruction; Jim Crow laws; sharecropping; the 13th, 14th, and 15th Amendments; Ida B. Wells; and the Tulsa race riot. With considerations for your grade level, limit your exploration to specific accounts and images, if needed. On the other hand, supplement with additional areas of study if students wish to dig deeper. Additional key figures, events, and institutions to consider include Emmett Till (key for connections to the Black Lives Matter movement), the Tuskegee Institute, the Ku Klux Klan, the Scottsboro boys (including the Broadway musical "Scottsboro Boys" by Kander and Ebb), *Plessy v. Ferguson, Brown v. Board of Education*, the Harlem Renaissance, and the March on Washington.

Procedure

As a class, listen to the song "Scottsboro Boys" by Leadbelly and follow along with the lyrics. Ask students to speculate about the composer's purpose in creating the song and its meaning. Accept a variety of responses, and then inform students that they will return to the song at the end of the lesson.

Print copies of the following images and accounts of events for a matching activity. Divide students into small groups and direct them to examine each written account and image. Using context clues, students will match each account with the aligning image.

As a whole class, discuss the written accounts and images, confirming their alignment. Use the information included in the accounts and the images to open a class discussion about laws, rules, power, and authority. Throughout the presentation of information, allow students to ask questions and share perceptions.

1. Emancipation:

President Abraham Lincoln's primary concern near the beginning of the Civil War was to protect and uphold the United States. He wrote, "My paramount object is to save the Union, and not either to save or destroy slavery" (Basler, 1953, p. 389). However, as the war continued, the situation began to look bleak for the Union cause, and Lincoln realized that he needed to end slavery to win the war. He issued a preliminary proclamation on September 22, 1862, then signed and released the complete Emancipation Proclamation on January 1, 1863. The Emancipation Proclamation granted freedom to slaves in Confederate states (Snyder, 2018).

Figure 4.1 shows the Roberts and Alvord edition of the Emancipation Proclamation.

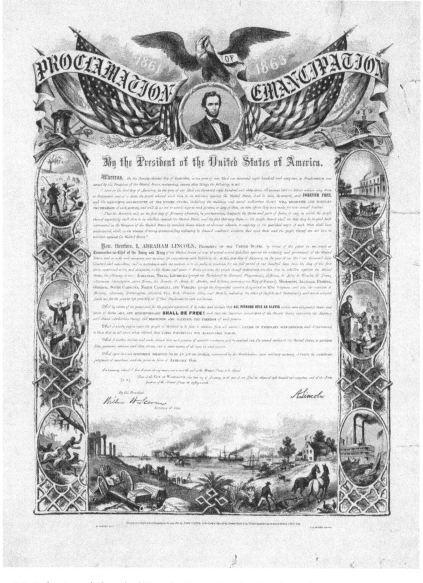

Figure 4.1 Roberts and Alvord edition the Emancipation Proclamation, 1864.
© The Library of Congress.

2. Reconstruction:

Reconstruction generally refers to the period in United States history immediately following the Civil War in which the federal government set the conditions that would allow the rebellious Southern states back into the Union. After Lincoln's assassination in April of 1865, President Andrew Johnson alienated Congress with his Reconstruction policy. He supported White supremacy in the South and favored pro-Union Southern political leaders who had aided the Confederacy during the war. Southerners, with Johnson's support, attempted to restore slavery in substance, if not in name. (Public Broadcasting System, 2002)

Figure 4.2 shows an allegorical artwork depicting the reconciliation of the North and the South during Reconstruction. Amid the many symbols and figures in the artwork, the US government is represented as the large structure in the center of the image that is literally being reconstructed.

Figure 4.2 *Reconstruction*, by J. L. Giles, New York; printed by F. Ratellier, 1867.
© The Library of Congress.

3. Jim Crow:

"Jim Crow" was a label given to a set of laws that enforced racial segregation. These laws were passed between 1876 and 1965. Essentially, these laws amounted to government-sanctioned oppression, leading to unfair treatment, inferior accommodations, and unequal economic, educational, and social opportunities. Various Jim Crow laws ordered the segregation of schools, transportation, restrooms, restaurants, and drinking fountains for Whites and Blacks. "Jim Crow" was a fictional character in the song "Jump Jim Crow." The song was made famous by Thomas Dartmouth "Daddy" Rice, who promoted stereotypes and performed in blackface (King, 2015).

Figure 4.3 shows a sign designating a segregated waiting room in a Greyhound bus terminal in Memphis, Tennessee.

Figure 4.3 A Greyhound terminal in Memphis, Tennessee, 1943.
© Esther Bubley/The Library of Congress.

4. Sharecropping:

Sharecropping was common in the Southern United States during the Reconstruction era. After the Civil War, many landowners did not have money to pay farm workers, and most former slaves were willing to work but did not have land. Sharecropping was the economic arrangement between them. A "cropper" was assigned a section of land to farm, and at the end of the season, a "share" of the profits went back to the land owner; however, it was very difficult for workers to make a living wage and the status quo between Blacks and Whites was largely maintained (Griffin & Hargis, 2012).

Figure 4.4 shows sharecroppers during the Reconstruction period.

5. The 13th, 14th, and 15th Amendments:

The Thirteenth, Fourteenth, and Fifteenth Amendments to the Constitution were adopted after the Civil War to guarantee Black rights. The Thirteenth Amendment abolished slavery,

Figure 4.4 Cotton picking scenes on Roger Williams Plantation in the Delta, new Drew, Mississippi, 1940.
© The Library of Congress.

the Fourteenth granted citizenship to people once enslaved, and the Fifteenth guaranteed Black men the right to vote. These amendments were designed to protect the civil liberties of recently freed slaves. (Public Broadcasting System, 2002)

Figure 4.5 shows the 15th Amendment of the US Constitution.

6. Ida B. Wells:

In March of 1892, Ida B. Wells, a journalist and former Memphis school teacher, started a crusade against lynching after three friends of hers were brutally murdered by a Memphis mob. Tom Moss and two of his friends, Calvin McDowell and Henry Stewart, were arrested for defending themselves against an attack on Moss' store. Moss was a highly respected figure in the Black community, a postman as well as the owner of a grocery store. A White

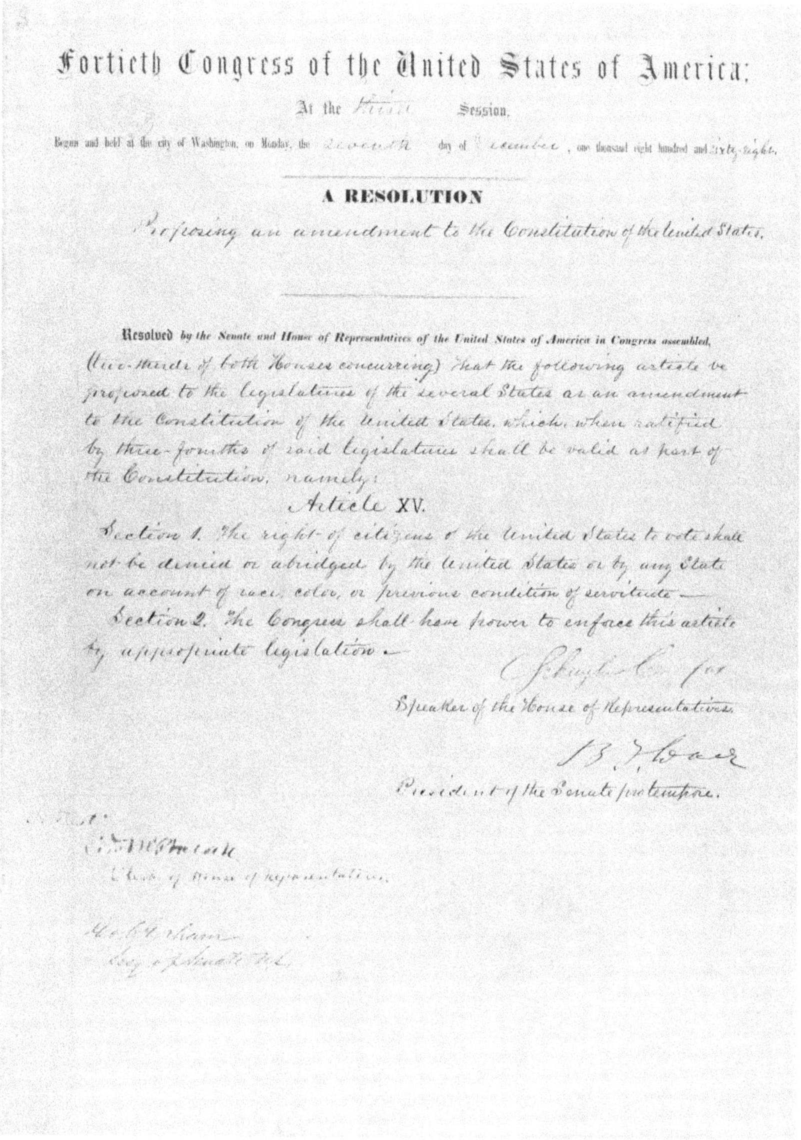

Figure 4.5 Fifteenth Amendment of the United States Constitution, 1870.
© National Archives of the United States/Wikimedia.

competitor, enraged that Moss had drawn away his Black customers, hired some off-duty deputy sheriffs to destroy the store. (Public Broadcasting System, 2002)

Figure 4.6 shows Ida B. Wells with her children.

7. Tulsa race riot, 1921:

By 1921, Tulsa was booming thanks to the discovery of oil, and many African Americans had also prospered. Most Black people lived in the racially segregated "Greenwood" section of the city, which contained stores, shops, hotels, banks, newspapers, schools, theaters, and restaurants. Greenwood had several wealthy Black entrepreneurs and was sometimes

Figure 4.6 Ida B. Wells with her children.
© Unattributed/Free-Images.com.

called the "Black Wall Street" of America. By 1921, membership in the Ku Klux Klan was rapidly spreading throughout America and an active chapter had been formed in Tulsa. The riot was triggered over a Memorial Day weekend report in two White newspapers that a Black youth had tried to assault a young White female elevator operator. (Public Broadcasting System, 2002)

Figure 4.7 shows a scene after the Tulsa race riot.

Following the class discussion of the Jim Crow era, divide students into small groups. Give each group a printed copy of the lyrics of one of the following songs: "Jim Crow Blues" by Cow Cow Davenport, "Scottsboro Boys" by Leadbelly, or "Jim Crow Train" by Josh White.

Direct students to collaborate with their group as they interpret the lyrics and determine ways their assigned text highlights or clarifies social, political, or economic

Figure 4.7 Ruins after the race riots, Tulsa, Oklahoma, 1921.
© The Library of Congress.

situations. Ask students to theorize how the creator of their song felt about those situations. Allow each group to explain their conclusions to the class, and then listen to each of the three songs together, following along with each respective set of lyrics.

Conclude with a class discussion exploring ways the musical elements of each piece (instrumentation, tempo, rhythmic drive, dynamics, etc.) enhance or detract from the meanings of the songs.

Assessment

- Following groups' analysis of "Jim Crow Blues," "Scottsboro Boys," or "Jim Crow Train," ask each group to present their conclusions to the class. Assess students' ability to synthesize and appropriately connect historical, social, political, and/or economic content to their assigned song. Note students' capacity for considering their songwriter's perspective and empathizing with the given circumstances.
- At the end of the lesson, ask students to complete a table group exercise. At each table, place a set of index cards, each listing one of the following topics from the lesson: Emancipation; Reconstruction; Jim Crow laws; sharecropping; the 13th,

14th, and 15th Amendments; Ida B. Wells; and the Tulsa race riot. Students draw cards and describe their selected topic using key details and terms.

Lesson 4.3: Crossroads blues part 2, blues structure, lyrics, and culture

Grade Level: Intermediate or upper elementary
Essential Question: How are the ideas of symbolism, transformation, and choice exhibited in music and in culture?

Objectives

- As a class, students will analyze 12 bar blues harmonic structure and AAB lyric form in existing blues songs and in one example of children's literature.
- First as a class and later individually, students will create blues verses demonstrating correct usage of the AAB lyric formula and incorporating given themes. Students will perform class-constructed verses with an accompaniment created by singing or playing pitched percussion instruments on the roots of chords aligned with 12-bar blues harmonic structure. Students will share their individual verses with the class and modify them by employing musical borrowing techniques.
- Students will analyze the lyrics of "Cross Road Blues," connecting themes from the text to events and ideas from regional history and culture by identifying and explaining specific instances when power and authority were exemplified by people, events, and symbols.

National Curriculum Standards for Social Studies addressed

- NCSSS 1: Culture: Social studies programs should include experiences that provide for the study of culture and cultural diversity.
- NCSSS 2: Time, Continuity, and Change: Social studies programs should include experiences that provide for the study of the past and its legacy.
- NCSSS 4: Individual Development and Identity: Social studies programs should include experiences that provide for the study of individual development and identity.
- NCSSS 5: Individuals, Groups, and Institutions: Social studies programs should include experiences that provide for the study of interactions among individuals, groups, and institutions.
- NCSSS 7: Production, Distribution, and Consumption: Social studies programs should include experiences that provide for the study of how people organize for the production, distribution, and consumption of goods and services.

C3 Framework for Social Studies State Standards addressed

- C3 Dimension 1: Developing questions and planning inquiries
- C3 Dimension 2: Economics
- C3 Dimension 4: Communicating conclusions and taking informed action

National Core Arts Standards for Music addressed

- MU:Cr1: Generate and conceptualize artistic ideas and work
- MU:Cr2: Organize and develop artistic ideas and work
- MU:Cr3: Refine and complete artistic work
- MU:Pr6: Convey meaning through the presentation of artistic work
- MU:Re9: Apply criteria to evaluate artistic work
- MU:Cn10: Synthesize and relate knowledge and personal experiences to make art

Materials

- Recorded musical examples
  - "St. Louis Blues" by W. C. Handy, sung by Billie Holiday on the album *The Jazz Playlist, Part 12*
  - "Cross Road Blues" by Robert Johnson, on the album *Robert Johnson: The Complete Recordings*
  - "Blues Backing Track" from GuitarFriendly.net (RealPlayer audio file)
- Printed lyrics
  - "St. Louis Blues" by W. C. Handy
  - "Cross Road Blues" by Robert Johnson
- Instrument or app for producing given pitches
- Optional: Pitched percussion instruments for students
- Books
  - *Last Day Blues* by Julie Danneberg
  - *Black Cat Bone: The Life of Blues Legend Robert Johnson* by J. P. Lewis

Procedure

Blues is a musical genre first developed by African Americans living in the Southern United States before the turn of the 20th century (Oliver & Kernfield, 2003). Introduce students to the harmonic structure and AAB lyric form of 12-bar blues (with no focus on themes present in the text). Use the first two verses of W. C. Handy's "St. Louis Blues" to demonstrate. A version that clearly exposes the structure is a

1940 recording sung by Billie Holiday, found on the album *The Jazz Playlist, Part 12*. The counting information included here refers to Holiday's recording. First, project the lyrics of "St. Louis Blues" and ask students to follow along as they listen to the recorded performance. While students listen, label each line with the letter A or B, revealing the AAB structure of each verse.

Verse 1:

I hate to see that evenin' sun go down,	A
I hate to see that evenin' sun go down,	A
'Cause my baby, he has left this town.	B

Verse 2:

If I'm feelin' tomorrow like I feel today,	A
If I'm feelin' tomorrow like I feel today,	A
I'll pack my trunk and make my get-away. (Handy, 1914)	B

Now that students are more familiar with the sound of the piece, listen again to determine the harmonic structure. Traditional 12-bar blues follow a very predictable pattern. The "12 bars" refer to the 12 measures that comprise each verse. Billie Holiday's version opens with a four-measure introduction, which is separate from the 12-bar structure. "St. Louis Blues" is written in 4/4, so count the introduction by saying, "*one* two three four; *two* two three four; *three* two three four; *four* two three four." The very next beat marks the start of the first 12-bar section and the beginning of the first verse. To show that the verse is 12 measures long, direct students to count the beats in the same way they counted the introduction, extending their counting for 12 measures. You may continue beyond the first verse by restarting the counting for each repetition, demonstrating that each verse is exactly 12 measures long. Table 4.2 shows the pattern for counting beats in 12-bar blues aligned with the AAB lyric structure.

The three chords that make up the conventional harmonic structure of 12-bar blues are the I chord, the IV chord, and the V chord. The Roman numerals refer

Table 4.2 Counting 12-Bar Blues

Counting Beats in 12-Bar Blues				Lyric Structure
1 2 3 4	2 2 3 4	3 2 3 4	4 2 3 4	A
5 2 3 4	6 2 3 4	7 2 3 4	8 2 3 4	A
9 2 3 4	10 2 3 4	11 2 3 4	12 2 3 4	B

Courtesy of author.

to the scale degrees that mark the roots of those chords. In the key of C major, the pitch C is the root of the I chord. Counting up the scale four pitches (CDEF) brings us to the pitch F, which is the root of the IV chord. One pitch higher than F is G, the root of the V chord. Table 4.3 shows the chords that make up 12-bar blues.

The traditional 12-bar blues harmonic structure is evident in "St. Louis Blues." Billie Holiday's rendition of "St. Louis Blues" was recorded in C major, making it simpler for students to perform the chord structure along with the recording. Using a pitch pipe app, piano, or other pitched instrument, allow students to hear the three pitches they will sing (C, F, and G). After they have heard each pitch, ask them to match the pitch with their singing voices, singing "one" for C, "four" for F, and "five" for G. Play the recording again and direct students to sing the roots of the I, IV, and V chords (C, F, and G) in time with the music. Table 4.4 aligns the counting of 12-bar blues form, structure, and pitch names.

If you have pitched instruments available (bells, Boomwhackers, recorders, etc.), students can play along with the recording. Practice to make sure students can play the roots of the I, IV, and V chords (C, F, and G) and then ask them to accompany the song with instruments, just as they accompanied with voices. You may keep using the Billie Holiday recording from earlier in the lesson; however, there are many recordings of "St. Louis Blues" from which to choose, including a video recording of

Table 4.3 Chord Structure of 12-Bar Blues

I	I	I	I
IV	IV	I	I
V	IV	I	I

Courtesy of author.

Table 4.4 Counting and Structure of 12-Bar Blues Aligned With Pitch Names

Singing the Harmonic Structure of 12-Bar Blues			
1 2 3 4 I ("one") C	2 2 3 4 I ("one") C	3 2 3 4 I ("one") C	4 2 3 4 I ("one") C
5 2 3 4 IV ("four") F	6 2 3 4 IV ("four") F	7 2 3 4 I ("one") C	8 2 3 4 I ("one") C
9 2 3 4 V ("five") G	10 2 3 4 IV ("four") F	11 2 3 4 I ("one") C	12 2 3 4 I ("one") C

Courtesy of author.

W. C. Handy himself playing the instrumental-only version on the Ed Sullivan Show in 1949.

As time allows, follow the same steps to guide students as they analyze the 12-bar harmonic structure and AAB lyric form in additional 12-bar blues examples. Suggestions include B. B. King's "Stormy Monday" and Robert Johnson's "Dead Shrimp Blues" and "Sweet Home Chicago."

Read the picture book *Last Day Blues* by Julie Danneberg. Note that the poetic structure does not follow AAB format. As a class, create two verses in AAB lyric form using themes from the book.

Divide students into small groups and ask them to analyze the 12-bar harmonic structure found in "Blues Backing Track" (same format as previous examples). Invite students to perform the accompaniment along with the recording, singing the roots of the chords or playing any pitched percussion instruments available. Perform the entire piece: "Blues Backing Track," added percussion/vocal accompaniment, and newly created AAB lyrics.

Share a brief biography of the life of blues musician Robert Johnson, such as the one found in the picture book *Black Cat Bone: The Life of Blues Legend Robert Johnson* by J. P. Lewis. Download, print, and pass out the lyrics of Johnson's "Cross Road Blues." While students listen to the song, they will work with a partner to identify connections between the themes in the song and the associated social, economic, and political environment, drawing on recollections from the previous lesson and discussion. Additionally, ask students to scrutinize the lyrics for possible double meanings and symbolism.

Discuss the prospective intentions or purposes behind the use of hidden meanings in song lyrics, asking groups to provide specific examples to support their perspectives. Consider the metaphorical meaning of a crossroad, using the lyrics and recording as jumping-off points for a class discussion of symbolism, transformation, choice, power, and authority.

Ask individual students to envision a possible "crossroad" or injustice people face in their lives today. Students may choose to explore a variety of contemporary social issues such as immigration, gender identity, poverty, etc. Direct them to write one verse of a blues song from a contemporary perspective that follows AAB lyric form, includes at least one example of symbolism, and highlights a crossroad.

When students' verses are completed, collect them and spread them around the room. Invite students to walk around, read the various verses, and locate something in another stanza that they can "borrow." When students return to their seats, they must modify their original verses to incorporate the newly borrowed material, then share with the class. Drawing on examples from students' modified verses, discuss the transformation and borrowing that was especially common in early blues writing. (Blues singers would often alter their existing songs to incorporate new musical ideas or lyrics they encountered. They also frequently recycled lyrics from other songs when composing new pieces.) Conclude the discussion by connecting symbolism present in students' blues lyrics to the historical examples the class examined. In some instances, historical examples of blues lyrics can be read literally, and in others, they can be interpreted more broadly as a commentary on the day-to-day experiences and struggles that the Black community faced.

Assessment

- Through informal discussion and observation, determine if students are able to correctly analyze 12-bar blues form and AAB lyric structure.
- Assess student performances of 12-bar accompaniment, checking that the pitches students perform (singing or playing) align with the roots of the given chord structure of 12-bar blues; verify that the class-created verses correctly demonstrate AAB lyric structure and incorporate themes given in the book *Last Day Blues*; check that students' individually created lyrics follow AAB form and contain at least one instance of symbolism.
- Ask students to write short responses to various prompts related to blues music and culture. Possible prompts:
  - How are the ideas of transformation, choice, power, and authority related to Robert Johnson's "Cross Road Blues" and the culture of the times?
  - How is symbolism shown in blues music? Why might blues songs contain hidden meanings?
  - How do the lyrics in your "crossroad" composition relate to historical content?
  - Describe the process of transforming your lyrics and explain how transformation relates to blues composition. How might transformation apply to other topics?

Lesson 4.4: Górecki's *Symphony No. 3* and the Holocaust

Note to teachers: This lesson contains material that may be disturbing to some students. Adjust, shorten, or otherwise adapt the material to fit your students' needs.
Grade Level: Upper elementary
Essential Question: What was the Holocaust and how can a piece of music memorialize an event from history?

Objectives

- Following a presentation with images, historical narration, and class discussion, students will demonstrate their understanding of the timeline and key events of the Holocaust, as well as the concepts of conflict, tension/release, and cause/effect, by accurately recreating timelines.

- Students will analyze and accurately describe the musical components of tempo, dynamics, instrumentation, and mood in Górecki's *Symphony No. 3*. Additionally, students will respectfully and empathetically describe connections between musical elements and events relating to the Holocaust.

National Curriculum Standards for Social Studies addressed

- NCSSS 2: Time, Continuity, and Change: Social studies programs should include experiences that provide for the study of the past and its legacy.
- NCSSS 6: Power, Authority, and Governance: Social studies programs should include experiences that provide for the study of how people create and change structures of power, authority, and governance.
- NCSSS 9: Global Connections: Social studies programs should include experiences that provide for the study of global connections and interdependence.
- NCSSS 10: Civic Ideals and Practices: Social studies programs should include experiences that provide for the study of the ideals, principles, and practices of citizenship in a democratic republic.

C3 Framework for Social Studies State Standards addressed

- C3 Dimension 2: History
- C3 Dimension 3: Evaluating sources and using evidence

National Core Arts Standards for Music addressed

- MU:Pr4: Select, analyze, and interpret artistic work for presentation
- MU:Re7: Perceive and analyze artistic work
- MU:Re8: Interpret intent and meaning in artistic work
- MU:Cn11: Relate artistic works and ideas with societal, cultural, and historical context to deepen understanding

Materials

- Recorded musical example: *Symphony No. 3,* Op. 36: I. Lento, by Henryk Mikolaj Górecki
- Printed portion of lyrics: Górecki's *Symphony No. 3,* Op. 36: I. Lento
- Printed score: First eight pages of *Symphony No. 3,* Op. 36: I. Lento, by Henryk Mikolaj Górecki
- Book: *The Children We Remember* by Chana Byers Abells

Procedure

Softly start the recording of Górecki's *Symphony No. 3,* 1st movement. Continue to play the recording in the background while students view images and listen as you read the narration. This lesson is envisioned as the first lesson in a social studies unit focusing on the Holocaust, providing elementary students a reflective first encounter with the related timeline of events, as well as a review of the social studies concepts of conflict, tension/release, and cause/effect. Students will not be expected to take notes but will simply experience the presentation as a prompt for later discussion.

- For many centuries, misunderstandings, ignorance, and hate could be found in the way Jewish people were treated. Throughout history, they were considered by some to be the enemy. "Anti-Semitism" is the term for the belief that Jewish people are not as good as others. In the late 1800s, Jewish people began to be persecuted not only because of their religion but also because they were now identified as the Jewish race (Gross, 2006).
- Adolph Hitler lived in Germany (see Figure 4.8) and he fought in World War I. After the war, he went home and found that Germany was having problems.

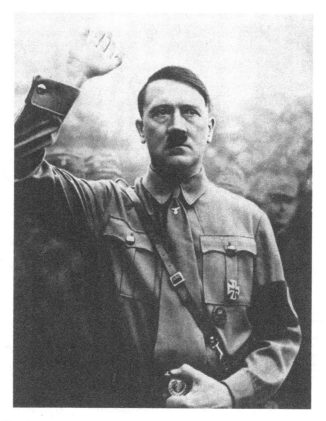

Figure 4.8 Adolf Hitler, 1940.
© The Library of Congress.

Many groups formed that claimed to know the answers and offer solutions. Hitler joined one of these groups, called the Nazis. The Nazis claimed Germany had lost World War I because the Jews had weakened the government. They claimed that since Jews were a separate race, they couldn't be Germans (Davies, 2000).

- Hitler was a powerful speaker. He blamed Jews for the lost war and he presented himself as the one man with the answers. In the early 1930s, the Nazi Party grew so much and became so popular that on January 30, 1933, the German government appointed Hitler as their chancellor (see Figure 4.9).
- With the invasion of Poland on September 1, 1939, World War II began. Figure 4.10 shows German soldiers near the beginning of the war. In less than a month, the Polish government had surrendered. Even though Jews had been in Poland for thousands of years, they now were not wanted. In Poland, Jewish people made up about 30% of the population. They lived in cities but mostly in towns, villages, and rural areas. Many of them spoke Yiddish instead of Polish, so their language, as well as their clothing and traditions, revealed their heritage (Bartov, 1996).
- When Germans first took over Poland, Jewish children were barred from school, Jews were forced to wear yellow stars (see Figure 4.11), and Jewish businesses were subjected to looting and vandalism (Davies, 2000). Gypsies, homosexuals, and people with incurable diseases were also persecuted.

Figure 4.9 Ceremony opening the 1933 Reichstag session when Hitler was named chancellor of Germany.

Figure 4.10 German troops parade through Warsaw, Poland, September, 1939.
© The National Archives and Records Administration/Free-Images.com.

- The first step in the German army's plan was to make all Jews move to what they called "ghettos" (see Figure 4.12). Jews were forced to leave their things behind and go to certain areas that were always the worst and most run down. They were forced to have 10 or 20 people live in one bedroom, or else they lived on the streets. Many Jews died on the freight trains on their way to the ghettos, and many people died of starvation in the ghettos. In 1940, 90 people starved in the ghettos. In 1941, 11,000 people starved. At its worst it was 500 people each week. Many people who didn't die of starvation died from cold or disease (Cole, 2003).
- Jewish people were brought to Polish ghettos as part of Hitler's "Final Solution." His horrible idea was to kill them all. Germans set up most of their concentration camps in Poland (see Figure 4.13). The reasons were that nearly all of Europe's Jews were there, because the army could use converted Polish army barracks for the camps, and the camps were close to railway lines. These were horrible places, designed for the extermination of Jews. Auschwitz was one of these camps (see Figure 4.14). To get Jewish people to go there, the German army tricked or forced them. People were told that they were going to a place

Figure 4.11 Yellow Jude Star.
© Naci Yavuz/Shutterstock.com.

Figure 4.12 A Jewish boy surrenders in Warsaw.
© United States Holocaust Museum/Free-Images.com.

Figure 4.13 Auschwitz-Birkenau railroad.
© Alex Guevara/Shutterstock.com.

with plenty of food, jobs, and doctors, and that it would be safer. Those were all lies (Cole, 2003).

- When they got there, the people would be divided into two groups (see Figure 4.15). The first group was people who were healthy enough to work. The second group—old people, sick people, and children—were sent to be killed. Families were split up. Everything that they had left was taken from them (Davies, 2000).

- The people who were chosen to work lived for a few more days, or weeks, or months. People who survived the camp have said that while it is possible to describe the camp, the feelings of living through it can never be made real to those who did not experience it. The people in these camps lived knowing that any day they might get beaten or be selected to be killed. What happened during the Holocaust is almost unimaginable, but it was real. We talk about Auschwitz in memory of those who did not survive. We also talk about it to make certain that nothing like it ever happens again. Figure 4.16 shows a portion of the Holocaust Memorial in Washington, DC.

Keep the recording of Górecki's *Symphony No. 3* playing; read aloud the children's story, *The Children We Remember,* by Chana Byers Abells.

Stop the recording at 12:50. Debrief with students about the material they just experienced. It is likely that listening (even if passively) to Górecki's music colored

Figure 4.14 Auschwitz-Birkenau concentration camp.
© JacekAbramowicz/Pixabay.

Figure 4.15 Selection and separation of prisoners at the Auschwitz-Birkenau concentration camp railway station, ca. 1944.
© Everett Historical/Shutterstock.com.

Figure 4.16 Holocaust Museum glass wall with names of Holocaust victims, Washington, DC, 1980–2006.
© Carol M. Highsmith/The Library of Congress.

their perceptions and impressions. Allow students to share their perceptions of the events and their feelings about the material. Ask students questions about the time-line of events, conflicts, and instances that displayed a cause/effect relationship.

Give a brief overview of Górecki's life. Inform students that the music they have been listening to was written by the Polish musician Henryk Górecki. He was born in 1933, the same year that Hitler came into power; he was six years old when the war began. Górecki grew up in Katowice, a small Polish village near Auschwitz. Górecki lived through World War II and wrote his *Symphony No. 3* to memorialize those who lost their lives during the Holocaust (Thomas, 2001; Moore, 2011).

Project the score of the first movement of Górecki's *Symphony No. 3* on a large screen. Direct students to visually analyze the music, paying special attention to dynamics and instrumentation. Show the first eight pages of the score, allowing students to examine only the first half of the initial arch structure, and then have students predict what occurs in the rest of the section. In the first section of the first movement, an overall arch exists in the dynamics (the piece starts very softly, then gradually crescendos to loud, then gradually decrescendos back to soft) and the instrumentation (the piece opens with one instrument part, then instruments are gradually added up to the climax, then instruments are gradually removed). This arch structure should be easy for students to perceive.

The first movement opens with a canon. A canon is similar to a round, but when new parts enter, instead of echoing the previous musical material exactly, they usually echo at a different pitch level. Direct students to listen as they follow along with the score to aurally and visually identify when different instruments enter. Ask students to take notes as they listen, recording their perceptions of the rhythm, tempo, melody, dynamics, instrumentation, harmony, and overall mood. They should keep in mind what they've learned about the Holocaust and consider why Górecki may have wanted the music to sound the way it does. It should help that they have heard the piece once already. Listen to a few segments with students.

After listening, discuss students' observations of musical elements that impact the work's mood: rhythm, tempo, melody, dynamics, and instrumentation. Regarding the harmony, mention that this piece opens with a special type of minor called Aeolian, which is based on church modes from Renaissance music. Table 4.5 provides teachers with an overview of the elements that work together to create a reflective, meditative mood in the first section of the first movement of Górecki's *Symphony No. 3*; a slow tempo and an overall arch to the dynamics and instrumentation (build-up of tension followed by relaxation). All timings are based on the recording of Górecki's *Symphony No. 3* by the London Sinfonietta, conducted by David Zinman.

Introduce the sections of the symphony that contain singing. Górecki had a hard time picking texts to use for his symphony. When he finally completed his work, he titled it *Symphony No. 3, the Symphony of Sorrowful Songs*. Górecki used Polish words for all three movements. The first movement incorporates a mother's prayer from a 15th-century collection of sacred songs at the Holy Cross Monastery at Lysa Góra in Poland. The second movement uses the prayer a Polish girl scratched inside a Gestapo prison. The third movement uses folk poetry from the province of Opole, which is close to Górecki's hometown in Poland. The poem was written by a mother mourning her son who died in World War I (Griffith, 2015). The lyrics for movements two and three are available online if your class wishes to explore further.

Project a portion of the first movement's lyrics and ask a volunteer to read them aloud:

> *My son, my chosen and beloved*
> *Share your wounds with your mother . . .*
> *Although you are already leaving me, my cherished hope.* (Górecki, 1992)

Table 4.5 Overview of Elements in the Opening Section of Górecki's *Symphony No. 3*

Time	Tempo	Dynamics	Instrumentation
0:00	*lento*	*pp*	Bass II part enters
1:01		*pp+*	Bass I part is added
2:02		*p*	Cello II part is added
3:04		*p+*	Cello I part is added
4:08		*mp*	Viola II part is added
5:10		*mp+*	Viola I part is added
6:09		*mf*	Violin II part is added
7:10		*f*	Violin I part is added
8:05		*f+*	Violins divide
9:06		*f*	First violins stop doubling
10:03		*mf*	Second violins begin unison playing
11:45		*p*	Basses drop out
12:50			Unison Es

Courtesy of author.

Listen to the segment of the first movement of Górecki's *Symphony No. 3* in which the soprano sings about her son who has died (start the recording at 12:50—the singing starts about 30 seconds later). In the recording, the text is sung in Polish, but students might want to follow along with the English translation. While they listen, ask them to connect what they hear with what they know about this composition, the composer, and the history of the time. How do they describe the sound of the singer's voice? How would they describe the dynamics? Why do they suppose the opening notes the soprano sings blend seamlessly with the notes played by the strings immediately beforehand?

Assessment

- Ask groups of students to work together, using resources available to them in the classroom, to create timelines of the Holocaust. Timelines should include major events, conflicts, and key details. In addition, they should include Górecki's birth on their timeline. Through informal class discussion, determine if students are able to appropriately explain and converse knowledgably about the information included in their timelines.

- Collect each student's written log describing musical elements of the first section of *Symphony No. 3*. Check for accurate descriptions of various musical elements including tempo, dynamics, instrumentation, and mood. In addition, through informal class discussion, determine if students are able to empathetically and respectfully explain the relationship between the events of the Holocaust and Górecki's symphony.

Extension

Allow students to explore and locate a text on which to base their own original composition. Ideas to get their research started include "The Diary of a Young Girl" by Anne Frank and "I Never Saw Another Butterfly," a collection of poetry and art created by Jewish children during their time living in the concentration camp Theresienstadt. You might also choose to have students examine other persecuted populations or groups facing discrimination.

Inventory of ideas

The following collection of ideas contains additional lesson topics, specific teaching strategies, and recommended activities.

1. Explore social studies and music with pen pals. Many teachers partner with educators from other states or countries to arrange pen pal exchanges between their students. Exchanges such as these allow students to practice their writing skills and learn about new regions in ways that are relevant to them. Extend students' musical understandings by exploring the music associated with the region in which the students' pen pals live. As a culminating activity, "meet" the pen pals via an online platform, and sing songs from each other's regions.

2. Read the children's book *Follow the Drinking Gourd* by Jeanette Winter. This picture book is based on a true story and there are many recordings of the accompanying song. In addition to singing the song, an analysis of the text will allow students to identify different landmarks and symbols that helped slaves on their journey to freedom in the north, creating a natural connection between language arts, music, and geography.

3. Create an imaginary road trip to travel to a variety of national parks and monuments around the United States. Listen to and sing Willie Nelson's "On the Road Again," and then analyze the style, lyrics, and structure. Explore the "See America" campaign, a movement to encourage people to connect and reconnect with American National Parks. Through an analysis of vintage parks posters, visual arts standards could be easily incorporated into this lesson as well. Figures 4.17, 4.18 and 4.19 show examples of vintage National Parks posters.

Figure 4.17 See America, Visit the National Parks, 1936.
© The Library of Congress.

4. Explore the importance of perspective in the recounting of specific historical events. Examine the song "Sixteen Tons" by Merle Travis, performed by Tennessee Ernie Ford, about the life of a coal miner, based on first-hand accounts of working in Kentucky coal mines. Utilize primary historical documents to find perspectives similar to and different from the perspective from which the song was written.

5. Listen to music that is representative of a specific time period or culture as a conversation starter. For example: (a) use the song "Winds of Change" by Klaus Meine, performed by the German band the Scorpions, to introduce a unit about the Cold War and the falling of the Berlin Wall; (b) use Billie Holiday's "Strange Fruit" to open a discussion of race relations and African American lynchings in the 1930s; or (c) listen to the song "Pretty Girl," a new Native American round dance song written and sung by Roger White Jr., an Assiniboine from

Figure 4.18 Grand Canyon National Park, a free government service, 1938.
© The Library of Congress.

the Red Bottom Clan of the Fort Peck Reservation in Montana. The following list includes additional songs for listening, analyzing, and performing.

Patriotic songs
- "America," text by Samuel Francis Smith; tune, Traditional
- "America the Beautiful" by Katherine Lee Bates
- "Battle Hymn of the Republic," text by Julia Ward Howe; tune, Traditional
- "God Bless America" by Irving Berlin

Figure 4.19   Yellowstone National Park, Ranger Naturalist Service, 1938.
© The Library of Congress.

- "Hail to the Chief" by James Sanderson
- "The Star-Spangled Banner" by Francis Scott Key
- "Yankee Doodle," Traditional
- "Yankee Doodle Dandy" by Robert Buckner
- "You're a Grand Old Flag" by George M. Cohan

Songs that describe specific social studies topics
- "Arlington" by Dave Turnbull and Jeremy Spillman, performed by Trace Adkins (national cemeteries, pride, and tributes)

- "Another Day in Paradise" by Phil Collins (homelessness)
- "America" by Neil Diamond (immigration)
- "Biko" by Peter Gabriel (anti-apartheid, racism)
- "Black and White" by Three Dog Night (racism)
- "A Change Is Gonna Come" by Sam Cooke (great migration)
- "Citizenship" by Red Grammer (citizenship)
- "Don't Drink the Water" by Dave Matthews (colonization of Native American land)
- "Don't Laugh at Me" by Allen Shamblin and Steve Seskin (bullying)
- "Everything Possible" by Fred Small (identity, sexual orientation)
- "Eyes on the Prize" by Sweet Honey in the Rock (civil rights)
- "Homeless" by Paul Simon (homelessness in South Africa)
- "Immigration Man" by Graham Nash and David Crosby (immigration)
- "Invisible" by Hunter Hayes (bullying)
- "It's Not Easy Bein' Green" by Joe Raposo (racism, identity)
- "Mr. Cab Driver" by Lenny Kravitz (racism)
- "Pressure Drop" by Toots Hibbert (natural disaster)
- "Saltwater" by Julian Lennon (climate change)
- "The Taxman" by the Beatles (taxation)
- "We Shall Not Be Moved" by Mavis Staples (civil rights)
- "Where We Going to Go?" by David Todd (climate change)

Songs that describe specific events in history
- "Alabama" by John Coltrane (written following Martin Luther King Jr.'s eulogy at a memorial service for four young girls who were killed in a church bombing in 1963)
- "The Battle of New Orleans" by Jimmy Driftwood (Revolutionary War)
- "North to Alaska" by Tillman Franks and Johnny Horton (Alaska gold rush)
- "When Johnny Comes Marching Home" by Patrick Gilmore (American Civil War)
- "Wreck of the Edmund Fitzgerald" by Gordon Lightfoot (shipwreck in Lake Superior)

Orchestral and choral compositions with social studies connections
- "Across the Bridge of Hope" by Jan Sandstrom (music) and Sean McLaughlin (text) (poem written by 12-year-old boy from Northern Ireland who was later killed when a bomb exploded)
- *Mass No. 10* "Mass in the Time of War" by Franz Joseph Haydn (French Revolution)
- "Metropolis Symphony" by Michael Daugherty (expressing American pop culture)

- "The Peacemakers" by Karl Jenkins (work for choir featuring texts by Gandhi, Martin Luther King, Nelson Mandela, and others)
- *Sinfonia da Requiem* by Benjamin Britten (originally commissioned by Japanese government, but written for Britten's parents; embodies an anti-war message)
- *A Survivor from Warsaw* Cantata by Arnold Schoenberg (tribute to Holocaust victims)
- *Symphony No. 1* by John Corigliano (memorializes AIDS victims; influenced by the NAMES Project AIDS Memorial Quilt)
- *Symphony No. 2* by Alexander Borodin (depiction of heroic figures from ancient Russia)
- *Symphony No. 2* "Song of a New Race" by William Grant Still (racism, identity, elitism)
- *Symphony No. 3* "Eroica" by Ludwig van Beethoven (first dedicated to Napoleon Bonaparte, then retitled "Eroica" by Beethoven, likely for its overall heroic quality)
- *Symphony No. 3* "The Great National" by Muzio Clementi (includes British national hymn "God Save the King")
- *Symphony No. 4* "For Peace" by Claudio Santoro (includes a choral setting of a portion of the poem "Poem of Peace" by Antoineta Dias de Morias e Silva)
- *Symphony No. 6* "Gettysburg" by Roy Harris (inspired by Lincoln's "Gettysburg Address")
- *Symphony No. 7* "Leningrad" by Dmitri Shostakovich (Nazi invasion of Russia in 1941)
- *Symphony No. 8* "The Journey" by Einojuhani Rautavaara (human lifespan; passages)
- *Symphony No. 9* "Symphony of Hope" by Andrzej Panufnik (racial and religious tolerance)

Musicals with social studies connections
- *1776* by Sherman Edwards and Peter Stone (US Declaration of Independence)
- *Billy Elliot* by Elton John and Lee Hall (classism, identity, and gender roles)
- *Hamilton* by Lin-Manuel Miranda (life of American founding father Alexander Hamilton, American Revolution, immigration)
- *My Fair Lady* by Alan Jay Lerner and Frederick Loewe (portrayals of classism and gender inequality)
- *Newsies* by Alan Menken and Jack Feldman (child labor, economics, reform)
- *Oliver* by Lionel Bart, based on the novel *Oliver Twist* by Charles Dickens (poverty, classism, privilege)

- *Ragtime* by Stephen Flaherty, Lynn Ahrens, and Terrence McNally (racism, immigration, gender equality, economics)
- *South Pacific* by Richard Rodgers and Oscar Hammerstein (racism, sexism, prejudice)
- *West Side Story* by Leonard Bernstein and Stephen Sondheim (racism, immigration, musical adaptation of *Romeo and Juliet*)

6. Consider the relationship between the lyrics, instrumentation, and mood of the song "Rosie the Riveter" by Redd Evans and John Jacob Loeb with the World War II cultural icon of Rosie the Riveter as a symbol of American feminism and the influence of women in American economics (also see Lesson 2.1).

7. Read and dissect the poem "The Colossus" by Emma Lazarus, which is found inside the pedestal of the Statue of Liberty. Study and rehearse the song "Give Me Your Tired, Your Poor" by Barbara Silberg, then audio-record students singing the piece. As a class, design and create a video presentation that applies geographic knowledge, highlights various motivations for immigration, portrays the impact of immigration over time, and utilizes the class-created audio recording to accompany the film. Through this project, students will communicate the results of their research and rehearsal with others using digital tools.

8. Compare and contrast Woodie Guthrie's "This Land Is Your Land" with Irving Berlin's "God Bless America." Rehearse and perform both pieces. As a class, explore the history of America in the 1930s and investigate the significance and meaning of each song.

9. Compare and contrast the meaning and effect of two different versions of the song "Wavin' Flag" by K'naan, a Somali-Canadian artist. The original describes the Somalian people's desire for freedom and gives an unfiltered portrayal of their struggles. The song was chosen as Coca-Cola's promotional anthem for the 2010 FIFA World Cup and was revised and remixed as "Wavin' Flag (Coca-Cola Celebration Mix)."

10. Go on an exploration of your classroom, lunchroom, playground, or other "environment." Collect and define the sounds you encounter using musical terms such as pitch (high/low), tempo (fast/slow), harmony (consonant/dissonant), and timbre (tone quality).

11. Research the origin of familiar melodies contained in symphonic works, for example, *Appalachian Spring* by Aaron Copland, *New World Symphony* by Antonin Dvorak, "Negro Folksongs in Counterpoint: No. 5, Swing Low, Sweet Chariot" by Florence Price, and "American Rhapsody" by Ernst von Dohnányi. This lesson will allow students to explore ways that people create, learn, share, and adapt to culture.

12. Research work songs and locate examples of songs representing people from a variety of professions (sailors, lumberjacks, postal workers, cowboys, miners,

railroad workers, and farmers). Explore ways the music was connected to each occupation, aided workers in completing tasks, eased burdens, and developed a sense of community. In groups, have students create either songs or chants to accompany their daily work and perform their compositions for the class.

13. In a social studies unit focused on identifying events and democratic values associated with the civil rights movement, listen to, analyze, and sing Bob Dylan's "Blowin' in the Wind." Explore Dylan's possible motivation for asking rhetorical questions about war, peace, and freedom in the text of his song and his possible motivation for incorporating the melody of the African American spiritual "No More Auction Block." As a class, discuss the ways individuals can act as actively engaged citizens and use their voices to bring about positive change.

14. Listen to and analyze the song "Video Killed the Radio Star," performed by the Buggles. Explore the concept of cause and effect, especially focusing on the impact of technology on the music industry. Examine technology that is now outdated (floppy discs, pagers, etc.) and analyze reasons technology becomes obsolete.

15. Listen to a recording of the Dubliners performing "The Rising of the Moon," an Irish ballad whose lyrics describe a battle that occurred during the Irish Rebellion of 1798. Create a spiral timeline using the lyrics of the song, and then create a second spiral timeline after exploring primary source documents related to the battle. Through this lesson, students can analyze, evaluate, and compare information presented in diverse formats, identifying parts of a text that show the authors' points of view.

16. In groups, have students identify and investigate 10 major historical events that have taken place in their lifetimes. As a class, consider the structure and content of Billy Joel's "We Didn't Start the Fire." Have small groups create lyrics for new verses that incorporate their own histories and align with Joel's original structure, melody, and rhythm. Finally, have small groups perform for the class.

17. Encourage students to identify similarities and differences between their lifestyles and the lifestyles of people living in another part of the world. Explore music from both regions, listening for elements that are the same and elements that are different. Read a book together such as *Same, Same, but Different* by Jenny Sue Kostecki-Shaw or *This Is How We Do It: One Day in the Lives of Seven Kids From Around the World* by Matt Lamothe to open the conversation. Ask your students to write a journal entry from the perspective of another part of the world and use sensory details to accurately describe a typical day in that place.

18. Assist your students in identifying candidates running for political office. You might choose to focus on local, regional, state, or national elections. Invite students to identify their candidate of choice, research their candidate's views

and background, and work together in small groups to create campaign songs and posters for their nominee.

19. Any time your students explore a specific region or culture, take time to listen to and sing the music associated with that region or culture:

   - If your students complete "state projects" and create online presentations, encourage them to include official state songs as a part of those presentations.
   - Students might explore geography by checking the labels of their clothes and shoes, identifying areas of the world where those items were produced, and learning about those locations. Incorporate music by studying examples of songs from those regions.
   - Take your students on virtual field trips. For example, if your students travel to Hawaii (see Figure 4.20) on a Google journey, study the song "Aloha 'Oe," written by Hawaii's Queen Lili'uokalani in the late 1870s.

Figure 4.20 Illustrated map of Hawaii.
© Mio Buono/Shutterstock.com.

5

Music and Science

Introduction

Our world today depends on people who can think logically *and* creatively, and experiences connecting music and science promote both these types of reasoning. Lessons that integrate music and science also encourage active student engagement and offer opportunities for students to perceive connections, make observations, synthesize disparate information, formulate conclusions, and thoughtfully reflect. Teachers can meaningfully integrate music and science by incorporating tools of inquiry across both disciplines and by emphasizing the concepts and process skills shared by both. When students explore concepts, skills, and processes the disciplines share, their understandings in music and science will be enhanced.

One key connection between music and science is their shared focus on inquiry. Both disciplines emphasize rational and empirical thinking, and both disciplines also favor healthy skepticism, encouraging questioning and confirmation of results. This focus on inquiry has huge benefits for student learning, as concepts students discover for themselves are more meaningful than concepts that have simply been presented by a teacher. It is not always easy or efficient to allow student exploration to guide lessons. For example, in music, teachers sometimes miss out on opportunities for students to grow as reflective musical performers. In any given piece, teachers could simply tell their students how to sing a particular phrase. They could also, perhaps even more quickly, demonstrate how the particular phrase should be sung. Alternatively, if the students are allowed to work through the different phrasing possibilities, analyze the chord tones and nonharmonic tones, discover the melodic spans, and determine the levels of rhythmic activity, they will arrive at a phrasing decision that makes musical and personal sense to them. Their inquiry would definitely shine through during a performance. This is as true in science as it is in music. For example, in any given scientific observation exercise, it is likely more efficient for a teacher to direct students to observe key elements and simply inform them about the features that are present; however, allowing students to make their own observations, analyze what they encounter, work through the categorization of information, and share their findings with others results in a richer learning experience.

The Chapter 5 lessons and inventory of ideas promote active engagement in learning, explore high-level concepts, draw on a wide variety of musical examples, and focus on valid connections between music and science.

Integrating Music Across the Elementary Curriculum. Kristin Harney, Oxford University Press (2020). © Oxford University Press.
DOI: 10.1093/oso/9780190085582.001.0001.

Common links between music and science

A common strategy for connecting music and science is to explore "big ideas" that the two disciplines have in common, utilizing the tools of each discipline to examine shared concepts. Enduring ideas that might be explored in music and science include:

Balance
Beauty
Change
Classification
Cause and effect
Cycle
Development
Diversity
Energy
Flexibility
Force
Frequency
Habit
Hierarchy
Instinct
Interdependence
Intuition
Inquiry
Measurement
Models
Motion
Observation
Pattern
Prediction
Repetition
Stability/instability
Structure
Synergy
Systems
Transformation

National standards

It is important for teachers to address standards in music and science when designing lessons that integrate the two disciplines. Including standards from each discipline promotes a balance between music and science and helps to avoid one subject serving the other. Regarding calls for integration, the National Core Arts Standards for Music unambiguously emphasize integration, specifically inviting students to explore ways that other disciplines connect with music. The Next Generation Science Standards (NGSS) do not explicitly promote music integration; however, broad themes included in the standards suggest many meaningful curricular connections with music. For example, NGSS Crosscutting Concepts facilitate students' exploration of science concepts across the four primary domains of Life Science, Earth and Space Science, Physical Science, and Engineering Design. Just as those broad concepts are a way of linking the domains of science, they are also useful for connecting with disciplines outside science. Additionally, NGSS performance expectations include connections to the Common Core State Standards at every grade level, offering more avenues for possible music integration. The NGSS were developed through a collaborative process and were released in 2013. They are broadly based on the National Academy of Science's *Framework for K-12 Science Education*. The following boxes specify the standards that are addressed in the Chapter 5 lessons and inventory of ideas:

- Box 5.1, Next Generation Science Standards
- Box 5.2, National Core Arts Standards

Box 5.3 offers a framework for structuring Chapter 5 lessons and activities.

Box 5.1 Next Generation Science Standards Included in Chapter 5 Sample Lessons (L) and Inventory of Ideas (I)

Life Science	LS1	From Molecules to Organisms: Structures and Processes	L5.1
			L5.2
			L5.3
			L5.6
			I3
			I5
			I9
			I10
			I15
	LS2	Ecosystems: Interactions, Energy, and Dynamics	L5.1
			L5.6
			I1
			I4
			I12
			I14
			I16

	LS3	Heredity: Inheritance and Variation of Traits	L5.2
			I7
			I9
			I10
	LS4	Biological Evolution: Unity and Diversity	L5.1
			L5.2
			L5.4
			L5.6
			I7
			I9
			I13
Earth & Space Science	ESS1	Earth's Place in the Universe	L5.4
			I2
			I10
	ESS2	Earth's Systems	L5.3
			L5.4
			I2
			I6
			I13
			I14
	ESS3	Earth and Human Activity	L5.1
			L5.6
			I3
			I7
			I8
Physical Science	PS1	Matter and Its Interactions	L5.4
			L5.5
			I4
			I6
			I15
			I17
	PS2	Motion and Stability: Forces and Interactions	I1
			I7
	PS3	Energy	L5.3
			L5.5
			L5.6
			I1
			I4
	PS4	Waves and Their Applications in Technologies for Information Transfer	L5.3
			L5.5
			I12
			I15
			I17

Engineering	ETS1	Engineering Design	L5.1
Design			L5.5
Introduction			I3
			I5
			I10
			I11
			I14
			I16

Next Generation Science Standards: For States, By States. NGSS Lead States, 2013, The National Academies Press.

Box 5.2 National Core Arts Standards for Music Included in Chapter 5 Lessons (L) and Inventory of Ideas (I)

MU:Cr1 (Create)	Generate and conceptualize artistic ideas and work	L5.1
		L5.2
		L5.5
		I3
		I5
		I9
		I16
		I17
MU:Cr2 (Create)	Organize and develop artistic ideas and work	L5.3
		L5.6
		I4
		I5
		I16
		I17
MU:Cr3 (Create)	Refine and complete artistic work	L5.1
		L5.5
		L5.6
		I5
		I13
		I17
MU:Pr4 (Perform)	Select, analyze, and interpret artistic work for presentation	L5.1
		L5.2
		I6
		I7
		I11
		I14

MU:Pr5 (Perform)	Develop and refine artistic techniques and work for presentation	L5.1 L5.4 I5 I10 I15
MU:Pr6 (Perform)	Convey meaning through the presentation of artistic work	L5.3 L5.6 I4 I7 I12 I13
MU:Re7 (Respond)	Perceive and analyze artistic work	L5.1 L5.5 I1 I3 I6 I10 I14
MU:Re8 (Respond)	Interpret intent and meaning in artistic work	L5.4 L5.6 I2 I8 I12
MU:Re9 (Respond)	Apply criteria to evaluate artistic work	L5.2 L5.5 I1 I9 I11 I15
MU:Cn10 (Connect)	Synthesize and relate knowledge and personal experiences to make art	L5.2 L5.3 L5.5 L5.6 I3 I4 I8 I9 I11 I13 I16

MU:Cn11 (Connect)	Relate artistic ideas and works with societal, cultural, and historical context to deepen understanding	L5.1 L5.4 I2 I6 I7 I15 I17

Box 5.3 Framework for Chapter 5 Lessons and Ideas

This chapter is designed to support K–5 educators as they integrate music and science. The lessons are designed to be fully taught by classroom teachers; however, the plans may also facilitate partnerships and collaboration between classroom teachers and music specialists. All lessons and activities have been reviewed by practicing teachers, and most have been field-tested in elementary classrooms. Chapter 5 lessons are labeled as primary, intermediate, or upper elementary, but all the plans and activities are adaptable to a variety of grade levels and are intended as tools for you to meet your students' needs. Some of the lessons may need to be spread over two or more class periods. Please adjust, adapt, or expand however works best for you and for your students.

Lesson 5.1: Ebola, the infectious disease and the song

Grade Level: Intermediate or upper elementary
Essential Questions: How can scientists and musicians change an environment to meet people's needs? How are the transmission of disease, the transmission of music, and the transmission of ideas related?

Objectives

- Following class discussion, a demonstration modeling the spread of infectious disease among a population, and a musical and textual analysis of the song "Ebola in Town," students will correctly identify a variety of methods by which infectious diseases like Ebola are spread.

- Students will demonstrate proper handwashing techniques and describe the relationship between handwashing and the transmission of infection.
- Students will sing the chorus of "Ebola in Town," performing with accurate rhythms, pitches, and enunciation.
- Students will create rhythmic accompaniments and dance sequences to accompany "Ebola in Town" that align with the style and tempo of the song.
- Students will identify a contemporary science-based issue and compose a song to inform others about the issue they selected, then perform their composition with in-tune, rhythmically accurate singing and clear enunciation.

Next Generation Science Standards addressed

- LS1: From Molecules to Organisms: Structures and Processes
- LS2: Ecosystems: Interactions, Energy, and Dynamics
- LS4: Biological Evolution: Unity and Diversity
- ESS3: Earth and Human Activity
- ETS1: Engineering Design

National Core Arts Standards for Music addressed

- MU:Pr1: Generate and conceptualize artistic ideas and work
- MU:Pr3: Refine and complete artistic work
- MU:Pr4: Select, analyze, and interpret artistic work for presentation
- MU:Pr5 Develop and refine artistic techniques and work for presentation
- MU:Re7: Perceive and analyze artistic work
- MU:Cn11: Relate artistic ideas and works with societal, cultural, and historical context to deepen understanding

Materials

- Supplies
  - Lotion
  - Glitter
- Recorded musical example: "Ebola in Town" by Samuel "Shadow" Morgan, Edwin "D-12" Tweh, and Kuzzy of 2Kings
- Printed lyrics: Last verse and chorus of song "Ebola in Town"

Procedure

Before you begin this lesson and away from the view of your students, rub lotion on your hands, sprinkle some glitter into your palm, and then rub your hands together to distribute the glitter on your palms. As you progress through the lesson, move around the room naturally, perhaps opening a window, adjusting the lights, closing a door, looking in a cupboard, writing on the board, pulling down a screen, or sharpening a pencil. You will be distributing glitter on every surface you touch. As you get closer to the handwashing portion of the lesson, your touching can become more obvious and you might touch various students' desks, adjust your glasses, or scratch your cheek. Depending on when your students notice you have glitter on your hands, you can either stop the lesson and address the glitter right then, or you can politely disregard their comments and continue ("Oh, thank you, I was working on a project earlier," then lightly wipe your hands with a tissue as you carry on). You might also select a few students to secretly spread the glitter around the room during the lesson.

Overview of Ebola virus disease

Ask students to describe or define what they know about Ebola and list their responses on the board. Throughout history, health epidemics have had major impacts on human existence.

Ebola virus disease (EVD) is an uncommon but deadly disease that can affect people, monkeys, gorillas, and chimpanzees. The virus that causes EVD was discovered in 1976 in what is now the Democratic Republic of Congo, and there have been numerous outbreaks of the disease since then. The World Health Organization announced a Public Health Emergency of International Concern related to Ebola in Western Africa when tens of thousands of people became infected in 2014. The outbreaks have been concentrated in parts of sub-Saharan Africa. The virus forcefully attacks a person's blood and quickly spreads throughout the body. Many people die soon after contracting the virus. Symptoms include fever, severe headache, chest pain, muscle pain, cough, rash, gastrointestinal issues, unexplained bleeding, and shock (World Health Organization, 2019). Figure 5.1 shows a magnified image of Ebola virus particles.

Transmission of infection

Ask students to describe ways they think that viruses like Ebola or even the common cold are spread, and again, list their responses on the board. Regarding Ebola, scientists believe that infected bats transmit the virus to humans, either directly or by infecting other animals that people hunt for meat (World Health Organization, 2019). Once a person has been infected, the virus can spread from person to person through direct contact with blood or bodily fluids. This means that if people touch the blood, urine, saliva, sweat, tears, or other body fluid of an infected person, then touch their eyes, nose, mouth, or broken skin, they can become infected too. Symptoms may appear between 2 and 21 days after contact. A person who is infected with Ebola and displaying symptoms of the disease can transmit it to others.

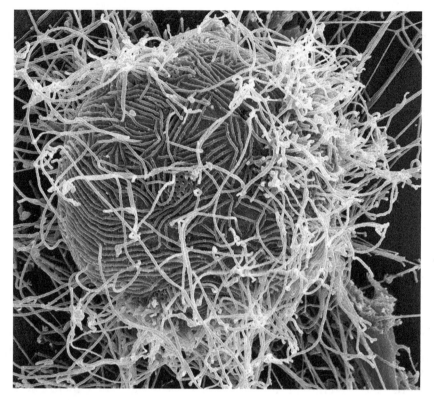

Figure 5.1 Microscopic view of Ebola virus particles, 2014.
© National Institute of Allergy and Infectious Diseases, National Institutes of Health/Flickr.

Preventing the transmission of disease

Next, discuss preventative measures and ask students to describe specific actions that help prevent viruses from spreading. These include staying home when you are sick (quarantine), handwashing, covering coughs/sneezes, vaccination, and wearing masks.

If people will be in an area impacted by Ebola, they are advised to avoid contact with blood and body fluids, with items that might have blood or body fluids on them, and with bats, primates, and meat from unknown sources. According to the American Centers for Disease Control and Prevention (n.d.), the most valuable thing people can do to prevent the spread of infections, illnesses, and deadly viruses like Ebola is proper handwashing.

If you haven't already, take time to explain why you have glitter on your hands—to model how viral and bacterial infections can spread. Invite students to walk around the classroom to observe as many places that glitter has been left behind as they can. During their walk, play the song "Ebola in Town" by Samuel "Shadow" Morgan, Edwin "D-12" Tweh, and Kuzzy of 2Kings.

After a brief review of their observations, relate the spread of glitter around the room to the spread of viruses. We can't see viruses, but if we have them on our hands, we leave them everywhere we touch, just like the glitter.

Wipe your hands on a tissue or paper towel, and then show your students how much glitter still remains. Next, rinse your hands in cold water, and again show that most of the glitter is staying put. Finally, wash your hands thoroughly with soap and warm water to remove all traces of the glitter. People often touch their eyes, noses, and mouths, even without realizing it, so as the Centers for Disease Control and Prevention recommends, removing germs through handwashing is essential for keeping us healthy.

Review proper handwashing techniques with your class (use warm water and soap; scrub palms, backs of hands, fingers, thumbs, wrists, and under fingernails for 20 seconds; rinse with warm water; and dry with a single-use towel or air dryer). Singing a song such as the "ABCs" while scrubbing will help students attain the correct 20-second time recommendation. Allow everyone to wash their hands.

The song "Ebola in Town"

At the beginning of 2014, many people in Liberia were not taking the Ebola out-break seriously. Liberian songwriters Samuel "Shadow" Morgan, Edwin "D-12" Tweh, and Kuzzy of 2Kings wanted to help spread the word that Ebola was a real and very dangerous disease, so they wrote and produced "Ebola in Town," an awareness song explaining to people about the Ebola virus and how to avoid becoming infected. Typical awareness songs are slow and serious, but Morgan, Tweh, and Kuzzy chose an upbeat, danceable rhythm for their hip-hop-style song. Street DJs began playing and promoting the song, and it became an almost instant hit in Liberia.

Tell students they heard the song during their previous walk around the class-room, but that you will play it again so they can focus on the music. Download and project the lyrics for the last verse and chorus of "Ebola in Town." Listen to approx-imately the last minute of "Ebola in Town" while students follow along with the lyrics. Explain that the kissing mentioned in the song describes a cheek kiss greeting. Close physical contact is common in Liberian culture. Finger-snap handshakes, hugging, touching, and double cheek kisses are customary, even between strangers (Olukoju, 2006).

Ask students to identify strategies for protecting against the spread of the Ebola virus that were described in lyrics. Have students imagine what it would be like to not be able to shake anyone's hand, hug anyone, or even give a high five to a friend.

After analyzing the lyrics, rehearse the song and prepare for a final per-formance. Listen to "Ebola in Town" again, and ask students to tap, clap, or snap to the beat. Ask students to create an instrumental accompaniment or body percussion ostinato (a repeating rhythm) that aligns with the music. As students become comfortable, invite them to sing along on the chorus, then the verses. Work to correctly perform the rhythm of the chorus, including longer sounds, rests, and instances where phrases jump in ahead of the beat such as on the lyrics "don't touch your friend" (Morgan, Tweh, & Kuzzy, 2014). Invite groups of students to create dance sequences that fit the upbeat music and possibly reflect the lyrics. Finally, perform the entire song by singing, playing, and dancing.

Simon "Shadow" Morgan, Edwin "D-12" Tweh, and Kuzzy of 2Kings wrote the awareness song "Ebola in Town" to inform people about Ebola and to persuade them to change their behavior to stay safe. They intended for their song to transmit information and hoped that the song would be popular, so that as many people as possible might be helped. Assist your students in identifying other contemporary science–based issues such as antibiotic resistance, clean drinking water, pollution, obesity, impact of microplastics, and clean energy. Guide small groups to research issues they select, then compose short awareness songs to inform others. Depending on grade level, time, and expertise, students' songs might be vocal only or might have instrumental accompaniment. Students might use existing songs ("Twinkle Twinkle," "Mary Had a Little Lamb," etc.) as frameworks for their compositions. As a culminating activity, invite each group to perform for the class.

Assessment

- Ask students to reflect on the lesson and write a response to the following prompts: Why can the term "infectious" describe the Ebola virus and the song "Ebola in Town"? Can a virus and a song be contagious? What is the relationship between the transmission of disease and the transmission of ideas through music? Collect students' reflections and check for accuracy of information, key details regarding viruses, and evidence of musical analysis.
- Ask students to demonstrate self-awareness by honestly appraising their current handwashing habits on a scale of 1 to 5.
- Observe small group performances of awareness songs. Assess the lyrics for accurate information and alignment with a contemporary science–based issue, and listen for in-tune, rhythmically accurate singing and clear enunciation.

Extensions/adaptations

- Compare and contrast "Ebola in Town" with Liberian visual art that has been created in response to the Ebola outbreak. For example, explore the work of artist Leslie Lumeh, who created Ebola posters for UNICEF.

- For older students or students who may not need a review of handwashing techniques, you might elect to focus on another prevention strategy such as vaccinations or food safety, or you might explore infections or epidemics more thoroughly.

Lesson 5.2: Saint-Saëns's *Carnival of the Animals* and animal classification

Grade Level: Primary or intermediate
Essential Question: How do scientists and musicians classify various items and entities within their disciplines?

Objectives

- Students will listen and evaluate the musical characteristics of various segments of Camille Saint-Saëns's *Carnival of the Animals* to make informed guesses about the animals represented in each movement.
- Students will correctly classify five types of vertebrates based on their identifying characteristics.
- Students will demonstrate body movements that align with the musical characteristics of *Carnival of the Animals* as they move to interpret the characteristics of various animals.
- Students will apply scientific criteria regarding various animals' characteristics to evaluate how successful Saint-Saëns was in representing those animals through music.

Next Generation Science Standards addressed

- LS1: From Molecules to Organisms: Structures and Processes
- LS3: Heredity: Inheritance and Variation of Traits
- LS4: Biological Evolution: Unity and Diversity

National Core Arts Standards for Music addressed

- MU:Cr1: Generate and conceptualize artistic ideas and work
- MU:Pr4: Select, analyze, and interpret artistic work for presentation
- MU:Re9: Apply criteria to evaluate artistic work
- MU:Cn10: Synthesize and relate knowledge and personal experiences to make art

Materials

- Recorded musical example: *Carnival of the Animals* by Camille Saint-Saëns
- Animal Classification Logs (Table 5.1)
- Musical Classification Logs (Table 5.2)
- Objects and/or artifacts for five categories of vertebrate animals

Procedure

Scientists sort animals into groups that share various characteristics, a process called classification. First, have students study the difference between vertebrates (animals with a spine) and invertebrates (animals without a spine) and classify representative examples from each group.

Vertebrates	Invertebrates
Dog	Spider
Eagle	Honeybee
Goldfish	Worm
Snake	Octopus
Frog	Snail

Next, introduce the five classes of vertebrates most commonly studied in elementary school: mammals, birds, fish, reptiles, and amphibians. Introduce stations where students will explore different characteristics of each class of animal and collect evidence for classifying them. At each station, you may display artifacts that represent each group. Artifacts might include animal skins, skulls, a bird's nest, feathers, a living goldfish, a turtle shell, and a living frog. Each station could also include resources such as books, photos, fact sheets, and web resources about each group.

Pass out an Animal Classification Log to each student (see Table 5.1). As they visit each vertebrate station, students will record their observations, collecting evidence the class will use in developing a list of characteristics for each vertebrate group. Students will also sketch and label a representative animal from each class.

Following students' individual work, project a blank Animal Classification Log and fill it in as a class, using group consensus and discussion to determine the common attributes and characteristics for each class of vertebrates. Your log may include the following information (Pennock & Wood, n.d.):

Mammals
- Drink milk when they are born
- Have hair or fur on their body

Table 5.1 Animal Classification Log

Vertebrate Class	Observations and Sketches
Mammal	
Bird	
Fish	
Reptile	
Amphibian	

Courtesy of author.

- Are warm-blooded
- Give birth to live young
- Include people, dogs, cats, bears, bats, mice, dolphins, and whales

Birds
- Have feathers
- Hatch from hard-shelled eggs
- Are warm-blooded
- Include robins, ducks, eagles, seagulls, owls, parrots, flamingos, and hawks

Fish
- Live in water
- Breathe with gills
- Have scales and fins
- Are cold-blooded
- Most lay eggs
- Include sharks, salmon, tuna, stingrays, trout, clownfish, and goldfish

Reptiles
- Have dry, scaly skin
- Most hatch from soft-shelled eggs on land
- Are cold-blooded
- Include snakes, lizards, turtles, crocodiles, and alligators

Amphibians
- Hatch from eggs in the water
- Are born with gills
- Have smooth, moist skin
- Develop lungs and can live on land
- Are cold-blooded
- Include frogs, toads, and salamanders

As scientists classify animals, so can musicians classify music. If students are not yet familiar with instruments of the orchestra, or as a review, display images and play short excerpts of the flute, clarinet, xylophone, glockenspiel, piano, and instruments of the string family (violin, viola, cello, and bass). Students will also need grade-level appropriate terms to describe tempo (fast/medium/slow or allegro/andante/largo), dynamics (loud/medium/soft or forte/mezzo forte/piano), rhythmic quality (choppy/smooth or marcato/staccato/legato), and pitch (high/low). Say, "Just like we can classify animals based on their various characteristics, we can classify musical examples based on their musical characteristics."

Introduce the French composer Camille Saint-Saëns, who was born in Paris, France, in 1835. Explain that in French-speaking countries, the name Camille is a common name for boys. From a very young age, Saint-Saëns was extremely skilled in music. He was known in his lifetime as a teacher, performer, and composer of music. He was also known for being very good-natured. In 1886, Saint-Saëns wrote a set of short movements that musically represented the characteristics of different animals. The collection is titled *Carnival of the Animals*. During Saint-Saëns's lifetime, he did not permit the collection to be published, but since his death in 1921, audiences around the world have been able to enjoy this composition (Fallon, Ratner, & Harding, 2001).

Pass out a Musical Classification Log to each student (see Table 5.2). As they listen to excerpts from various movements of *Carnival of the Animals*, students will have two primary tasks. One is to speculate what animal they think Saint-Saëns is portraying in each movement and sketch that animal in their log. The second is to record any musical observations that informed their decision-making process, collecting evidence the class will use in developing a list of characteristics for each movement of the piece. Their observations may include notes about each movement's instrumentation, tempo, dynamics, rhythmic quality, and pitch. Posting a list of these terms may be helpful to students.

As with the animal classification, following students' individual musical analysis, project a blank Musical Classification Log and fill it in as a class, using group consensus, discussion, and perhaps relistening to portions of the music to determine the common attributes and characteristics of each movement of *Carnival of the Animals*. The titles listed are Saint-Saëns's own names for those movements. Your log may include the following information:

1. "Introduction and March of the Lion"
   - String family and pianos
   - Stately march tempo and strong rhythmic accents (marcato) sound like a lion walking proudly
   - Loud, low rumbles on pianos mimic the sound of a roaring lion
   - The division between the introduction and the march is very clear at about the 0:30 point

2. "Hens and Roosters"
   - Violin, viola, pianos, and clarinet
   - Fast, repeated rhythmic theme that sounds like chickens pecking and scratching as they eat
   - A very fast "cock-a-doodle-doo" melody can be heard in the pianos and the clarinet

3. "Tortoises"
   - String family and piano
   - Soft, smooth, slow melody played by low strings mimic the movement of a tortoise

Table 5.2 Musical Classification Log

Musical Example	Observations and Sketches
1.	
2.	
3.	
4.	
5.	
6.	
7.	
8.	
9.	
10.	

Courtesy of author.

- The melody is a slow version of Jacques Offenbach's well-known, and very fast, piece "Can Can," again highlighting a tortoise's slow, deliberate movements
- Repeated high chords in the piano provide accompaniment

4. "The Elephant"
   - Double bass and piano
   - Melody is very low and heavy; along with the moderate tempo, it sounds like an elephant lumbering along
   - Piano plays a waltz-like higher accompaniment

5. "Kangaroos"
   - Pianos
   - A bounding, bouncy figure is the main rhythmic aspect of the piece, signifying the hopping of kangaroos
   - When chords ascend, they get louder and speed up; when they descend, they get softer and slow down

6. "Aquarium"
   - Violin, viola, cello, pianos, flute, and glockenspiel (sometimes played by glass harmonica)
   - Smooth, soft flute melody sounds like fish gliding through the water
   - Peaceful runs and arpeggios in the piano sound like bubbles in the water
   - Someone will probably say this is from Disney's *Beauty and the Beast*. It is not in *Beauty and the Beast.*

7. "Characters with Long Ears" (donkeys)
   - Violins
   - The violins alternate playing upwardly sweeping harsh, high, and loud pitches with low descending pitches in sets of two, imitating the sound of a donkey saying hee-haw

8. "The Cuckoo in the Depths of the Woods"
   - Pianos and clarinet
   - The pianos create the setting, using a moderate tempo and mostly soft dynamics, emulating a forest
   - The clarinet repeats only two notes, copying the sound of a far-away cuckoo bird's call (in the score, Saint-Saëns wrote that the clarinet should play from off-stage)

9. "Aviary"
   - String family, pianos, and flute
   - Fast, trilling, light, high, running notes in the flute copy the sound of a single songbird

- The piano and strings play the accompaniment and mimic the background noises, fluttering, and hectic activity that can be found in an aviary

10. "The Swan"
    - Pianos and cello
    - Slow, smooth, soft cello melody imitates the movement of a swan elegantly gliding across the water
    - The faster, but still gentle sounds of the piano accompaniment could represent the faster movements of the swan's feet under the water

Note: There are 14 movements in Saint-Saëns's *Carnival of the Animals*. This lesson only includes information about 10 of the movements.

Next, divide your class into 10 groups. Assign each group an animal from one of the movements of *Carnival of the Animals* that they studied. As a group, have students write about where their animal lives (habitat), what it eats (diet), how it moves (including speed), how it breathes, its size and other physical characteristics, and its classification. Members of the group will work collaboratively to create, rehearse, and present a set of body actions that aligns with the musical characteristics of their assigned movement of *Carnival of the Animals* and represents characteristics of their assigned animal. Students present with the recording.

Finally, based on the cataloguing and classification of animal characteristics, direct students to evaluate how well Saint-Saëns portrayed the animals in his composition *Carnival of the Animals* through his choice of specific musical characteristics. Use group consensus techniques to arrive at an answer for each movement of the piece.

Assessment

- Collect students' Animal Classification Logs and Musical Classification Logs. Check for representative evidence and sketches for each vertebrate class and each musical movement of *Carnival of the Animals*.
- Pass out 3-2-1 exit tickets. Ask students to reflect on the lesson, then write three things they learned, two things they would like to study further, and one question they still have.

Lesson 5.3: Steady beat, heartbeat, tempo, and rate

Grade Level: Primary or intermediate
Essential Question: What are the relationships between (1) steady beat in music and heartbeat in science and (2) tempo in music and heart rate in science?

Objectives

- Students will accurately move to the steady beat of "Stayin' Alive" by the Bee Gees and tap, clap, or pat to maintain a steady beat at a variety of other tempos.
- Students will locate their pulses and correctly measure and record their resting heart rates and exercise-elevated heart rates.
- Students will examine the concept of steady beat from a unique perspective, reflecting about the importance of maintaining a steady beat during cardiopulmonary resuscitation (CPR) and evaluating their ability to maintain the tempo required for proper CPR.

Next Generation Science Standards addressed

- LS1: From Molecules to Organisms: Structures and Processes
- ESS2: Earth's Systems
- PS3: Energy
- PS4: Waves and Their Applications in Technologies for Information Transfer

National Core Arts Standards for Music addressed

- MU:Cr2: Organize and develop artistic ideas and work
- MU:Pr6: Convey meaning through the presentation of artistic work
- MU:Cn10: Synthesize and relate knowledge and personal experiences to make art

Materials

- Stopwatch
- Stethoscope (optional)
- Recorded musical example: "Stayin' Alive" by the Bee Gees
- Printed lyrics for chant "Engine Engine Number Nine"

Procedure

Steady beat practice

Play the first minute or so of "Stayin' Alive" by the Bee Gees and challenge students to show the steady beat in a nonlocomotive, but aerobic way (not traveling through space, but active) like jumping jacks, marching in place, or jogging in place. This activity will not only allow students to demonstrate their ability to perceive a steady beat and perform it accurately but also elevate their heart rates, making the next activity easier.

Defining and finding pulse

Explain to students that, in general, a pulse is a rhythmic beating and that one type of pulse is the rhythm of our heartbeats. Tell students that they will each find their own pulses. First, students need to locate their pointer and middle fingers. Those two fingers are used to measure pulse, not the thumb. The two primary areas for checking one's own pulse are the wrist and the neck. As one location may be easier than the other for students, make sure to model checking in both places. To measure pulse in your neck, place two fingers on the side of your neck, next to your windpipe. To check your pulse on your wrist, use the same two fingers and place them on the inside of the wrist, just down from the fold of the wrist, on the thumb side.

Walk around the room and help each student locate a pulse. Consider acquiring a stethoscope for students who might struggle with this activity. Explain to students that the throbbing they sense is the feeling of blood moving through the body because their hearts are pumping.

Ask students to continue checking their pulses while you engage them in a discussion about heart rates.

- Which people check pulses? Medical professionals check their patients' pulses, sometimes parents or adults at school will check your pulse, sometimes you check your own pulse, and sometimes people use technology to help them keep track of their heart rates.
- What can a pulse tell you? Your pulse can give you information about how fast your heart is beating, the rhythm and strength of your heartbeat, and how fit you are. There are many other reasons that medical professionals would check your pulse.

Determine resting heart rate

By now, students' pulses should have had time to return to their resting rates. Explain to students that "resting heart rate" refers to the total number of beats the heart generates during one minute at rest. Tell students to find their pulses and to look at you when they have found them. When students are ready, you will say "count." Tell them to silently start counting the beats of their heart. When they hear you say "stop," they should freeze on the last number they counted. You can have students count for 60 seconds, count for 30 seconds and multiply by two, or count for 15 seconds and multiply by four. Have them record their resting heart rates.

Exercise and recalculate heart rate

Have students dance, march, or vigorously move to at least one minute of "Stayin' Alive" by the Bee Gees. At the conclusion of their minute, immediately begin the process to determine heart rate, following the same steps as earlier. Ask students to record their heart rate after exercise.

You might repeat the data collection cycle, calculate class averages, graph results, or ask students to evaluate and summarize their findings. You might also consider listening to some heart rate examples with a metronome or a metronome app to allow students to experience heart rates aurally, rather than just kinesthetically. Engage students in a discussion about what the beating heart is doing for the body and why the rate speeds up and slows down.

Defining beat in music

Remind students that they already have a working definition for pulse. In music, the pulse is called the beat. If they hear the word "beat" in music, they can think of it as the "steady beat." A steady beat doesn't have variation in it. Show them the following notation and ask if they think it represents a steady beat.

It doesn't, because it has variation; it isn't constant. Does the pattern repeat? Yes, but it is not a steady beat because it has missing sounds in there. If your heart is following that notation (thump thump thump pause, thump thump thump pause), you're not going to be feeling well. When you don't hear any rests or missing sounds, it is a steady beat, like this one:

Defining tempo in music

Tempo can be defined as the rate or speed of a musical example. It is how fast or slow we perceive a piece to be. If you think back to our earlier heartbeat example, we labeled the heartbeat as a steady beat because it is constant and doesn't have any missing sounds or rests. Of course, your heart can beat faster or slower, but it's still maintaining a steady quality. It might be a fast steady beat at some times and a slow steady beat at others. Even while the heart is accelerating or decelerating, it still has a steady quality.

Put it all together

The following musical example highlights steady beat and tempo. Invite students to read the chant together:

> Engine, engine number nine,
> Going down the railroad line.
> If the train goes off the track,
> Will I get my money back?

Direct students to read the chant again, this time keeping a steady beat with their hands patting on their laps. If you notice students patting on every syllable (the rhythm pattern), you can stop them and start the steady beat first. Pat once for each beat.

| | | |

If students are patting really loudly, have them bring it down. A softer steady beat allows them to really hear the words of the chant. Also, once the steady beat starts to get louder, students tend to get faster and faster until the beat runs away from them. Once a quiet steady beat is established, read the chant together, maintaining the patting throughout:

| | | |
En - gine,   en- gine   num- ber   nine,

| | | |
Go- ing   down the   rail- road   line.

| | | |
If   the   train goes   off the   track,

| | | |
Will   I   get my   mo- ney   back?

A musical chant like "Engine Engine Number Nine" can also be used to clarify the concept of tempo. Performing a well-known chant at a slow speed and then a fast speed easily demonstrates the contrasting tempos for students. Slowing the tempo down promotes accurate patting of the steady beat, and speeding the tempo up, while not necessarily a way to enhance accuracy, is often fun for students. Additionally, when the tempo alternately becomes ultra-slow then ultra-fast, it's easy for students to hear and feel how the steady beat is affected.

Rhythm is one of the essential building blocks of music. Opportunities for students to explore rhythms, express what they know, and demonstrate what they can do can be challenging and enjoyable aspects of your classroom routine.

Lead a follow-up discussion asking students to reflect on connections between tempo and heart rate and between steady beat and heartbeat or pulse. Finally, ask if anyone can identify the song that was used for the steady beat exercise during the lesson ("Stayin' Alive" by the Bee Gees). Ask for ideas about why that song was chosen. Student responses may vary, but lead the discussion to highlight that to correctly perform CPR, you need to maintain a steady beat. The song "Stayin' Alive" has 103 beats per minute, which aligns with the recommended compressions per minute for CPR. A study found that thinking of the song "Stayin' Alive" while giving CPR created a "mental metronome" that helped people to perform CPR more accurately (Hafner, Sturgell, Matlock, Bockewitz, & Barker, 2012). The main lyrics in the chorus, "stayin' alive," are appropriate for CPR too. Ask students to infer why a song with a much slower or much faster tempo would be unsuitable for CPR. Play the song a final time and invite students to mimic the action of CPR to the beat of the music. Direct them to evaluate their own rate of speed to determine if they are maintaining a proper tempo for CPR.

Assessment

- Observe students while they move and tap, confirming that they can maintain a steady beat that aligns with a variety of given tempos, including that of "Stayin' Alive" and the spoken chant "Engine, Engine, Number Nine."
- Assess students' ability to accurately perceive, measure, and record their resting heart rates and exercise-elevated heart rates.
- Ask students a variety of short yes/no questions about the lesson and direct them to answer silently with a thumbs up or thumbs down to show their answers. This activity allows the students to reflect about their learning and allows the teacher to informally assess student understanding. Questions might address the steps for finding pulse; definitions of resting heart rate, heartbeat, tempo, and steady beat; or aural identification of rhythmic examples as steady or unsteady.

Extension

The American Heart Association and the American Red Cross recommend that people sing "Stayin' Alive" by the Bee Gees while performing CPR, but that song may be unfamiliar to your students. Ask students to find additional contemporary musical examples that could work for CPR (songs with tempos of approximately 103 beats per minute).

Lesson 5.4: Layering and preservation: "Pompeii" the song, Pompeii the city, and Mount Vesuvius

Grade Level: Upper elementary
Essential Question: How are layers and preservation revealed and described in the physical world and in music?

Objectives

- Students will analyze and interpret maps and diagrams and accurately describe layers of the earth, plate tectonics, the borders of continental plates, and volcanic features and activity.
- Students will aurally distinguish and label the musical layers (texture) of the song "Pompeii."
- Students will accurately sing and/or play rhythms in layers, maintaining part independence and appropriate balance between the layers.

- Students will replicate the process of casting, following specified steps, collecting data, and making observations about their experiences.
- Students will demonstrate empathy for victims of the Pompeii explosion and describe applications for their scientific and musical knowledge.

Next Generation Science Standards addressed

- LS4: Biological Evolution: Unity and Diversity
- ESS1: Earth's Place in the Universe
- ESS2: Earth's Systems
- PS1: Matter and Its Interactions

National Core Arts Standards for Music addressed

- MU:Pr5: Develop and refine artistic techniques and work for presentation
- MU:Re8: Interpret intent and meaning in artistic work
- MU:Cn11: Relate artistic ideas and works with societal, cultural, and historical context to deepen understanding

Materials

- Images
  - Cross-section of the layers of the earth (Figure 5.2)
  - Earth's continental plates (Figure 5.3)
  - Cross-section of a volcano (Figure 5.4)
  - Mount Vesuvius exploding (Figure 5.5)
  - Map of southern Italy (Figure 5.6)
  - Victims of the Pompeii eruption (Figure 5.7 and Figure 5.8)
- Recorded musical example and printed lyrics
  - "Layers of the Earth" by Joseph Bitetto (optional)
  - "Pompeii" by Bastille
- Casting supplies
  - Gallon milk jug or individual milk cartons
  - Craft sand
  - Vegetable oil
  - Various objects to cast
  - Plaster of Paris

Procedure

Start by asking students what they know about volcanoes. Direct students to analyze and interpret maps to describe features of the earth that affect volcanic activity.

Display a cross-section of the layers of the earth (see Figure 5.2), labeling and discussing the inner core, outer core, mantle (magma), and crust.

Next, discuss the role of plate tectonics in causing volcanic eruptions, noting that the points where two plates meet are the most likely places for volcanoes to occur. Figure 5.3 shows the earth's continental plates.

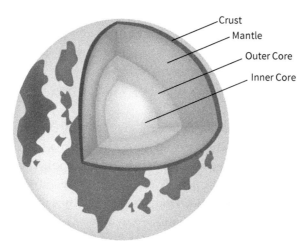

Figure 5.2 Layers of the earth.
© Sakurra/Shutterstock.com.

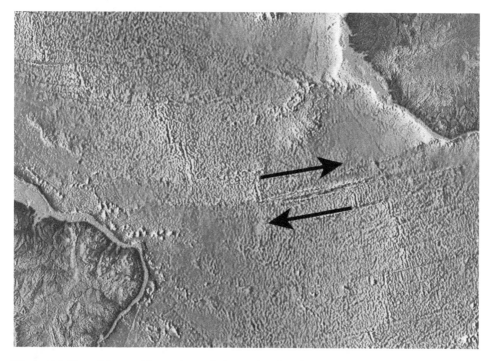

Figure 5.3 Map of the earth's continental plates, showing the Romanche Trench, 2006.
© National Oceanic and Atmospheric Administration (NOAA)/Wikimedia.

Draw or project a cross-section of a volcano, labeling the magma chamber, vents, and the crater. An example is shown in Figure 5.4. There are numerous songs and videos available that provide overviews of these elements and events. One example is "Layers of the Earth" by Joseph Bitetto.

Explain that in some volcanic eruptions, huge amounts of hot, pressurized gas explode from a vent and force a column of volcanic ash into the air. Volcanic ash, sometimes called volcanic dust, is made up of powder-sized to sand-sized fragments of igneous rock. Ashfall deposits occur as particles fall out of the air. A thicker ashfall deposit occurs close to the vent, but smaller particles can be carried on the wind for long distances. Although very fine, volcanic ash is a coarse material that can cause respiratory problems, irritate the eyes and skin, affect water supply systems, harm plants and animals, cause buildings to collapse, and damage aircraft and other mechanical equipment.

Pyroclastic flows result from the most explosive volcanic eruptions. In these cases, a mass of ash and superheated gas rushes down the mountain at temperatures that can reach over 1,000°F and speeds over 100 miles per hour. These flows instantly destroy every living thing in their path (Wei-Hass, 2018). Figure 5.5 shows an image of Mount Vesuvius erupting. Mount Vesuvius is an example of a volcano with a pyroclastic flow. Have students locate Mount Vesuvius on a historical map of southern Italy (see Figure 5.6).

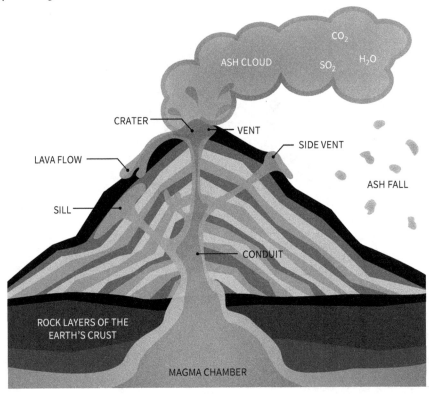

Figure 5.4 Cross-section of volcano.
© VRVector/Shutterstock.com.

Figure 5.5 Mount Vesuvius, active, 1880.
© The Library of Congress.

Share information about Mount Vesuvius and Pompeii, or direct students to research the topic in preparation for group presentations or class discussion. Twenty thousand people once lived in the shadow of Mount Vesuvius in the Italian port city of Pompeii, but in the year 79 AD, the volcano erupted. During the initial ashfall, most people had time to escape the city, but for the approximately 2,000 people who chose to remain behind, there was no chance for survival. Because of Pompeii's proximity to the volcano, when the pyroclastic flow reached the city, the superheated poisonous gas killed people instantly, capturing the victims in the exact final moment of their lives. The volcanic ash that continued to fall then preserved their remains and left the city buried under about 16 feet of ash (Hamilton, 2012).

Archeologists have uncovered the city of Pompeii and we can now see it just like it was on the day of the eruption. Buildings, art, and artifacts were preserved, giving us a picture of everyday life in the ancient Roman city. Organic material that was preserved in the ash decayed away over the centuries, leaving natural molds. Scientists filled the molds with plaster, dried the casts, then removed the ash from the casts to reveal the forms of Mount Vesuvius's victims (Cocco, 2012).

Complete a sand-casting activity to better understand the process that scientists underwent when casting Pompeii's three-dimensional cavities in the ash. First, mix

Figure 5.6 Southern Italy, 1851.
© Tallis, J. & F./The David Rumsey Historical Map Collection.

fine craft sand with vegetable oil until the sand sticks together. Cut off the top of a milk jug, fill it with the craft sand mix, and densely compress it. Alternately, prepare milk cartons for each student. Press various items such as a pencil, ruler, index finger, crayon, etc., straight down into the sand and then carefully pull straight out. Mix plaster of Paris, following instructions on the package. Spoon plaster into the sand molds and allow to cure. Remove the casts from the sand and brush off excess sand to reveal three-dimensional castings of your objects. Figures 5.7 and 5.8 show casts from two victims of the Pompeii explosion.

Listen to the song "Pompeii" by the British band Bastille and follow along with the lyrics. Ask students to identify elements from the song that directly or indirectly reference the impact of volcanoes on people and places. They will likely make note of lyrics that mention the falling walls of the city, ash clouds, darkness, people caught in the pyroclastic flow, and feelings of despair.

In their inquiry, students might not have concentrated on the musical elements in "Pompeii" that align with scientific characteristics of volcanoes. For example, although students have examined the importance of the earth's layers in the creation of volcanoes, they may not have taken note of the distinct layering in the song "Pompeii." In music, layers are described in terms of texture and refer to the number of distinct melodic, rhythmic, or harmonic components that are performed simultaneously. Typically, when more layers are present in a piece (thicker texture), it results

Figure 5.7 Pompeii victim of the eruption of Mt. Vesuvius, sitting.
© k6gmf6/pixabay.

in a richer, fuller sound. Table 5.3 shows the layers present at different points during the song "Pompeii." All timings align with Bastille's official music video recording.

To more easily perceive the musical layers, have the class view a video recording of one of Bastille's acoustic performances of "Pompeii." Students will be able to see when one, two, three, or four people are performing independent parts at any point during the song.

Students can then perform the song "Pompeii" in layers. This can be accomplished in a variety of ways: (1) adding vocal layers to the recording by singing along only on certain sections of the piece such as the "And the walls" (Bastille, 2013, track 1) or the "But if you close your eyes" (Bastille, 2013, track 1) sections; (2) performing two layers simultaneously by dividing into two groups and singing the "But if you close your eyes" section along with the chant part or the "And the walls" section; or (3) performing in groups with the recording, choosing some to be the "chant" singers, some to be percussionists, some to sing the lead vocal part, etc. After students have rehearsed and feel comfortable singing in layers and maintaining part independence, audio- or video-record their performance.

Figure 5.8 Pompeii victim of the eruption of Mt. Vesuvius, close-up.
© Jebulon/Free-Images.com.

Table 5.3 Layers Present in Bastille's "Pompeii"

Timing	Layers	Description
0:00	One	Following some windy sound effects, "Pompeii" opens with a vocalized, repetitive, chant-like section. Technically, there are multiple people singing on different pitches, but for simplicity, we will label the chanting collectively as a single layer.
0:20	Two	The accompaniment layer enters, played by a synthesized keyboard using a slightly different rhythm than the chanting singers.
0:32	Three	("I was left") The chanting singers drop out and are replaced with a single vocalist singing the main melody; keyboard continues; a drum part enters that highlights one portion of the keyboard rhythm.
0:47	Three	("And the walls") The drums take off on a new energetic rhythm, while keyboard and vocalist continue.
1:02	One	("But if you close your eyes") As the vocalist begins the chorus, all instruments drop out for two seconds.
1:04	Four	Instantly, the chant layer, keyboards, and drum re-enter; vocalist continues.
1:19	Four	("How am I gonna be") Vocalist, keyboard, and drums continue; backup singers move to harmony chords.
1:27	Two	("We were caught") Vocalist and keyboard.
1:34	Three	Drums re-enter; vocalist and keyboard continue.

Table 5.3 Continued

Timing	Layers	Description
1:45	Four	Backup singers enter, echoing words of lead vocalist.
1:55	One	Drum solo.
1:57	One	("But if you close your eyes") Again, as the vocalist begins the chorus, everyone else drops out for two seconds.
1:59	Four	Vocalist, chant, keyboard, drums.
2:14	Four	("How am I gonna be") Vocalist, keyboard, and drums continue; backup singers move to harmony chords.
2:21	Three	Chant, keyboard, drums.
2:29	Two	("Oh, where do we begin") Vocalist and keyboard.
2:36	Three	Backup singers enter, echoing vocalist; keyboard continues.
2:44	Four	("And the walls" + "Oh, where do we begin") Lead vocalist and backup singers sing different parts; drums enter; keyboard continues.
2:57	One	Drum solo.
2:59	One	("But if you close your eyes") Again, as the vocalist begins the chorus, everyone else drops out for two seconds.
3:01	Four	Vocalist, chant, keyboard, drums.
3:16	Four	("How am I gonna be") Vocalist, keyboard, and drums continue; backup singers move to harmony chords.
3:24	Five	Vocalist, keyboard, drums, backup singers on harmony, chant.
3:31	Two	Chant, keyboard.
3:45	One	Chant.

Courtesy of author.

Guide students to reflect about preservation. In the city of Pompeii, layers of ash preserved the city and its victims. The recording of the class singing preserved their performance. In both instances, the preservation served to document a specific event and allowed for deferred observation and analysis.

Assessment

- During class discussions, activities, and analysis of maps and diagrams, evaluate students' responses for accurate descriptions of the layers of the earth, plate tectonics, the borders of continental plates, and volcanic features and activity.
- Observe students' performance of "Pompeii." Listen for balance between the parts when students perform in layers and watch for part independence of performers (students stay on their assigned part without being pulled to another).

- Direct students to complete partner assessment interviews to encourage empathy for a peer's ideas and for the victims of the Pompeii disaster. Students interview a partner, record his or her responses, then write whether or not they agree with their partner's perspective, justifying their positions with clear rationales. Possible interview prompts include:
  - One line in the song "Pompeii" is a question that reads, "How am I gonna be an optimist about this?" (Bastille, 2013, track 1). What happened after the Pompeii explosion was horrible for the people living there at the time. Is it possible to take away anything positive from the event? What and how?
  - How can you apply what you learned about layers of the earth, layers of music, and texture to other things? Use key details and facts in your answer.
  - How can you apply what you learned about preservation and documentation in science and music to other things? Use key details and facts in your answer.

Literature extension

Because the lyrics of the song "Pompeii" are a dialogue between two victims in the eruption of Mount Vesuvius in 79 AD, explore the idea of poetic dialogue in the song, and then have students create their own dialogues. Discuss similarities between life in Pompeii and students' lives—people working, families at home, friends playing, etc.—and show images of artifacts from Pompeii to support these conclusions. Ask students to write a dialogue between two characters who might have been in Pompeii on the day Mount Vesuvius erupted. Their characters could be a worker and a boss, a mom and dad, a boy and his friend, etc. As in the lyrics of "Bastille," students should include key details that support historical events and human emotions.

Lesson 5.5: Creating musical instruments: Explore the properties of sound and apply the engineering design process

Grade Level: Primary
Essential Question: How are sounds made and what makes sounds different from each other?

Objectives

- Students will collaboratively investigate the properties of sound at a variety of stations, collecting evidence to show that vibrating materials can make sound, that sound can make materials vibrate, that sounds can be louder or softer, and that sounds can be higher or lower.

- Students will accurately record observations to describe and share evidence regarding the properties of sound using correct terminology related to vibration, pitch, and dynamics.
- Students will create and perform on musical instruments, demonstrating that the instruments they designed and built produce sound by vibrating, can produce more than one pitch, and can be played at more than one dynamic level.

Next Generation Science Standards addressed

- PS1: Matter and Its Interactions
- PS3: Energy
- PS4: Waves and Their Applications in Technologies for Information Transfer
- ETS1: Engineering Design

National Core Arts Standards for Music addressed

- MU:Cr1: Generate and conceptualize artistic ideas and work
- MU:Cr3: Refine and complete artistic work
- MU:Re7: Perceive and analyze artistic work
- MU:Re9: Apply criteria to evaluate artistic work
- MU:Cn10: Synthesize and relate knowledge and personal experiences to make art

Materials

- Books of your choice that introduce students to science of sound concepts using elementary-appropriate language. Recommended titles:
  - *Polar Bear, Polar Bear, What Do You Hear?* by Bill Martin Jr. and Eric Carle
  - *Zin! Zin! Zin! A Violin* by Lloyd Moss and Marjorie Priceman
  - *Sounds All Around* by Wendy Pfeffer and Anna Chernyshova
  - *Roadwork* by Sally Sutton and Brian Lovelock
- Station 1 supplies
  - Rubber bands
- Station 2 supplies
  - Drums in a variety of sizes (borrow from music teacher; create by cutting the openings off thick balloons and stretching them over empty coffee cans, soup cans, and tuna cans; or create them by stretching cellophane over different-sized bowls)
  - Bowl of salt or sand
  - Drumstick or pencil

- Station 3 supplies

Teacher-constructed string telephone (two paper cups with holes poked in the bottom; approximately 20 yards of string or fishing wire; attach each end of the string through the bottom of a cup; use paper clips like washers to secure the string and keep it from being pulled through the holes)

- Station 4 supplies
  - Four to six glasses or small glass jars, each filled with a different amount of water
  - Metal spoon
- Station 5 supplies

Four to six opaque plastic bottles, canisters, or eggs, each filled with a different material such as beans, rice, seeds, beads, buttons, or pennies

- Station 6 supplies

Variety of musical instruments (borrow from music teacher or create your own) such as egg shaker, maraca, triangle, wood block, rhythm sticks, sand blocks, tambourine, ukulele, hand bell, finger cymbals, drum, castanet, jingle bell, guiro, cabasa, etc.

- Station 7 supplies
  - Tuning fork
  - Dishpan or large bowl filled with water
- Variety of construction materials for student use: Paper, scissors, glue, tape, rulers, metal cans, shoe and cereal boxes, forks, spoons, straws, balloons, rubber bands, paper towel and toilet paper rolls, wooden dowels, wooden craft sticks, empty plastic canisters, plastic eggs, ribbon, paper plates, paper bowls, paper cups, funnels, plastic tubes, egg cartons, jar lids, plastic and metal bottle caps, nails, screws, washers, string, fishing line, piano wire, beans, seeds, beads, buttons, pipe cleaners
- Bluetooth speaker

Procedure

Read one or more books with class

Introduce the science of sound by reading aloud an elementary-level picture book on the topic (see materials section). Brainstorm with students about different sounds in the world and ask them to characterize each sound they identify as primarily loud or soft (dynamics) and high or low (pitch). Ask students to define vibration (a repeating back-and-forth movement) and direct them to place their fingers over their voice boxes. As they hum, sing, or speak, the larynx (voice box) vibrates and the vibrations make sounds. Students can feel the vibrations through their fingers. Experiment with different sounds (high/low and soft/loud) and observe the different feelings that result. Engage the class in a brief discussion of vibration, dynamics, and pitch to reinforce their understandings.

Properties of sound classroom stations

Invite students to investigate about the properties of sound by visiting a variety of stations. Introduce each station to the whole class and then divide students into small groups to visit each station. Direct students to collect and record evidence to address two main questions: (1) Do vibrating materials make sound? (2) Do sounds make materials vibrate? Students will record their evidence and perceptions in a journal or on a teacher-created template. Responses may be any age-appropriate combination of drawings, labels, or words. Directions for students follow with notes for teachers in italics:

Station 1. Rubber bands

Set out a variety of rubber bands for student use.

In pairs, one student stretches a rubber band between two hands and one student plucks the band with a finger. Allow each group member to take a turn in each role. Note any vibrations you can see or feel and any sounds you hear. Experiment and observe how the results change if the rubber band is stretched more or less. Record your observations.

Station 2. Drums

Set out drums in a variety of sizes (see materials section), a small bowl filled with salt or sand, and a drumstick.

Sprinkle a small amount of material on the head of each drum. Lightly tap the drum with a drumstick or pencil and observe the motion of the salt or sand. Depending on the size of the drum and material of the drum head, it may be possible to get the drum head to vibrate by vocalizing (humming or singing) near the drum. Does the size of the drum make a difference in the vibrations you see? Does the size of the drum make a difference in what you hear? Record your observations.

Station 3: String telephone

Set out a string telephone prepared by the teacher (see materials section). This station may work best in a long hallway.

Pairs of students stand at each end of the string telephone. Pull the string taut. One partner hums, sings, speaks, or whispers into one cup; the other partner holds one cup up to his or her ear. Switch roles. Describe what you observed. What happens if the string is not taut? What happens if someone pinches the string? Record your observations.

Station 4: Glass xylophone

Set out a glass xylophone (see materials section) and a metal spoon.

Take turns gently tapping the glasses or jars with the spoon. What do you hear? Which glasses produce higher pitches? Which glasses produce lower pitches? Why does this happen? Record your observations.

Station 5: Shaker fillings

Set out a number of opaque canisters or plastic eggs, each containing a different material (see materials section).

Take turns shaking each of the homemade shakers. Predict what is inside each one based on what you feel and hear. Record your thinking and your predictions.

Station 6: Producing sounds

Set out various musical instruments (see materials section).

Take turns playing each instrument. Collect data about different ways you can play each instrument (shaking, scraping, tapping, plucking, etc.), whether or not you can play more than one pitch (higher/lower), and whether or not you can play more than one dynamic (soft/loud). Record your observations.

Station 7: Tuning fork

Set out a tuning fork and a dishpan or large bowl filled with water.

Take turns tapping the tuning fork against the side of the table, then placing the end into a pan of water. The sound will create vibrations that are transferred into the water. Can you hear the tuning fork after you tap it? What do you see when you place it in the water? Record your observations.

Class discussion

Engage in a full-class discussion to review findings and conclusions from students' investigations of the properties of sound. Reinforce students' understandings with additional demonstrations.

1. Ask students to describe and share evidence demonstrating that vibrating materials can make sound (rubber bands; drums; string from the telephone; various instruments from Station 6; tuning fork). Use a slow-motion video app or the slow-motion feature on your phone to record a rubber band as it is plucked and a tuning fork as it is tapped. Viewing the resulting recording in slow motion will allow students to see the vibrations that accompany the sounds they heard. You could also video a guitar, ukulele, or violin string, or use videos of this process that are available online.

2. Ask students to share evidence showing that sound can make materials vibrate and to describe different ways they were able to visualize vibrations (the salt or sand from Station 2; string from the telephone; various instruments from Station 6; the water in Station 7). Place a Bluetooth speaker under a large drum from Station 2 and sprinkle salt on the drum head. Sync the speaker with your phone or other device and play a series of steady tones, low bass thumps, or a song the students know, and then view the resulting motion of the material on the drum head. There are also videos of sand vibrating on drum heads and metal plates available online.

3. Ask students to share evidence demonstrating that sounds can have different pitches (rubber bands stretched different amounts; different-sized drums; different amounts of water in glasses; different substances inside a shaker). Download an app that displays different soundwave frequencies when you speak or sing, giving visual evidence that sounds are higher or lower. The faster something vibrates, the higher the pitch; the slower something vibrates, the lower the pitch. Play a xylophone or straw pan flute. Guide students to determine that longer bars or longer straws sound lower and shorter bars or straws sound higher.

4. Ask students to share evidence that demonstrates that sounds can have different dynamic levels (drums, string telephone, glass xylophone, shakers, various instruments from Station 6). Download an app that uses a decibel meter to check volume and discuss safe decibel levels. Investigate the loudness of a variety of instruments and sounds. Download an app that shows the amplitude (size) of a soundwave when you speak or sing. The louder a sound is, the larger the amplitude; the softer a sound is, the smaller the amplitude.

Creating musical instruments

The primary goal of STEM education, composed of the disciplines of science, technology, engineering, and mathematics, is to increase STEM literacy. Activities that allow students to focus on the engineering design process are one way to address that goal. The steps in the engineering design process are typically defined as (1) identify a problem or need, (2) gather background information and research existing solutions, (3) brainstorm solutions and choose the most suitable idea, (4) sketch and explain the design, (5) make and test a physical model, (6) review and share results, and (7) redesign to improve the solution.

Guide students as they follow the steps to create an instrument. Their process may look something like the following:

1. Identify a problem or need: Create an instrument that makes a sound by vibrating, that can play more than one pitch, and that can be played at more than one dynamic level

2. Gather background information and research existing solutions: Re-explore or review instruments they previously played during their time at Station 6

3. Brainstorm solutions and choose the most suitable idea: Talk with a table partner to generate ideas and to narrow in on potential designs

4. Sketch and explain the design: Draw and label a plan for the new instrument; describe it to a table partner

5. Make and test a physical model: Use classroom supplies (see materials section) to build a musical instrument; decorate if desired; play the instrument to test its functionality and suitability

6. Review and share results: Play the instrument for peers; describe the ways it meets the identified problem
7. Redesign to improve solution: Suggest improvements to the design and continue the process

Assessment

- Collect students' journals and examine the illustrations, labels, and/or writing for accurate descriptions and representations of the properties of sound using correct terminology related to vibration, dynamics, and pitch; informally assess students' responses during class discussion and group work.
- Review students' progression through the engineering design process, observing their research, planning, creating, testing, dissemination of results, and self-analysis.
- Ask students to play and describe their instruments, demonstrating that they can produce a sound by vibrating, can change the pitch of their instrument, and can change the dynamic level of their instrument.

Extensions

- With older students, you might investigate the relationship between wave amplitude and volume and the relationship between wave frequency and pitch more thoroughly.
- Students can study the relationship between sound waves and the human ear. As students learn about the structure and function of the ear, they explore how sound waves are filtered and converted to electrical signals that are sent to the brain for interpretation.

Lesson 5.6: Butterflies as indicators of climate change

Grade Level: Primary
Essential Questions: What is climate change, how can scientists identify it, and how can musicians help inspire positive action?

Objectives

- Students will gather information from reputable sources, engage in class discussions about climate change and indicators of climate change, and analyze a simulation game, demonstrating their understanding of the impact of rising temperatures on ecosystems.

- Students will demonstrate an awareness of various musical concepts such as beat, melody, and expressive qualities in a variety of musical examples related to butterflies and climate change.
- Students will explore and identify human actions that can have a positive impact on the natural world, including climate change.
- Students will select one strategy for addressing climate change, create a plan for implementing the action, and compose a song or chant to inform an audience about the issue.
- Students will present a final version of their song or chant, performing with accurate rhythms, pitches, and enunciation, for the purpose of persuading audience members to take action.

Next Generation Science Standards addressed

- LS1: From Molecules to Organisms: Structures and Processes
- LS2: Ecosystems: Interactions, Energy, and Dynamics
- LS4: Biological Evolution: Unity and Diversity
- ESS2: Earth's Systems
- ESS3: Earth and Human Activity
- PS3: Energy

National Core Arts Standards addressed

- MU:Cr2: Organize and develop artistic ideas and work
- MU:Cr3: Refine and complete artistic work
- MU:Pr6: Convey meaning through the presentation of artistic work
- MU:Re8: Interpret intent and meaning in artistic work
- MU:Cn10: Synthesize and relate knowledge and personal experiences to make art

Materials

- Recorded music examples
  - "Life Cycle of a Butterfly (Metamorphosis Song)" by Jack Hartmann (optional)
  - "Butterfly Life Cycle: Metamorphosis" by Mr. R (optional)
  - "Butterfly's Day Out" by Mark O'Connor
  - "Ode to a Butterfly" by Nickel Creek
  - "Papillons" by Moriz Rosenthal
  - "Arctic Sea Ice" by Judy Twedt
  - "1,200 Years of Earth's Climate, Transformed Into Sound" by Chris Chafe

- Climate change children's book: *The Tantrum That Saved the World* by Megan Herbert and Michael E. Mann
- Climate change websites
  - "Climate Kids" produced by the National Aeronautics and Space Administration (NASA)
  - "A Students' Guide to Global Climate" produced by the US Environmental Protection Agency (EPA)
  - "Elementary Resources: Earth Science" produced by the National Oceanic and Atmospheric Administration (NOAA)

Procedure

Note to teachers: The life cycle of the butterfly is a familiar elementary school science unit. There are many songs for young children with butterflies as their theme. Two to consider singing with your class are "Life Cycle of a Butterfly (Metamorphosis Song)" by Jack Hartmann and "Butterfly Life Cycle: Metamorphosis" by Mr. R. You might also consider augmenting a unit about the life cycle of butterflies with this lesson exploring the role of butterflies as indicators of climate change. The Lesson 5.6 content can also exist as a stand-alone lesson or unit.

1. Introduce the topic of global climate change by reading aloud a book such as *The Tantrum That Saved the World* by Megan Herbert and Michael E. Mann. Depending on students' grade level, guide students to gather information about the topic as a whole class, in small groups, or individually by exploring sites such as "Climate Kids" produced by NASA, "A Students' Guide to Global Climate" produced by the EPA, and "Elementary Resources: Earth Science" produced by NOAA. Engage in an age-appropriate class discussion exploring climate change.

The terms "climate" and "weather" do not mean the same thing. "Weather" refers to locally occurring conditions (rain, snow, wind, storms, etc.) over a short period of time (hours or days). "Climate" refers to regionally or globally occurring conditions (average temperature, humidity, rainfall, etc.) over a long period of time (seasons, years, or decades). We are currently in a period of abrupt climate change: The average temperature of the earth has risen more than 1°F over the last century, in large part due to increased carbon dioxide in the atmosphere trapping heat from the sun. While one degree might not sound like much, consider that a one-degree difference in your body temperature can be the difference between being healthy and having a fever. Scientists predict that the average temperature of the earth could increase by as much as 10°F during this century (NASA, 2019). Additional evidence of climate change includes increasing the average temperature of the earth's oceans, retreating glaciers, and rising sea levels.

2. Connect the topic of climate change to the study of butterflies. Again, depending on grade level, consider inviting your students to research the topic in groups or as individuals prior to class discussion.

Butterflies act as indicators of climate change. It is hard for them to regulate their own body temperatures, so butterflies are very sensitive to changes in the temperature of their environment. Additionally, many butterflies and caterpillars prefer to feed on the nectar and leaves of specific plants, so they are affected when changes in temperature and rainfall impact plant life. For example, in the Rocky Mountains, the Mormon Fritillary butterfly population is declining because of early snowmelt in the region. Rising temperatures are causing the snow to melt earlier than usual—snow that usually acts as an insulator. Without the snow cover, plants are exposed to occasional frosts that kill the buds of their flowers. Without the nectar from those flowers, butterflies do not produce as many eggs. Intermittent frosts also are responsible for killing caterpillars, preventing them from forming chrysalises and metamorphosing into butterflies (Boggs & Inouye, 2012). Figure 5.9 shows a Mormon Fritillary butterfly.

To compensate for rising temperatures, some nonmigratory butterfly species such as the Edith's checkerspot butterfly and the Clodius Parnassian butterfly are slowly shifting their populations north or to higher elevations in search of cooler climates and in response to changes in the host plants on which they depend (Parmesan, 1996; Szcodronski, Debinski, & Klaver, 2018). If butterflies lay their eggs on plants that typically would have been green at the time the eggs hatched but now, because of warmer temperatures, are dried up, the caterpillars will not survive. A butterfly population might start to decline because of small changes to

Figure 5.9 Mormon Fritillary.
© Rob Santry/Flickr.

their habitat, even before scientists have noticed the changes. It appears that our climate is changing faster than the butterfly populations can adjust; some species of butterfly have already become extinct, and many more are listed as endangered. Figure 5.10 shows an Edith's checkerspot butterfly and Figure 5.11 shows a Clodius Parnassian butterfly.

Play a game of musical chairs to highlight the relationship between rising temperatures, plant health, and butterfly population. Set up a circle of chairs with one chair for each student in the class. Tell students that each chair represents a flower with nectar that butterflies like to eat and that each student will be a butterfly looking for food. Play a variety of butterfly-inspired musical pieces such as "Butterfly's Day Out" performed by Yo Yo Ma, "Ode to a Butterfly" by Nickel Creek, or "Papillons" by Moriz Rosenthal. While the music plays, students move around the circle, using their bodies to emulate the sounds they hear. When the music stops, they must sit in an available chair, signifying that the butterfly gets to eat the nectar from a healthy flower. Because you started with the same number of chairs (flowers) as students (butterflies) for the first round, each student will have a safe place to sit. Say, "When an ecosystem is healthy, there are enough resources to go around. Right now, there is enough nectar for all the butterflies to eat. What happens if there are changes to the habitat?" Invite student responses. Consider using an oversized "temperature" dial, and mimic turning up the temperature. Say, "When the temperature goes up just a little bit, some plants will die." Ask students to stand as you remove one

Figure 5.10 Edith's Checkerspot.
© Dennis Holmes/Flickr.

Figure 5.11 Clodius Parnassian.
© Dennis Holmes/Flickr.

or more chairs from the circle. Continue the musical chairs game. This time, when the music stops, one or more students will not have a place to sit. Say, "Because of climate change, some plants died, so not all the butterflies can find healthy flowers with nectar to eat. Those butterflies will not survive." Continue to play the game, turning up the temperature and removing chairs each round. Lead students in a class discussion summarizing the impact of increasing temperatures on butterfly species and how changes in butterfly populations indicate climate change. Conclude the activity with a detailed examination of the musical examples you utilized for the musical chairs game. Identify specific instruments; describe the styles; characterize melodies, rhythms, and harmonies; and speculate why the composers made the musical choices they did to exemplify butterflies. Note to teachers: Students can play this game as "caterpillars" looking for "healthy leaves" to eat as well.

Reinforce the understandings that humans have an impact on the natural world and that wildlife is affected by habitat changes. Review connections between specific actions and climate change, encourage a sense of climate stewardship, and highlight the positive impact that students can have by researching simple actions in people's everyday lives that help the earth. Students' list of actions may include the following ideas:

- Reduce, reuse, recycle
- Walk, bike, or carpool to school

- Create an idle-free zone in the school's loading area
- Unplug chargers when not in use
- Turn off lights when not in use
- Turn off computers when not in use
- Use energy-efficient light bulbs
- Plant a pollinator garden
- Plant trees
- Avoid single-use plastic when possible
- Turn down heat in winter; turn up air conditioning in summer

Historically, music has often been written to bring attention to various scientific issues. Music can help people start difficult conversations. Music can bring ideas to life in ways that tables, charts, or graphs cannot. Regarding climate change, music might inspire people to become energy conscious and take greater responsibility for their actions. Examine two examples of music driven by climate data: "Arctic Sea Ice" by Judy Twedt based on satellite data of the sea ice index, and "1,200 Years of Earth's Climate, Transformed Into Sound" by Chris Chafe, based on CO_2 and temperature data compiled by Hal Gordon, Kate Pennington, and Valeri Vasquez.

Spark a response by asking students to choose one action related to climate change and make a plan to implement it. Guide the class as they compose a song or chant to inform members of their school community about the climate change action they identified. Perform the song at a school assembly or on the school's morning announcements to inspire and motivate others to join the cause. For example, if the action on which your class decided to focus was turning off lights, they might volunteer to serve as "energy police" for the building (check with an administrator before implementing your plan). At regular intervals throughout the day, supervised student "officers" can check the school for violations. If they find lights that are left on but are not in use, they can issue a citation and leave a "ticket" for the rule breakers. The song they compose should draw attention to the importance of turning off lights and inform others of potential consequences. Ideally, their action plan and song will build enthusiasm and empower others to make changes. With guidance, a class of kindergarten students might compose a rhythmic chant like this:

> Turn off the lights when you leave the room.
> Turn off the lights, we'll be watching you.
> Turn off the lights, help save the earth.
> Turn off the lights, for what it's worth.
> Turn off the lights, every single time.
> Turn off the lights to avoid a fine!

Imagine the motivation for change if a class of fifth-grade students realized that five- and six-year-olds were going to be monitoring their light usage.

Assessment

- Informally assess students with a 3-2-1 activity. Ask students to talk with a partner, discussing three things they learned about climate change in the lesson, two things they would like to learn more about, and one question that they have. Circulate around the room to monitor students' responses.
- Evaluate students' verbal explanations of climate change and indicators of climate change, checking for accurate information, effective participation as speakers and listeners, and demonstrated understanding that people's actions can affect the world around them.
- Evaluate students' planning strategies, composition process, and preparation for and performance of their climate change strategy composition, observing the suitability of the interpretive decisions they made regarding musical and science content, sufficient detail, and effective organization.

Inventory of ideas

The following collection of ideas contains additional lesson topics, specific teaching strategies, and recommended activities.

1. Connect the ideas of force and motion in science and music. For the science portion of the lesson, your students might investigate the effect of pushing or pulling an object with more or less force. Then, to illustrate the tendency of music to be pulled toward a resolution, read a few statements that are missing the ending such as, "Today for lunch we are having. . . ." The unfinished quality makes listeners feel like they are being pulled toward a conclusion. Next, move on to musical examples. Hum the beginning of a few songs, sometimes stopping before the end of a phrase. Ask students to show thumbs down if they think the phrase seems unfinished or thumbs up if it sounds complete. Just as pulling on an object causes it to move, musical forces pull or move toward resolution. Conclude with another round of thumbs down/thumbs up with Chopin's "Prelude in E Minor, Op. 28, No. 4." This piece has lots of tension and subtle resolution of chords for aural analysis.

2. Listen to "Fingal's Cave" recorded by Natalie MacMaster and the Chieftans. Listen for transformation of the melodic and rhythmic motives over time. In various sections of the piece, the fiddle part is ornamented, elaborated on, passed around to other instruments, fragmented, and accented. Fingal's Cave is a sea cave on an island in Scotland. Connect the idea of transformation of musical themes to transformation of the Earth's surface. Study ways the surface of the earth changes and what causes those transformations, including water, ice, wind, and vegetation. Another musical version of Fingal's Cave to explore is Mendelssohn's "Hebrides Overture," a piece he composed in 1829

after visiting the cave. Direct students to sing a well-known melody and experiment with various rhythmic, melodic, and expressive transformations of the tune.

3. Some contemporary composers use "found sounds" to create music. Biologist and author David George Haskell's book *The Songs of Trees: Stories From Nature's Great Connectors* explores the biology of trees and their role today. Listen to sounds Haskell recorded when he visited 12 trees around the world. Listening examples can be heard on his website, dghaskell.com. Some recordings are environmental; some are amplified, like the sound of a chewing beetle larvae; and some recordings are digitized examples of data Haskell collected, allowing students to hear phenomena like a 24-hour hydration cycle. This topic suggests science connections such as structure and plant systems, and also links with visual art. Just as musical applications of science have allowed us to hear inside trees, visual arts applications of science allow us to see inside trees. Figure 5.12 shows a magnified cross section of a tree branch.

4. There are many connections between science and music that students can demonstrate with creative movement. One of the simplest ways for students to move creatively is to use walking as the basis for their movements. Clap, tap, play an instrument, or use recordings as the musical material to guide students' walks. They should gently step the pulse of the musical example, move with quiet feet, and travel through the space in the room. Direct students to freeze

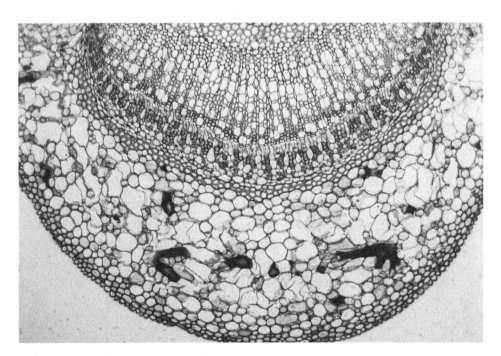

Figure 5.12 Magnified cross-section of a tree branch.
© Digital Photo/Shutterstock.com.

when you intermittently stop the music, encouraging the development of active listening and body control. Once students are comfortable with the basic walking format, you can add layers of difficulty to which they must adapt.

- Portray characteristics of various environments: Move like you're inside a dark cave; in a vat of sticky, thick liquid; a dry leaf blowing in the wind; or a green leaf attached to a tree. Suggested music: "Ride of the Valkyries" by Richard Wagner; "Spiegel im Spiegel" by Arvo Pärt; "Eine Kleine Nachtmusik" by Wolfgang Amadeus Mozart; and the fourth movement of the *New World Symphony* by Antonín Dvořák.
- Portray force: Move with different amounts of tension in the body; stretch, strain, relax, push, and pull. Suggested music: "Rocky Theme" by Bill Conti; "O Fortuna" from *Carmina Burana* by Carl Orff; "The Wang Wang Blues" performed by the Benny Goodman Sextet; and "Gymnopédie No. 1" by Erik Satie.
- Portray speed: Accurately move to various musical tempos. Suggested music: "Magnum Mysterium" by Morten Lauridsen; "Dance of the Sugar Plum Fairy" by Pyotr Ilyich Tchaikovsky; "Brandenburg Concerto No. 3" by Johann Sebastian Bach; and "Flight of the Bumblebee" by Nikolai Rimsky-Korsakov.
- Create a set of movements to portray science concepts such as the phases of the moon, the life cycle of a butterfly, dispersing seeds and pollination, etc.

5. Students often have a hard time memorizing sets of facts like the bones of the body. Help students to remember the bones of the body while connecting the idea that individual bones are discrete parts of the skeletal system and individual notes, phrases, and words are discrete parts of a song. Sing "Head, Shoulders, Knees, and Toes" and count the number of body parts sung (eight total parts). Pass out large sheets of butcher paper to groups of students. Trace one volunteer per group, and then ask students to identify their top eight most problematic bones to memorize. List the eight bones at the top of the paper, draw them in their correct spot on the butcher paper, and then sing "Head, Shoulders, Knees, and Toes" with the new lyrics, pointing to each bone as its name is sung (e.g., "mandible, clavicle, radius, ulna, radius, ulna . . .").

6. Ask students to devise a strategy for describing and classifying various materials based on their observable properties. You might begin with a set of rocks, photos of different land masses, water in different states, etc. Similarly, ask students to devise a strategy for describing and classifying different kinds of music with observable properties. Play excerpts of recordings and/or perform pieces representing various genres such as blues, jazz, gospel, swing, folk, rock, pop, hip-hop, and rap. Conduct both investigations, making observations, taking measurements, and recording findings.

7. There are many songs and musical examples with science as their subjects. Of course, students should sing and listen to these pieces, but rather than *only* sing

and listen, challenge students to examine conceptual connections such as observation, interaction, energy, structure, function, development, or change as well. Some possible songs to explore:

"Hibernate With Me" by Benjamin Scheuer
The Four Seasons by Antonio Vivaldi
"Where We're Going" by Hans Zimmer, from the movie *Interstellar*
"No GMO" by Paul Izak and Seeds of Love
"The Cyclone" by Ferde Grofé
"Space Oddity" by David Bowie, sung by Chris Hadfield from space
"Solid, Liquid, Gas" by They Might Be Giants
The Planets Suite by Gustav Holst
The Grand Canyon Suite by Ferde Grofé
"The Elements" by Tom Lehrer (tune from *The Pirates of Penzance*)
"The Blue Danube" by Johann Strauss II

8. One of the NGSS Performance Standards directs students to "obtain and combine information about ways individual communities use science ideas to protect the Earth's resources and environment" (Next Generation Science Standards Lead States, 2013). Study energy sources and their effect on the environment. Generate and compare various solutions that might reduce negative impacts of fuels derived from nonrenewable natural resources. Just as you studied ways members of a scientific community can help protect the earth, reflect about ways members of a musical community might use their skills and talents to protect the earth's resources as well. Rehearse and perform "Keep the Oil in the Ground" by Tubby Love to jump-start your conversation.

9. When studying organisms and habitats, challenge students to also consider the *sounds* that are present in specific habitats. What role does sound play in how organisms interact with their environment? Then, ask students to consider the impact of music on their local environment (home, school, community, etc.) and answer the following questions: How do people use music to control their environments? What are potential changes to an environment when music is added? How do we know if music is too loud? How do certain styles of music affect an environment? How are people impacted when their musical environment changes?

10. Students can closely observe patterns, gather information, and interpret data in science and music. For example, in a unit on weather, students might describe local weather patterns in two ways: (a) qualitative descriptions such as hot, cold, windy, etc., and (b) quantitative descriptions based on numerical data such as temperatures, wind speeds, hours of sunlight per day, or number of cloudy days per month. Use qualitative and quantitative analysis to describe

a song such as "Here Comes the Sun" by the Beatles. For example, after students listen to and sing the song, they might describe the tempo using terms such as "moderato," "allegretto," or "medium," or they might label the tempo as 120 beats per minute. Other musical elements to consider include structure, rhythmic and melodic patterns, song length, and text.

11. Lead a discussion about music preferences and usage. Do your students listen to music while studying at home? How many of them say that music helps them focus? How many of them say that music distracts them? What other responses arise? What are your students' favorite songs? During what percentage of a typical weekend day can your students hear music? How often do your students sing? Collect the data generated during the discussion in a grade-level appropriate manner. Alternately, consider having students keep music logs and collect data over a longer period of time. Display data in tables and other graphic displays.

12. Examine interdependent relationships between various entities. Depending on grade level, you might explore relationships between plants and their environment, humans and their environment, or frequency and wavelength. You might also explore relationships throughout an entire ecosystem. Similarly, analyze interdependent relationships in music such as the links between text and music, melody and accompaniment, rhythm and style, or harmony and mood. To start, consider exploring the easily observable relationship between lyrics and music in a song such as "Blue Skies," sung by Frank Sinatra. First read the words of the song, isolated from the music. Next, listen to an instrumental-only version of the piece. Finally, listen to the full song, discuss the synergy between the lyrics and the music, and sing the complete piece. You might also connect this activity to a discussion of cause and effect, examining the effect of listening to a song without all its component parts present.

13. Ask students to describe the climates of different places in the world. Encourage them to consider the impact that climate has on organisms in different regions. Similarly, explore the different "climates" or "atmospheres" that can be created with music in a classroom environment. What is the impact of different musical climates on the organisms (students) in the room? This activity offers the opportunity for students to experience a wide variety of musical examples.

14. In science, systems are often described in terms of their components. Direct your students to analyze and interpret information they observe about a system (the earth's systems, ecosystems, the solar system, systems of the body, measurement systems, etc.) to develop a model that defines and describes the various parts of the system. Musical systems (a piece of music) can also be described in terms of their component parts. When a piece of music is broken down into relatively simpler and smaller pieces, the focus is often on the way

the pieces (melody, rhythm, harmony, lyrics) are arranged and interact with each other. Ask students to identify a musical example to dismantle. Work together to define all the elements that make up the piece.

15. Explore the vocal mechanism, care of the voice, and healthy vocal production with students. Depending on grade level, investigate some of the components of the body that impact singing including the diaphragm, lungs, larynx (voice box), vocal cords, and pharynx (one of the most important resonating cavities). You might show images from a spectrograph, a device that analyzes sound and produces visual images (spectrograms) of the frequency content of sounds. Spectrographs are used in voice science research and as diagnostic tools in voice therapy clinics. Invite students to sing a well-known song together, focusing on maintaining a tall, relaxed posture; an energetic tone; and pure, open vowels. Unhealthy vocal production may result in a rough, harsh, or raspy-sounding voice; intermittent voice loss; problems singing high notes; or excess coughing and throat clearing. Explain that some teachers use a system or device to amplify their voices to reduce vocal hoarseness and fatigue. Amplification devices allow teachers to speak at a conversational level yet have their voices heard over loud teaching environments. If you or another teacher at your school uses an amplification device, allow students to try speaking and singing into it. Other modifications to everyday behaviors that improve vocal hygiene include vocal rest, sufficient hydration, decreasing or eliminating caffeine intake, adequate sleep, and avoiding repeated straining of the voice or screaming.

16. Explore connections between technology and music with your students. Handheld devices such as tablets and phones have uses in adaptive learning settings, supporting visual and auditory perception, and offering tactile stimulation through haptic feedback. Invention kits like Makey Makey and Nintendo Labo allow students to create and play electronic musical instruments, and applications such as GarageBand facilitate composition, encouraging students to experiment with and manipulate musical elements.

17. Recycling is the process of converting materials that would otherwise be trash into a usable product. Recycling is commonly explored in science classes, but there are musical applications for recycling as well.

   • Just as physical materials can be transformed in recycling, musical materials are often altered and adapted. Composers will often "borrow" some aspect of an existing song and transform or replicate it in their new piece. Examine examples of musical recycling such as the exact repetition of a portion of the song "Yankee Doodle" within the song "Yankee Doodle Dandy," or Aaron Copland's orchestration of the tune "Simple Gifts" in his composition *Appalachian Spring.*

   • Create recycled instruments and perform with them by accompanying an existing song or creating an ostinato, a musical pattern that is repeated (recycled). This activity also offers opportunities to connect with concepts related to sound, vibration, and waves. See Lesson 5.5 for additional connections. Figures 5.13 and 5.14 show examples of recycled instruments. Figure 5.15 is an 1883 design for an imaginary instrument of "found sounds" that was purely theoretical, the cat piano.

Figure 5.13 Metal bottle cap shakers.
© Rose Beerhorst/Flickr.

Figure 5.14 Plastic bottle cap percussion instrument.
© Dante Busquets/Shutterstock.com.

Figure 5.15 Cat piano, 1883.
© Museum of Imaginary Musical Instruments/Wikimedia.

6

Music and Mathematics

Introduction

The disciplines of music and mathematics provide students with tools to understand the world around them and promote the development of strong reasoning skills, encouraging students to think in rational, logical ways to solve problems and evaluate information. Drawing connections between music and math can also reinforce a more creative, intuitive approach to solving problems. Ideally, students' experiences in school show them that mathematical reasoning, measuring, counting, and calculating are natural things people do every day. Similarly, every student should have experiences acknowledging the fundamental importance of music in their lives.

Math is indispensable to music; musicians use numbers and patterns every day. Likewise, music enhances math, promoting interest and enjoyment, offering real-life scenarios for applying skills, and encouraging disciplined, focused concentration. Beyond these low-level connections, however, there are many opportunities to explore fundamental concepts that music and math share. For example, music and math both utilize symbols to represent abstract ideas. Making sense of symbols can sometimes be confusing to students. In music, looking and listening for patterns, shapes, repetition, contrast, and other structural elements helps students label what they experience in a concrete way. When the building blocks of musical composition become apparent to students, it can be like the proverbial light bulb going off. Musical analysis can be the key to unlocking some of the mystery surrounding music. When students feel they can approach music from the perspective of an "insider," it can be very empowering. Similarly, math can feel like a mystery to some students. Connecting the idea of symbolic representation in music and symbolic representation in math can help students better grasp the concept in both disciplines.

The Chapter 6 lessons and the strategies and activities included in the Chapter 6 inventory of ideas encourage students to think critically and creatively, engage in inquiry-based problem solving, collaborate with peers, and make meaningful, real-life connections between music and math.

Integrating Music Across the Elementary Curriculum. Kristin Harney, Oxford University Press (2020). © Oxford University Press.
DOI: 10.1093/oso/9780190085582.001.0001.

Common links between music and mathematics

A student may have procedural understandings in math and music, but integrating the two disciplines may help students solidify conceptual understandings in both. For example, a math student might know the procedures for adding fractions. A music student might know that to determine meter they listen for the steady beat, discern the strong beat, then count beat groups. Knowing the procedures does not equate to deep understanding though. "Simplification" is a concept that can be explored in music and mathematics that connects the two previous examples. Highlighting these types of higher-level connections and providing opportunities for students to explore complex concepts in math and music help them to construct and understand those concepts in both concentrated and multilayered ways, ultimately benefiting the whole child. Enduring ideas that can be explored in both disciplines include:

Balance
Complexity
Counting
Function
Levels
Line
Measurement
Part/whole
Pattern
Proportion
Range
Regularity
Relationships
Repetition
Ratio
Rules
Same/different
Shape
Simplicity
Structure
Subdivision
Symbol
Symmetry
Trend
Unit

National standards

Structuring integrated lessons that meet standards in music and math promotes a balance between musical and mathematical skills and concepts. The National Core Arts Standards (NCAS) for Music unambiguously call for students to integrate learning in music and other disciplines, with 2 of the 11 anchor standards labeled as "connecting" standards. The Common Core State Standards (CCSS) for Mathematics do not specify interdisciplinary connections with music, but there are numerous meaningful connections that can be made.

The CCSS for Mathematics focus on topics and key ideas, conceptual understandings, and sequentially organized principles (National Governors Association Center for Best Practices, Council of Chief State School Officers. (2010b). For example, ideas connected to understanding and using place value are found in the detailed cluster standards of every grade from kindergarten to fifth. The overarching CCSS domain associated with these ideas is CCSS.Math.Content. NBT: Number and Operations in Base Ten. To simplify labeling across grade levels and to allow teachers to adapt lessons and activities to their needs, the standards listed here are the CCSS domain standards. The following boxes specify the standards that are addressed in the Chapter 6 lessons and inventory of ideas:

- Box 6.1, Common Core State Standards for Mathematics: Mathematical Practices
- Box 6.2, Common Core State Standards for Mathematics: Mathematical Content
- Box 6.3, National Core Arts Standards for Music

Box 6.4 offers a framework for structuring Chapter 6 lessons and activities.

Box 6.1 Common Core State Standards for Mathematics (Mathematical Practices) Included in Chapter 6 Lessons (L) and Inventory of Ideas (I)

Mathematical Practices		
CCSS.Math.Practice.1	Make sense of problems and persevere in solving them	L 6.1
		I 7
		I 10
CCSS.Math.Practice.2	Reason abstractly and quantitatively	L 6.2
		I 8
		I 14

Mathematical Practices		
CCSS.Math.Practice.3	Construct viable arguments and critique the reasoning of others	L 6.1
		L 6.2
		I 6
		I 11
CCSS.Math.Practice.4	Model with mathematics	L 6.3
		I 4
		I 13
CCSS.Math.Practice.5	Use appropriate tools strategically	L 6.4
		I 2
		I 9
CCSS.Math.Practice.6	Attend to precision	L 6.4
		I 1
		I 3
CCSS.Math.Practice.7	Look for and make use of structure	L 6.2
		I 5
		I 13
CCSS.Math.Practice.8	Look for and express regularity in repeated reasoning	L 6.3
		I 5
		I 9

Box 6.2 Common Core State Standards for Mathematics (Mathematical Content) Included in Chapter 6 Lessons (L) and Inventory of Ideas (I)

CCSS.Math.Content.CC	Counting and Cardinality	L 6.1
		I 3
		I 5
		I 6
		I 14
CCSS.Math.Content.OA	Operations and Algebraic Thinking	L 6.1
		L 6.2
		L 6.3
		L 6.4
		I 6
		I 8
		I 14

CCSS.Math.Content.NBT	Number and Operations in Base Ten	L6.4
		I5
		I14
CCSS.Math.Content.NF	Number and Operations—Fractions	L6.3
		L6.4
		I3
		I4
		I7
CCSS.Math.Content.MD	Measurement and Data	L6.1
		L6.2
		L6.4
		I1
		I2
		I11
		I12
		I13
CCSS.Math.Content.G	Geometry	L6.2
		L6.3
		I7
		I8
		I10

Box 6.3 National Core Arts Standards for Music Included in Chapter 3 Sample Lessons (L) and Inventory of Ideas (I)

MU:Cr1	Generate and conceptualize artistic ideas and work	L6.2
(Create)		L6.4
		I8
		I9
MU:Cr2	Organize and develop artistic ideas and work	L6.3
(Create)		L6.4
		I6
		I8

MU:Cr3 (Create)	Refine and complete artistic work	L 6.3 L 6.4 I 8 I 9
MU:Pr4 (Perform)	Select, analyze, and interpret artistic work for presentation	L 6.1 I 5 I 13
MU:Pr5 (Perform)	Develop and refine artistic techniques and work for presentation	L 6.1 I 3 I 14
MU:Pr6 (Perform)	Convey meaning through the presentation of artistic work	L 6.3 L 6.4 I 1 I 9 I 14
MU:Re7 (Respond)	Perceive and analyze artistic work	L 6.2 L 6.4 I 2 I 7 I 11 I 12
MU:Re8 (Respond)	Interpret intent and meaning in artistic work	L 6.3 I 5 I 10
MU:Re9 (Respond)	Apply criteria to evaluate artistic work	L 6.1 I 6 I 13
MU:Cn10 (Connect)	Synthesize and relate knowledge and personal experiences to make art	L 6.1 L 6.4 I 4 I 8
MU:Cn11 (Connect)	Relate artistic ideas and works with societal, cultural, and historical context to deepen understanding	L 6.2 L 6.3 I 2 I 7 I 10

Box 6.4 Framework for Chapter 6 Lessons and Ideas

This chapter is designed to support K–5 educators as they integrate music and mathematics. The lessons are designed to be fully taught by classroom teachers; however, the plans may also facilitate partnerships and collaboration between classroom teachers and music specialists. All lessons and activities have been reviewed by practicing teachers, and most have been field-tested in elementary classrooms. Chapter 6 lessons are labeled as primary, intermediate, or upper elementary, but all the plans and activities are adaptable to a variety of grade levels and are intended as tools for you to meet your students' needs. Some of the lessons may need to be spread over two or more class periods. Please adjust, adapt, or expand however works best for you and for your students.

Lesson 6.1: Dots in mathematics and music: Part and whole relationships

Grade Level: Primary
Essential Question: How can numeric and musical data be represented visually?

Objectives

- Students will read and write rhythms using nontraditional notation, demonstrating an understanding of one-to-one correspondence by aligning each dot with one musical sound, and of part–whole relationships by accurately labeling specific points in their work.
- Students will accurately count objects in a set, represent quantities with manipulatives and dots, and compare sets of manipulatives.

Common Core State Standards for Mathematics addressed

- CCSS.Math.Practice.1: Make sense of problems and persevere in solving them
- CCSS.Math.Practice.3: Construct viable arguments and critique the reasoning of others
- CCSS.Math.Content.CC: Counting and Cardinality
- CCSS.Math.Content.OA: Operations and Algebraic Thinking
- CCSS.Math.Content.MD: Measurement and Data

National Core Arts Standards for Music addressed

- MU:Pr4: Select, analyze, and interpret artistic work for presentation
- MU:Pr5: Develop and refine artistic techniques and work for presentation
- MU:Re9: Apply criteria to evaluate artistic work
- MU:Cn10: Synthesize and relate knowledge and personal experiences to make art

Materials

- Blank paper
- Markers
- Small mathematics manipulatives

Procedure

Explore nontraditional rhythmic notation with your students. Dotting is a straightforward approach to rhythmic notation where each dot represents one sound or syllable (Richards & Langsness, 1984). This method is an intuitive way for students to record the rhythm of a song by simply using dots.

•	•	•	•	•	•	•	•	•	•
•	•	•	•	•	•	•	•	•	•
•	•	•	•	•	•				

The previous dots represent the rhythm of a well-known children's song, but it is almost impossible to tell which song it is just by looking at the lines of dots. Once the text is added, it becomes clear. Sing along:

•	•	•	•	•	•	•	•	•	•	•	•
Do	you	know	the	muf-	fin	man,	The	muf-	fin	man	the
•	•	•	•	•	•	•	•	•	•	•	•
muf-	fin	man?	Do	you	know	the	muf-	fin	man	who	lives
•	•	•	•								
on	Dru-	ry	lane?					(MacKarness, 1888)			

Next is a differently organized version of the same song. In this version, each syllable is still represented by a single dot, but now the song is arranged in practical chunks (Bennett & Bartholomew, 1997; Bennett, 2016). Sing along again:

```
 •  •  •          •   •   •  •        •   •   •  • •        •   •   •  •
```

Do you know   the muf-fin man,   the muf-fin man,   the muf-fin man,

```
 •  •  •          •  •  •  •   •   •   •  •   • •
```

Do you know   the muf-fin man who lives on Dru- ry lane?   (MacKarness, 1888)

This "chunked" organization of the dots is more user-friendly for the reader, simplifies things visually, and makes it easier to follow along. When young students record the rhythm of a song using dots, their dots will likely resemble the first example given. When you create a set of dots for students to read, they will be more successful if you take the time to organize the rhythm in logical chunks.

Your choice of songs to dot with students is practically unlimited. Here, the steps are described using "Yankee Doodle" as an example.

1. Sing. Even though the end goal is to create a set of dots representing the rhythm of a song, getting out a pen or pencil is not the first step. Students must internalize a song before they try to express the rhythm. Direct students to sing the first verse of "Yankee Doodle."

> Yankee Doodle went to town
> Riding on a pony.
> Stuck a feather in his cap
> And called it macaroni. (Lomax & Lomax, 1934)

2. Clap. Clapping along with a song allows students to put the rhythm of the piece in their body. Even though they are not yet actually physically writing the rhythm, they will feel where the dots will go. Have students sing "Yankee Doodle" again, clapping once for each syllable. In the following text, each X represents one clap.

X	X	X	X	X	X	X
Yan-	kee	Doo-	dle	went	to	town

X	X	X	X	X	X	
Ri-	ding	on	a	po-	ny	

X	X	X	X	X	X	X
Stuck	a	fea-	ther	in	his	cap

X	X	X	X	X	X	X
And	called	it	ma-	ca-	ro-	ni. (Lomax & Lomax, 1934)

3. Dot with fingertip. In this step, students tap from left to right on their paper, mimicking what they will do with their writing utensils. This allows them to plan where the dots will go and plan when they will need to jump back to the

beginning of a new line, and is good practice for tracking left to right. Again, have them sing "Yankee Doodle," this time tapping on a blank sheet of paper where the dots will go.

4. Sing and dot. The next step is for students to sing while they dot. Just like students sang and clapped, then sang and tapped with their fingers, they will sing while they dot. This reinforces the one-to-one correspondence and alignment of each dot with a specific sound. Thick-tipped markers are usually a good choice for this activity. Extra-sharp pencils or fine-tipped pens are not the best for dotting, because if students bounce their pencil on the paper, it probably will not show up well. As a result, some students may spend time coloring in each dot, rather than just tapping once per sound, and they will be behind the beat. Give each student a marker, then sing and dot "Yankee Doodle." You might need to slow the tempo slightly. Students' dots will likely look something like this:

. . . .

5. Read and sing. For the next step, ask students to go back and read what they wrote. They can close their marker and tap with the cap or use their fingertip to follow along.

. . . .

If students recorded the rhythm correctly, they should arrive at the end of their set of dots at the same time as they sing the last word of the verse. To young students, this sometimes seems revolutionary. Often, young students may say, "Wow! I got there at the same time. Let's try it again," because they really do not know if it will happen that way every time. Go ahead and have your students sing and read it again. Observations like these exemplify the development of understanding that written symbols can represent music. Students are beginning to grasp that there are standardized ways to record musical sounds. You can highlight this connection for students by choosing different dots in a song to highlight. In the song Yankee Doodle, for example, you might say, "We are going to freeze on the dot for the word 'town.' Let's sing from the beginning and freeze on that dot."

. . . .

After students have identified the dot that aligns with the word "town," ask them to draw a house around that dot. Figure 6.1 shows a student example.

Go back to the beginning and sing again to "check" if the dot for the word "town" is still the one with the house around it. (It is.) Then, move on to the next section. The next phrase in "Yankee Doodle" is "riding on a pony." Ask the students to count the number of syllables in the word "pony" (two). For this set of directions, you might say, "This time we're going to freeze on the two dots that stand for the word 'pony.'

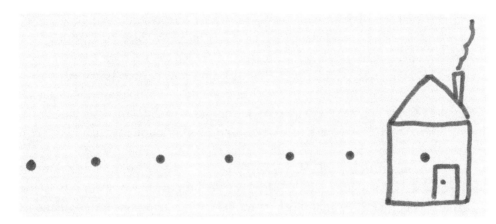

Figure 6.1 Student dotting example 1.
Image used with permission.

Figure 6.2 Student dotting example 1.
Image used with permission.

Those two dots are going to be the pony's eyes. Sing from the beginning, and then make a little pony around those two dots." Figure 6.2 shows another student example.

Reinforce student understanding of part–whole relationships by asking guiding questions such as "What does each dot represent?" (a single sound), "What do groups of dots represent?" (sections or parts of the song), and "What do all the dots and sections represent together?" (the whole song). Even though dotting is different than conventional music notation, recording rhythms in this way is usually intuitive for students and teachers, and is a valid way to read and write music.

Pass out a handful of small manipulatives (bear counters, cubes, base-10 blocks, buttons, colored chips, etc.) to each student. To help students move from rote counting (simply reciting numeral names in order ["one, two, three, four . . ."]) toward one-to-one correspondence counting (touching each object in a set once and saying its numeral name out loud), direct them to touch each of their manipulatives once and count them aloud to determine the total number of objects in their set.

Next, direct students to solve problems using counting skills. Besides counting the number of objects in a set, they can compare amounts in different sets using terms such as "more" and "less," match sets, determine whether numbers are odd or even, explain how numbers compare with the number 5 and the number 10, etc.

The following portion of the lesson reinforces the understanding that a number (in this case six, but you might use another) can be composed of smaller parts, laying the groundwork for understanding operations and carrying out mental calculations.

Pass out six identical manipulatives to each student. Explain that the six objects make up a single "group," and that they all "go together." None of the objects can be on their own or part of a smaller section. Ask each student to arrange the manipulatives in a single group that has exactly six components. You may want students to count their objects after arranging them to reinforce the idea that a number of objects remains constant, even when arranged differently. Direct students to leave their manipulative groupings intact at their places and "go on a walk" around the classroom to observe all the different object groups that were created by their peers. They will likely see arrangements resembling vertical, horizontal, and diagonal lines; circles; dice; and rough piles. Figure 6.3 shows possible manipulative arrangements.

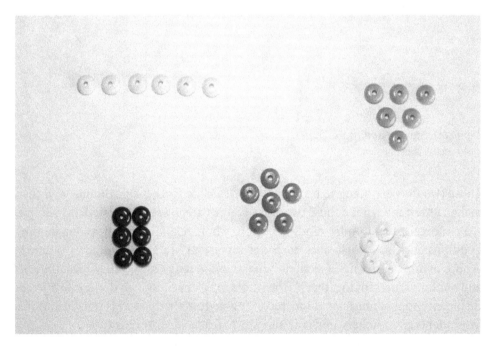

Figure 6.3 Mathematics manipulatives group 1, 2019.
Photo courtesy of Jennifer Versaevel.

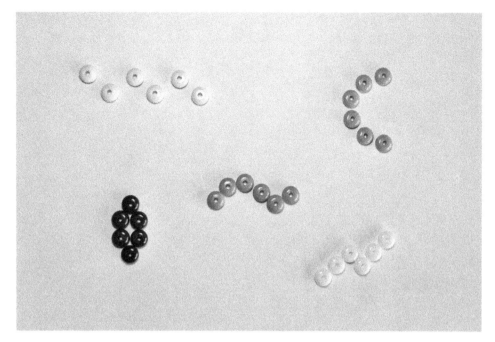

Figure 6.4 Mathematics manipulatives group 2, 2019.
Photo courtesy of Jennifer Versaevel.

When students are back at their spots, encourage them to verbalize the strategies they used to organize their groups. This will encourage reflective thinking and allow other students to consider new strategies.

Challenge students to arrange their manipulatives in a different way than anyone in the class had done previously, while still keeping them in a single group, then go on another observation walk. They may see arrangements such as zigzags, swirls, triangles, curves, or abstract forms. Again, ask students to share the strategies they used. Figure 6.4 shows additional manipulative groupings.

Next, review the definitions of "part" and "whole." If all six objects together represent the "whole," how could students arrange their manipulatives to visually separate the "whole" into multiple "parts"? Show one example, perhaps five manipulatives in a vertical line with one off to the side by itself. Model counting the arrangement both separately and together: "one, two, three, four, five, and one," then "one, two, three, four, five, six," to reinforce the "five plus one makes six" number relation. Challenge students to come up with a unique way to arrange their manipulatives to show "parts." Ask students to count their objects, counting each part separately and counting the whole. Again, walk around the room to observe. They may see two-part arrangements with manipulatives in sets of one and five, two and four, or three and three. They might also see arrangements with three or more parts. Finally, they may see creative arrangements such as two eyes with a four-object smile. Figure 6.5 shows manipulative groupings that demonstrate part–whole relationships.

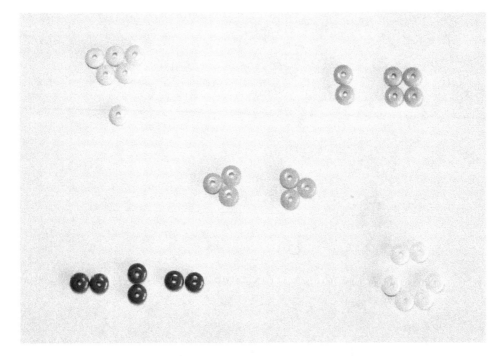

Figure 6.5 Mathematics manipulatives group 3, 2019.
Photo courtesy of Jennifer Versaevel.

Encourage students to reflect on and share connections they identified between counting and dotting. In this lesson, students practiced one-to-one correspondence and part–whole relationships in music and mathematics. In music, one dot represented one sound, and collectively, all the dots represented the rhythm of an entire song. In mathematics, each manipulative represented one numeral, and small sets of manipulatives added up to the whole. Manipulatives and dotting offer students a platform for discussing their mathematical and musical thinking, provide a framework for demonstrating understandings, and encourage students to investigate multiple ways to solve problems.

Assessment

- Observe students during the process of rhythmic dotting and assembling manipulative sets to check for accuracy and understanding.
- In a follow-up discussion, ask a variety of questions to encourage student self-reflection. Students will answer with their hands, holding up one, two, three, four, or five fingers to correspond with their self-perceived degree of understanding. Questions might address sets, groups, part–whole relationships, counting, or rhythmic notation.

Lesson 6.2: "Wide Open Spaces," structure, and pattern

Grade Level: Intermediate or upper elementary
Essential Question: How can patterns describe mathematical and musical phenomena?

Objectives

- Students will correctly organize and represent musical form by interpreting changes in harmony, text, dynamics, and instrumentation they perceive while singing and listening.
- Students will determine mathematical rules to classify and order themselves by size, number, or other property.
- Students will form generalizations based on relationships and properties they observe to discern patterns created by their peers.

Common Core State Standards for Mathematics addressed

- CCSS.Math.Practice.2: Reason abstractly and quantitatively
- CCSS.Math.Practice.3: Construct viable arguments and critique the reasoning of others
- CCSS.Math.Practice.7: Look for and make use of structure
- CCSS.Math.Content.OA: Operations and Algebraic Thinking
- CCSS.Math.Content.MD: Measurement and Data
- CCSS.Math.Content.G: Geometry

National Core Arts Standards for Music addressed

- MU:Cr1: Generate and conceptualize artistic ideas and work
- MU:Re7: Perceive and analyze artistic work
- MU:Cn11: Relate artistic ideas and works with societal, cultural, and historical context to deepen understanding

Materials

- Recorded musical example and lyrics: "Wide Open Spaces" by the The Chicks
- Printed lyrics of "Looby Loo"

Procedure

Rationale: Students are often asked to used pattern-based thinking to represent and understand mathematical phenomena. Pattern-based thinking is essential for students' musical analysis as well. Drawing connections between mathematical and musical patterns will reinforce students' understanding in both disciplines.

Engage students in a discussion about musical patterns. Musical elements including melody, rhythm, and form can be organized in patterns. This lesson focuses on patterns that are found in musical form. The form of a piece of music can be described as the way it is put together, the arrangement of its sections, or its structure. Depending on the situation, different levels of analysis are adopted; it is possible to label individual chords, single phrases, or entire symphonies. For this lesson, students will explore and label the main sections of the song "Wide Open Spaces" by the The Chicks to discern the large-scale formal structure of the piece.

Ask students how they might distinguish between different sections in a piece of music. Students might categorize differences between sections based on harmonic changes (brighter/darker or major/minor), changes in the text (verse/chorus), changes in dynamics (loud/soft), changes in tempo (fast/slow), changes in instrumentation, or a combination of these elements.

Musicians usually label large sections of music with capital letters, starting with the letter A for the first section. If there is an introduction, it can be labeled separately. An A section may be short or long, but it remains the A section until a musical change occurs. The new musical material that follows the A section is labeled with B, the next letter of the alphabet. If another change is noted and new material is heard, yet another letter is needed, so the section will be labeled with the letter C (ABC); however, if the change after the B section is a return to material that was heard previously, the new section will be labeled that corresponding letter, A (ABA).

One method elementary students regularly use when analyzing a song's form is text analysis. The lyrics of a song are often organized in sections that directly outline the structure of the piece. Singing "Looby Loo" while reading the lyrics clearly shows the song's ABA form

A   Here we go looby loo.
        Here we go looby light.
        Here we go looby loo.
        All on a Saturday night.

B   You put your left hand in.
        You put your left hand out.
        You shake it a little, a little, a little,
        And turn yourself about.

A   Here we go looby loo.
        Here we go looby light.

Here we go looby loo.

All on a Saturday night. (Fowke, 1969, pp. 18–19)

In some instances, watching a live performance or a music video can provide clues about the form of a piece of music. For example, in the movie *Mulan*, changes in the animation style directly align with the different musical sections in the song "A Girl Worth Fighting For."

An intuitive method for discerning musical form involves listening to music with a critical ear. Aural discrimination techniques allow students to listen for musical differences that mark the different sections of a piece of music. Challenge your students to try this method by aurally analyzing "Wide Open Spaces" together. Table 6.1 includes the timing associated with each section of the musical form and a

Table 6.1 Timing and Sections of "Wide Open Spaces"

Timing	Section	Sample Script
0:00	Intro	As you write "intro" on the board, say, "This is the introduction. What will the letter of the first section be?" (Students will respond with "A.") "Yes, the A section. When you think you hear something different than the introduction that we'll label as the A section, raise your hand."
0:21	A	Write an "A" on the board and say, "That's right. This is the A section. We could also label this as the verse."
0:43	A	Say, "Here's another section. What is it? It has different words than the first A section, but it has the same music. What should we label it?" (A) Write another A on the board.
1:03	B	Say, "Oh, here's another section. What are we in?" (B) "Yes, the music has changed." As you write "B" on the board add a note underneath it that reads "wide open" and say, "I'm going to write a note to myself so that I remember that the B section is the 'wide open' chorus part."
1:25	A	"What should we label this section?" (A) "Yes, this is another A section. Again, it has new words, but the same music." Write another "A" on the board, point to the form so far, and ask, "What section do we predict is coming?' (A)
1:45	B	"Based on the form so far, we predicted another A section, but what do you hear?" (B) "We hear the 'wide open' section, so it is another chorus." Write a "B" on the board.
2:08	C	"What is this? Have we heard anything like this before?" (No, or maybe a student will say it is like the introduction.) Since this is new musical material, what letter will we give it?" (C) Write a "C" on the board and say, "This is the C section, or you might call it the bridge or an interlude. What do we expect now?" (A)
2:29	A	Write another "A" on the board and say, "Yes, it is another A section. The instruments are a little different, but it is still a verse."
2:49	B	"What is this?" (B) Write a "B" on the board.
3:12	B	Say, "Another B" and write a final "B" on the board.

Courtesy of author.

sample script you might use. Start the recording and let it play until the end. Speak and write in time with the recording, notating the form on the board.

At the end of the recording, the following form should be written on the board:

Intro A A B A B C A B B

Draw students' attention to the circumstances surrounding their analysis of "Wide Open Spaces." They compiled the structure of the song in real time, listening for changes and labeling the distinct sections. They might look at the lyrics, watch the video, listen again, or sing along to double-check their conclusions, but point out that you don't always have to analyze printed music to determine the form of a piece of music. These strategies will allow students to discern the forms of vast numbers of songs and musical examples.

Engage students in a discussion about mathematical patterns. The patterns that students experience involve numbers, shapes, and words. Recognizing and creating patterns helps students to develop generalizations and to identify mathematical relationships. Just like in music, in mathematics we define the way patterns are organized as their structure.

For this lesson, students will explore and label the structural patterns that develop as a result of ordering students according to particular characteristics they possess. You might want to model this process using screenshots of images from the internet. For example, you could project four pictures: (1) person with blond hair, (2) person with gray hair, (3) person with gray hair, and (4) person with blond hair, demonstrating ABBA form.

Divide students into groups of four. Direct each group to quietly collaborate to determine a characteristic by which the members of their group might be classified. Examples are "sandals, sandals, tennis shoes, sandals" (AABA) and "eats hot lunch, eats cold lunch, eats hot lunch, eats cold lunch" (ABAB). Groups take turns coming to the front of the room where they arrange themselves according to their predetermined pattern. The remaining groups work together to predict and record the pattern they believe represents the structure of the arrangement. Each prediction group appoints a representative to explain and defend the rationale for the pattern they determined. Finally, the group in front will disclose the characteristic they featured and the pattern they are representing.

Assessment

- Following the group analysis of "Wide Open Spaces," ask students to verbally summarize the process they followed to determine the musical form and describe their results. Check their responses for accuracy.
- During the mathematical pattern activity, check to see if students' reasoning aligns with the patterns they created in their groups. Observe students as they discern patterns created by their peers, again checking for logical reasoning and clearly stated explanations.

Lesson 6.3: Fibonacci sequence in math and music

Grade Level: Upper elementary
Essential Question: How are mathematical sequences used in the natural and designed world?

Objectives

- Students will correctly identify, generate, and explain Fibonacci numbers; draw a golden rectangle; and construct a spiral.
- Students will individually and collaboratively assess the efficiency and effectiveness of the strategies they employed and reflect about ways they might apply their understandings in future learning scenarios.
- Students will compose and perform songs based on Fibonacci numbers. Tasks include creating lyrics with prescribed numbers of syllables; composing an organized, coordinated accompaniment; and performing compositions for the class.

Common Core State Standards for Mathematics addressed

- CCSS.Math.Practice.4: Model with mathematics
- CCSS.Math.Practice.8: Look for and express regularity in repeated reasoning
- CCSS.Math.Content.OA: Operations and Algebraic Thinking
- CCSS.Math.Content.NF: Number and Operations—Fractions
- CCSS.Math.Content.MD: Measurement and Data
- CCSS.Math.Content.G: Geometry

National Core Arts Standards for Music addressed

- MU:Pr2: Organize and develop artistic ideas and work
- MU:Pr3: Refine and complete artistic work
- MU:Pr6: Convey meaning through the presentation of artistic work
- MU:Pr8: Interpret intent and meaning in artistic work
- MU:Cn11: Relate artistic ideas and works with societal, cultural, and historical context to deepen understanding

Materials

- Musical examples

- "5678" by B. C. Manjunath (rhythmic konnakol composition)
- "Music for Strings, Percussion and Celesta" by Bela Bartok
- Graph paper
- Compasses (optional)
- Natural objects or photos of natural objects displaying Fibonacci numbers

Procedure

Introduce the Fibonacci sequence

Over 800 years ago in Pisa, Italy, a mathematician named Leonardo Bonacci (also known as Fibonacci) figured out a sequence of numbers that came to be called the Fibonacci sequence (Simonis, 1999). The sequence begins with the following numbers: 1, 1, 2, 3, 5, 8, 13 . . . . See if students can crack the code and find the next number. The solution: Each number can be calculated by adding the two numbers that precede it. The Fibonacci sequence is a sequence of numbers that continues forever: 1, 1, 2, 3, 5, 8, 13, 21, 34, 55, 89, 144 . . . .

Create a golden rectangle

Students can use the Fibonacci sequence to create a golden rectangle on graph paper where each unit represents one and the sides of each square are consecutive Fibonacci numbers. Give the following directions: Start by drawing around the perimeter of one square (see Figure 6.6).

Draw a square that aligns with the next number in the sequence (1) and place it adjacent to the first square (see Figure 6.7).

Draw a line along the longest length (two units) and use that line as one side of a square that does not include the existing squares. You now have a rectangle that is comprised of two 1×1 squares and one 2×2 square (see Figure 6.8).

These numbers represent the beginning of the Fibonacci sequence (1, 1, 2 . . .). To continue the process, draw a line along the longest length of the new rectangle that also includes the original 1×1 square. Use that line as one side of a new square. You now have a rectangle that is composed of two 1×1 squares, one 2×2 square, and one 3×3 square, again following the Fibonacci sequence (1, 1, 2, 3 . . .) (see Figure 6.9).

Continue the process, always connecting the new square to the side closest to the original 1×1 square (this creates the spiral around the center point). Draw students'

Figure 6.6 Fibonacci graph, step 1, 2019.
Image courtesy of Meta Newhouse.

Figure 6.7 Fibonacci graph, step 2, 2019.
Image courtesy of Meta Newhouse.

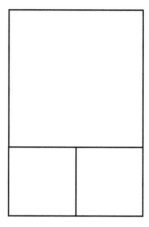

Figure 6.8 Fibonacci graph, step 3, 2019.
Image courtesy of Meta Newhouse.

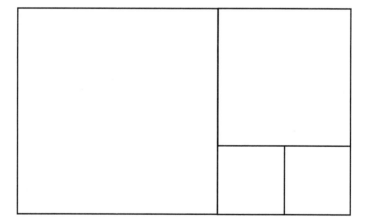

Figure 6.9 Fibonacci graph, step 4, 2019.
Image courtesy of Meta Newhouse.

attention to the fact that simply counting the number of units on one of the longest sides of the existing rectangle will always predict the next number in the Fibonacci sequence. (The length of the sides of each new square is the sum of the length of sides of the two squares before it.) Theoretically, you can continue forever, but realistically, you can continue as far as your graph paper will allow.

Relate the Fibonacci sequence to the golden rectangle

The golden ratio is based on Fibonacci numbers; the length and width of a golden rectangle form a golden ratio. As a decimal, the golden ratio is ≈ 1.61803398 . . . . When consecutive terms of the Fibonacci sequence are used as length and width of a rectangle, the ratio of the length to width gets closer and closer to this decimal value. These rectangles are called "golden rectangles" because of this property; if you cut a square off a golden rectangle, you're left with a smaller golden rectangle. Golden rectangles are thought to be the most perfect, beautiful rectangles that exist. Explore the ratios of the sides of the golden rectangles students have just drawn. Table 6.2 shows Fibonacci numbers that represent successive terms of the Fibonacci sequence, rectangle dimensions, the ratio of the length to width of the rectangles, and the decimal value of those ratios.

Draw the spiral in a golden rectangle

Direct students to take the golden rectangles they just drew and connect opposite corners of each square with an arc (see Figure 6.10). Students can draw arcs freehand or use a compass, making arcs in each square that have a radius that equals the size of the edge of that square. After constructing the spiral, ask students to write about the strategy they utilized and explain how it relates to the Fibonacci sequence.

Find the Fibonacci sequence in nature

Collect natural objects or photos of natural objects that can be related to the Fibonacci sequence. These might include flowers with their petals intact, pinecones, fruits and

Table 6.2 Fibonacci Sequence and the Golden Ratio

Fibonacci Numbers	Rectangle Dimensions	Ratio of Length to Width	Decimal Value
1, 1	1 × 1	1/1	1
1, 2	1 × 2	2/1	2
2, 3	2 × 3	3/2	1.5
3, 5	3 × 5	5/3	≈ 1.67
5, 8	5 × 8	8/5	1.6
8, 13	8 × 13	13/8	1.625
13, 21	13 × 21	21/13	≈ 1.615
21, 34	21 × 34	34/21	≈ 1.619
34, 55	34 × 55	55/34	≈ 1.618
55, 89	55 × 89	89/55	≈ 1.618

Courtesy of author.

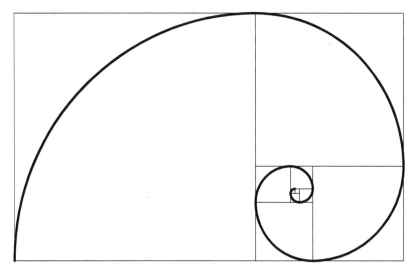

Figure 6.10 Golden spiral.
© Pyty/Shutterstock.com.

vegetables such as pineapples and cauliflower, nautilus shells, leaf arrangements, seed heads, or spiral galaxies (see Figures 6.11, 6.12, 6.13 and 6.14).

Ask students to draw a sketch and explain the connection between an object and the Fibonacci sequence. Students' explanations might note connections in the number of petals of a flower, the number of leaves of a plant around a stem, or the number of spirals they count on a pinecone or sunflower.

Fibonacci numbers can be found in the number of petals of many flowers and the number of leaves of many plants. For example, calla lilies have 1 petal, the carnivorous bladderwort has 2 petals, trilliums have 3 petals, hibiscus flowers have 5 petals, clematis flowers have 8 petals, and most daisies have 13, 21, 34, or 55 petals. The golden ratio also allows plants to be more efficient by using spirals that permit the most seed heads to fit in the least space. Many plants grow in spirals that radiate from the center, with some going clockwise, and some counterclockwise. If students count the spirals on pinecone specimens, they will usually find that the spirals in one direction are a number from the Fibonacci sequence and the spirals that grow in the other direction are a consecutive number from the sequence. For example, if a pinecone has 8 clockwise spirals, it will likely have 13 counterclockwise spirals (see Figure 6.15). The same is true for sunflowers and many other natural objects.

Find the Fibonacci sequence in music

Ask students what they think the Fibonacci sequence and music might have in common. Allow for several responses and engage the class in discussion. A simple way to connect the Fibonacci sequence and music is to locate Fibonacci numbers in musical contexts. Display a picture of one octave of a piano keyboard from C to C (see Figure 6.16) along with the beginning of the Fibonacci sequence.

Figure 6.11 Spiral design in a succulent plant.
© brackish_nz/Shutterstock.com.

Figure 6.12 Close-up of sunflower.
© Min C. Chiu/Shutterstock.com.

Figure 6.13 Nautilus shell cross-section.
© Lorna Roberts/Shutterstock.com.

Figure 6.14 Oxeye daisy.
© Aleksandra Antic/Shutterstock.com.

Figure 6.15 Close-up of the back of a pinecone.
© Bringolo/Shutterstock.com.

Figure 6.16 One octave on a piano keyboard.
© Ricardo de Paula Ferreira/Shutterstock.com.

Ask pairs or small groups of students to observe connections between the Fibonacci sequence and the keyboard. Students should discover that one octave contains 5 black keys (grouped in one set of 2 and one set of 3), 8 white keys, and 13 keys altogether. These are all Fibonacci numbers.

Depending on their musical background, students might note that the pentatonic scale includes 5 notes, major and minor scales have 8 notes, and the chromatic scale includes 13 notes. Again, these are Fibonacci numbers.

Some composers have directly used Fibonacci numbers to create their compositions—for example, B. C. Manjunath's rhythmic konnakol composition "5678" is based on the sequence 1, 1, 2, 3, 5, 8, 13, 21. Composer Bela Bartok structured his piece "Music for Strings, Percussion and Celesta" so that the important musical events occurred in measures associated with the Fibonacci sequence.

Beyond simple associations with Fibonacci numbers, many architects, visual artists, and musicians have used the golden ratio (1.618) as a way to structure their creations. For example, the Notre Dame Cathedral in Paris (see Figure 6.17) incorporates the golden ratio, and Leonardo da Vinci depicted the golden ratio in many of his paintings, including *The Last Supper* (see Figure 6.18).

Figure 6.17 Notre Dame Cathedral in Paris.
© TTstudio/Shutterstock.com.

Figure 6.10 *The Last Supper* by Leonardo da Vinci.
© Markus Baumeler/Pixabay.

The length of a musical composition can display a Fibonacci relationship if the climax or an important point of change is located at 61.8% of the piece, rather than at the middle or end. Bartok's previously mentioned "Music for Strings, Percussion and Celesta" is a good example of this concept. There are 89 measures in the entire composition and the climax falls in measure 55.

Perhaps composers gravitate toward the golden ratio naturally, placing climactic moments 61.8% of the way through their pieces, or perhaps they actually calculate the golden ratio. Either way, students can use mathematics to determine where 61.8% of any song lies.

If a copy of the score of a piece of music is available, students can count the total number of measures, then multiply that number by 0.618, using a calculator as needed. The result is the measure number that marks 61.8% of the way through the piece. For example, in a piece that is 32 measures long, they would predict that the climax or major event should occur around measure 20 ($32 \times 0.618 = 19.776$). Next, students should listen to the piece, following along on the score, to determine if that measure actually aligns with a high point or climax they can identify aurally.

If a recording of a piece is available, students can convert the total length of the song into seconds, then multiply that number by 0.618. Their answer will be the point (in seconds) that aligns with 61.8% of the way through the performance. Students will need to convert that number back into minutes, then listen to the recording to determine if that point aligns with a high point or climax.

Ask students to reflect about which of the previous two methods for locating the golden point of a song is more accurate and allow for a variety of responses. Direct students to think about variations in the tempo of performances that could shift the calculated solution slightly away from the actual golden point of a composition for various recorded examples, while the solution calculated from printed music will be consistent.

Students can also analyze a recorded song and aurally locate the climax, bridge, or other high point, then use the timing of that musical event to predict the total length of the piece using 0.618, assuming that the golden ratio is used. Similarly, if students have the musical skills necessary, they can analyze a printed score to locate the climax, count the measure number where the climax occurs, and predict the total number of measures in the piece.

Many pop songs align with the golden ratio, and students can explore any piece to which they have access. Some instrumental musical examples that fit include Khachaturian's "Sabre Dance"; John Powell's "Romantic Flight" from the movie *How to Train Your Dragon*; Chopin's "Mazurka No. 37 in A-Flat, Op. 59, No. 2"; Debussy's "Doctor Gradus ad Parnassum" from his *Children's Corner Suite*; "Ballade in G Minor Op. 118 No. 3" by Brahms; "Olympic Fanfare and Theme" by John Williams; and "Gonna Fly Now," also known as the "Theme From Rocky," by Bill Conti.

Create a song with Fibonacci numbers

Students will create lyrics about topics they choose with syllables that correspond to the first numbers in the Fibonacci sequence. Provide a blank framework to facilitate their writing and show the following set of lyrics as an example.

(1)   Oh.
(1)   My.
(2)   Goodness.
(3)   I don't know.
(5)   That sounds really hard.
(8)   I'm not sure I can write lyrics.
(13)   Wait—if I just line up the syllables, it's easy!

Next, students will compose music that aligns with their lyrics. They might create a rhythmic accompaniment involving snaps, pats, claps, or pencils used as drumsticks. They might use long, sustained tones to accompany their spoken text, perhaps striking metal bowls of various sizes or asking a partner to hum elongated pitches. They could also choose to create a melody that aligns with their text, singing each word of the lyrics with a specific pitch they determine. Overachievers might choose to place a climax at 61.8% of the way through their compositions.

Assessment

- Ask each student to perform their composition for the class. Assess the lyrics for alignment with Fibonacci numbers and musical accompaniments for coordination with texts.

- During discussions and activities, monitor students' ability to correctly recognize, generate, and explain Fibonacci numbers, golden rectangles, and spirals.
- Engage students in a think-pair-share activity to review the natural and designed objects that followed the Fibonacci sequence students encountered.
  - First, ask students to individually write responses to the following questions:
    - Do you agree that a common thread of beauty can be identified in the sounds and images you explored? Why or why not?
    - If the Fibonacci sequence and the golden ratio are fundamental building blocks of beauty in nature, does applying the ratio to designed objects such as musical compositions, architecture, and art help people to create things of beauty? Why or why not?
    - How might you apply your understanding of the Fibonacci sequence in the future?
  - Direct students to examine their ideas with a partner, and then engage in a full-class discussion.
  - Collect students' papers to check each individual's perspective and ideas.

Music extension

Explore connections between Fibonacci numbers and the frequencies of individual pitches or the relationships between various musical intervals in cycles per second. For example, the note frequency for middle C is 264 Hz and the frequency for the A above middle C is 440 Hz, a ratio of 3/5 that uses Fibonacci numbers.

Lesson 6.4: Create an amusement park ride and theme song

Grade Level: Primary or intermediate
Essential Question: How do people interpret information, solve problems, and present data in music and mathematics?

Objectives

- Students will rehearse and sing the song "it's a small world" with expression and technical accuracy.
- Students will collaboratively design and illustrate an amusement park ride, meeting criteria by including required elements.
- Students will work together to determine the processes required for various calculations associated with their amusement park attractions by applying the mathematics they know and considering available tools.

- Students will use place value understandings and properties of operations to calculate quantities, percentages, perimeter, and area, correctly expressing answers as whole numbers, fractions, or decimals, depending on the operations performed.
- As a class, students will visually and aurally analyze the formal structure and aurally analyze the rhythmic structure of "it's a small world."
- As a whole class and in collaborative groups, students will create new lyrics that align with the rhythmic and formal structure of "it's a small world," describing and promoting their theme park rides.
- Students will perform for and with the class, aligning new texts with the original structure and accurately singing melodies and rhythms.

Common Core State Standards for Mathematics addressed

- CCSS.Math.Practice.4: Model with mathematics
- CCSS.Math.Practice.5: Use appropriate tools strategically
- CCSS.Math.Content.OA: Operations and Algebraic Thinking
- CCSS.Math.Content.NBT: Number and Operations in Base Ten
- CCSS.Math.Content.NF: Number and Operations—Fractions
- CCSS.Math.Content.MD: Measurement and Data

National Core Arts Standards for Music addressed

- MU:Cr1: Generate and conceptualize artistic ideas and work
- MU:Cr2: Organize and develop artistic ideas and work
- MU:Cr3: Refine and complete artistic work
- MU:Pr6: Convey meaning through the presentation of artistic work
- MU:Re7: Perceive and analyze artistic work
- MU:Cn10: Synthesize and relate knowledge and personal experiences to make art

Materials

- Audio and video recordings: "it's a small world" (note: this title is always printed using only lowercase letters)
- Printed lyrics of "it's a small world"
- Poster boards and other art supplies

Procedure

Listen to an audio recording of "it's a small world" while following along with the lyrics. Ask students to turn to a partner and discuss why they think the song was created. It is likely that a majority of students will know that it is the song from the Disney ride of the same name. Originally, the idea was to have multiple national anthems playing in succession as people traveled through the attraction, but the result was aural chaos. In 1963, when brothers Richard and Robert Sherman walked through the mock-up of the attraction, they knew there needed to be one cohesive song playing throughout the ride. Together, they wrote "it's a small world" for the attraction (Watts, 1997). Figure 6.19 shows a view from inside the "it's a small world" ride.

Engage students in a discussion about amusement parks and amusement park rides, and then watch and listen to a video of the ride "it's a small world," allowing students to aurally and visually experience the ride. Next, sing the song as a class, rehearsing as needed to perform with rhythmic and melodic accuracy and with appropriate expressive qualities such as voice quality, dynamics, and tempo.

Divide students into collaborative groups to design their own amusement park rides. Begin with a variety of prompts to guide students' initial brainstorming about their attractions. To guide students in their thinking, ask for the following details:

Figure 6.19 View from inside the "it's a small world" ride.
© Whitenep/Wikimedia.

What is the theme of the ride?

Does the ride tell a story or allow riders to have a unique experience?

What will people see?

What will people hear?

What will people feel?

Will the ride be interactive? If yes, in what way?

Is the ride based on water, air, or land travel?

Will people travel through the attraction in boats, cars on rails, trams, baskets suspended in the air, or some other type of vehicle?

How many people can ride in each vehicle at a time?

How many total vehicles can run simultaneously?

How long will the ride take in minutes?

How much will it cost each person to ride?

Using poster boards and art supplies, each group will sketch their amusement park attractions, illustrating various components such as the name of their ride, ticket booth or other entrance to the ride, the line/waiting area, the entire path of the ride showing the total number of vehicles in motion, and the exit. Play the song "it's a small world" as students work.

In their groups, challenge students to work to determine the mathematical processes required to calculate how many people can ride the attraction per hour. The illustration of their ride may facilitate their reasoning. Guide them to discover the steps:

- First, determine the total number of possible trips per hour for one vehicle.
- Next, use place value understandings and properties of operations to multiply the total number of trips per hour by the total number of vehicles that can run simultaneously, and, finally, multiply that product by the number of people who can ride in each vehicle. For example, if one vehicle can make 10 trips through the ride each hour and you have 3 cars that can each hold 4 people, 120 people can ride your attraction per hour ($10 \times 3 \times 4 = 120$).
- Students will next perform operations with multidigit whole numbers and decimals to hundredths to calculate how much they will earn per hour, again working together to determine what calculations are required to find their answer.
- Multiply the total number of people who can ride the attraction each hour by the amount they will charge each person.
- You might ask students to research and provide a variety of estimates, including the total cost of materials required to build their ride, the amount required to pay all construction workers, the rent and taxes on the land, the salaries for all ride operators, and the expected profit after 1 year, 5 years, or 10 years.
- Combine all the groups' rides to create an entire theme park. Calculate the percentage of rides that fit different categories—thrill rides, roller coasters,

etc.—and express results as fractions. Determine the perimeter of the whole park, and calculate the total area.

Refocus students' attention on the song "it's a small world." As a class, aurally and visually analyze the song's structure (verse, chorus, verse, chorus, verse, chorus) and aurally analyze the rhythm of the text by counting the syllables in each line of the chorus and each verse. (The chorus has a rhythmic syllabic structure of 7, 7, 7, 5, and each verse has a rhythmic syllabic structure of 10, 10, 12, 7.)

Using the existing melody, structure, and rhythm of the song "it's a small world," create a new theme song that will feature each amusement park attraction. As a class, create a new chorus with lyrics that align with the 7, 7, 7, 5 syllabic structure students previously analyzed. The thematic content of their chorus lyrics might describe theme parks in general, focus on the overall atmosphere, describe the setting, or include a marketing strategy to promote the overall theme park. Lyrics that align rhythmically with the chorus of "it's a small world" can be sung with the original tune.

Invite students to work in their collaborative groups to create one verse, composing lyrics that align with the rhythm of the verses of "it's a small world" (syllables in groups of 10, 10, 12, and 7), and describe the ride they designed. Lyrics that align rhythmically with the verses of "it's a small world" can be sung with the original tune.

Perform the entire song together, adhering to the structure of "it's a small world" that the class previously analyzed (verse, chorus, verse, chorus, etc.). Each collaborative group will sing their verse for the class. The entire class will sing the newly composed chorus immediately following each verse.

Assessment

- While each collaborative group sings their verse, listen for in-tune, rhythmically accurate singing and lyrics that align with the original song's structure. Check that the whole class sings the newly created chorus each time it returns.
- Collect students' illustrated amusement park rides and compare their designs with the answers they calculated regarding the number of passengers who can ride their attraction, the amount they will earn each hour, the percentage of rides that fit different categories, the perimeter of the park, and the total area. Check that answers are correctly expressed as whole numbers, fractions, or decimals, depending on the operations performed.

Inventory of ideas

The following collection of ideas contains additional lesson topics, specific teaching strategies, and recommended activities. The first four ideas focus on movement. Movement is a useful tool for highlighting connections between math and music.

Clap, tap, play an instrument, or use recorded musical examples as students musically move to demonstrate their understanding of concepts in music and math.

1. Connect the idea of size and range of numbers to the size and range of movements (bigger, smaller, growing larger, smallest to biggest, moving in high/medium/low planes, etc.). Ask students to move to a musical example and demonstrate the terms you call out.

2. Interpret multiplication and division (math) and augmentation and diminution (music) as scaling (moving twice as fast, moving twice as slow, subdividing the beat). Ask students to walk to a musical example with a steady beat, and then demonstrate the term you call out by adjusting the speed with which they walk.

3. Direct students to align their steps with different patterns of beats. For example, in a song that would be counted as "1, 2, 3, 4, 1, 2, 3, 4," have them step only on the 1s and 3s (odd numbers). Next, ask them to step only on the 2s and 4s (even numbers). For an additional challenge, they can try stepping the 1s and 3s while clapping the 2s and 4s.

4. Ask students to walk around the space while you play a recording. When you pause the music, call out a number between 2 and 10. The students stop and form a group that aligns with the number you called. For older students, state a qualitative category such as eye color when you stop the music. Students will determine the ratio of people in each group and express their answer as a percentage or fraction.

5. There are many songs and musical examples with math as their focus. Listen to these pieces and sing them with your students to encourage mathematical understanding and memorization of information, but also challenge students to examine conceptual connections between music and math such as pattern, repetition, shape, and structure. Some possible songs to explore:
   - "Infinity" by They Might Be Giants
   - "Subitize Rock" by Jack Hartman
   - "The Square of the Hypotenuse" by Danny Kaye
   - "The 3 R's" by Jack Johnson
   - "That's Mathematics" by Tom Lehrer
   - "One and One Makes Two" by Johnny Cash and June Carter Cash
   - "If I Had a Million Dollars" by Steven Page and Ed Robertson

6. Phrases in music can be counted, but also felt musically. Play a musical example such as the traditional Irish tune "Fisher's Hornpipe" or an instrumental version of the American folk tune "Turkey in the Straw" and ask students to walk with a steady beat. Stop the music and divide students into groups. Direct students to make estimates and then check their guesses to determine the number of beats in each phrase. One strategy to test phrase length is to trace a rainbow shape with your arm from one side of your body over the top of your head to the other side. The number of counts to complete one rainbow

represents the number of beats in one phrase. Groups will work to build consensus regarding the number of beats per phrase. Typical responses are 4, 8, 16, and 32 beats. Discuss what these numbers all have in common and try making a rainbow phrase shape that matches each number (they all work). If a group has suggested another response, guide students to try moving their arms to that number in order to "feel" that it doesn't align with the musical phrase structure. Ask students to walk again, this time demonstrating their understanding of eight-beat phrase lengths. Students will count to eight over and over on the steady beat, aligned with each musical phrase. Every time they return to beat one, they will turn and walk in a new direction, showing the beginning of each new phrase.

7. While musicians don't typically think in terms of fractions while they are reading music and performing ("Oh, this dotted quarter rest equals 3/8 of a measure . . ."), mathematical relationships are present and can be explored by students. They can add and subtract beats within a measure; examine the numerical divisions of time; mathematically determine relationships between intervals, scales, and chords; or analyze rhythmic subdivisions. Figure 6.20 shows the relative values of whole notes, half notes, quarter notes, and eighth notes. The exploration of part–whole relationships in music aligns nicely with the study of part–whole relationships regarding money. Just as you could divide a circle into halves, quarters, and eighths to represent note values, you could divide a circle into quarters, 10ths, etc., to represent the values of various coins.

8. Ask students to categorize shapes based on their attributes, guiding them to recognize that all shapes with shared attributes are not identical; for example, a rectangle, a square, and a rhombus are all quadrilaterals. Reinforce that in music, different sections of a piece may be related, but not identical. For example, even though the different verses of a song each have their own unique words, they are still all classified as verses. This categorization of shapes and sections can then be connected to the idea of combining shapes and ordering sections. In mathematics, shapes may be combined to create more complex

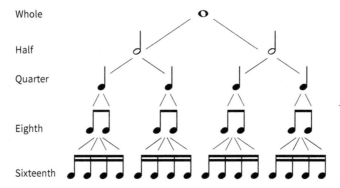

Figure 6.20 Relative values of whole notes, half notes, quarter notes, and eighth notes.
© Olha Polishchuk/Shutterstock.com/

shapes, that is, joining two squares to make a rectangle. In music, students can compose a musical example that follows a specific structure. Divide classroom instruments into separate categories, ask students to create short rhythmic patterns for each, and choose a specific arrangement for the composition. For example, students might decide on the following structure, displaying rondo form:

A section: Drums
B section: Triangles
A section: Drums
C section: Sand blocks
A section: Drums

If you think of the composition as having five sections, the students assigned to play drums perform their rhythmic pattern during sections one, three, and five; the students assigned to play triangles perform their rhythmic pattern during section two; and students assigned to play sand blocks perform their rhythmic pattern during section four. Students could also display their composition using shapes: A: circle; B: triangle; A: circle; C: square; A: circle.

9. Explore repetition in music and math with trains. Choose a train song such as "I've Been Workin' on the Railroad" or "Marrakesh Express" by Crosby, Stills, and Nash. In both examples, there are words, sections, melodic ideas, and rhythms that repeat. Listen and sing to identify examples of repetition with students. Create a rhythm or sound to perform at repeated intervals the class determines (e.g., at the beginning of each phrase or every time you hear the word "Dinah," students will clap their hands). A possible choice of instrument is the triangle, which, when muted, sounds like a hammer on a railroad spike. Next ask students to study pictures of trains and railroads. Direct them to identify repeating patterns and shapes they observe, then classify them according to their properties.

10. Explore lines of symmetry and parallel lines in music and math. Inspect various two-dimensional shapes to determine if they are symmetrical. Explain that line of symmetry is the imaginary line that divides a shape so that each remaining half is a mirror image of the other. In music, a common symmetrical organization is rondo form. Listen to and analyze various musical examples in rondo form such as the third movement of Bach's "Violin Concerto in E Major," the third movement of Mozart's "Horn Concerto No. 4 in E-flat Major, K. 495," or the third movement of Beethoven's "Piano Concerto No. 5 in Eb Major, Op. 73." Two examples where rondo form might be more easily recognized by students include Aaron Copland's "Hoe-Down" from the ballet *Rodeo*, and "Every Breath You Take" by the Police. The connection between parallel lines in math and music is a little less strict. In math, parallel lines are straight lines that lie in the same plane, never cross, and go on indefinitely. In music, parallel

motion refers to two separate voices or instrument parts (lines) that move together in the same direction and keep the same interval between them. Figure 6.21 shows two sets of railroad tracks running parallel to each other, and Figure 6.22 shows two parallel voices in music.

11. Make direct comparisons between objects with a specific attribute in common. For example, in mathematics, students could compare lengths. In music, students could compare dynamics. Following their analysis, ask students to describe how the measurements relate (identify the longest and the shortest line segments, discern which song is softest and which song is loudest, etc.).

12. Explore units of measures and iteration to examine the idea that the smaller the unit of measure, the more iterations of that unit will be needed to reach a certain length or weight. In music, filling a four-beat measure requires only one whole note, but if 16th notes are the unit of measure, it will take 16 to fill that same four-beat measure. In math, this can be highlighted by measuring the length of an object twice using two different units of measure (centimeters and inches, centimeters and millimeters, etc.). In music and in mathematics, ask students to describe how the measurements for each unit are related. Students can also examine relative sizes of measurement units within single systems of units in music (i.e., *largo, adagio, andante, allegro,* and *vivace*) and math (i.e., mm, cm, m, km).

Figure 6.21 Two sets of railroad tracks run straight and parallel to a vanishing point on the horizon.
© Kenneth Keifer/Shutterstock.com.

Figure 6.22 Two parallel voices in music.
Courtesy of author.

13. Use graphs and line plots to display data, simplify a complicated situation, and help students interpret results. Use a variety of musical material as the data for various graphs. For example, your students could sing a variety of songs and identify the number of times the choruses repeat, vote on their favorite musical selections, or test the pitch of various lengths, tensions, and diameters of strings on a guitar, ukulele, or violin, then graph the results.

14. Explore different ways of counting in music and mathematics. In math, students can count by 5s, 10s, and 100s as they expand their understanding of the base-10 system. In music, students can take turns acting as a conductor to set the tempo and count the class in for any song they will sing acapella (i.e., "one, two, ready, go"). Students can also rhythmically count beats along with a recorded example (i.e., "ONE, two, three, four, ONE, two, three, four," etc.).

References

Anderson, G. (2013, October 16). Armstrong, Louis. *Grove Music Online*. Retrieved from https://www.oxfordmusiconline.com.

Arthur Roger Gallery. (2016). Ida Kohlmeyer. Retrieved from http://arthurrogergallery.com.

Barrett, J. R. (2001). Interdisciplinary work and musical integrity. *Music Educators Journal, 87*(5), 27–31.

Barrett, J., McCoy, C., & Veblen, K. (1997). *Sound ways of knowing: Music in the interdisciplinary curriculum*. New York, NY: Schirmer.

Bartov, O. (1996). *Murder in our midst: The Holocaust, industrial killing, and representation*. New York, NY: Oxford University Press.

Basler, R. P. (Ed.). (1953). *Collected works of Abraham Lincoln* (Vol. 5). New Brunswick, NJ: Rutgers University Press.

Bastille. (2013). Pompeii. On *Bad Blood* [Digital album]. London, UK: Virgin.

Bates, K. L. (1897). America: A poem for July 4. *American Kitchen Magazine, 7*, 151.

Bates, K. L., & Ward, S. A. (1919). America the beautiful. In *National Songs of the Allies* [Notated music]. Boston, MA: Silver, Burdett & Company.

Beamer, K., & Duarte, K. (2009). I palapala no ia aina – documenting the Hawaiian Kingdom: A colonial venture? *Journal of Historical Geography, 35*(1), 66–86.

Bennett, P. D. (2016). Questioning the unmusical ways we teach children music. In C. R. Abril & B. M. Gault (Eds.), *Teaching general music: Approaches, issues, and viewpoints* (pp. 286–387). New York, NY: Oxford University Press.

Bennett, P. D., & Bartholomew, D. R. (1997). *Songworks I*. Belmont, CA: Wadsworth.

Bierley, P. E. (1984). *The works of John Philip Sousa*. Columbus, OH: Integrity Press.

Boggs, C. L., & Inouye, D. W. (2012). A single climate driver has direct and indirect effects on insect population dynamics. *Ecology Letters, 15*(5), 502–508.

Bosley, K. (1997). Finlandia. In *Skating on the sea: Poetry from Finland*. Newcastle, UK: Bloodaxe Books, 196.

Burkhart, C. (2005). The phrase rhythm of Chopin's A flat major Mazurka, Op. 59, No. 2. In D. Stein (Ed.), *Engaging music* (pp. 3–12). New York, NY: Oxford University Press.

Burkholder, J., Sinclair, J., & Magee, G. (2013, October 16). Ives, Charles. *Grove Music Online*. Retrieved from https://www.oxfordmusiconline.com.

Burnaford, G. (2007). *Arts integration frameworks, research & practice: A literature review*. Washington, DC: Arts Education Partnership.

Centers for Disease Control and Prevention. (n.d.). What is Ebola virus disease? U.S. Department of Health and Human Services. Retrieved from https://www.cdc.gov/vhf/ebola/about.html.

Chute, J. (2001). Torke, Michael. *Grove Music Online*. Retrieved from https://www.oxfordmusiconline.com.

Cocco, S. (2012). *Watching Vesuvius: A history of science and culture in early modern Italy*. Chicago, IL: University of Chicago Press.

Cole, T. (2003). *Holocaust city: The making of a Jewish ghetto*. New York, NY: Routledge.

Dahlström, F., & Hepokoski, J. (2001). Sibelius, Jean. *Grove Music Online*. Retrieved from https://www.oxfordmusiconline.com.

Davies, I. (Ed.). (2000). *Teaching the Holocaust: Education dimensions, principles, and practice*. New York, NY: Continuum.

Fallon, D., Ratner, S., & Harding, J. (2001). Saint-Saëns, (Charles) Camille. *Grove Music Online*. Retrieved from https://www.oxfordmusiconline.com.

Finnish Club of Helsinki. (n.d.) The music: Finlandia. From *Jean Sibelius* [Website]. Retrieved from http://www.sibelius.fi/english/.

Fowke, S. [Collector]. (1969). Here we go looby loo. In *Sally go round the sun*. Garden City, NY: Doubleday.

Fowler, C. (1992, April 5). The case for music education. *Washington Post,* p. 7.

Górecki, H. (1992). *Symphony No 3, Op. 36: I. Lento - Sostenuto Tranquillo Ma Cantabile* [Recorded by the London Sinfonietta, David Zinman, Conductor]. On *Symphony No. 3* [CD]. Nonesuch Records.

Griffin, L. J., & Hargis, P. G. (Eds.). (2012). *The new encyclopedia of Southern culture: Vol. 20: Social class.* Chapel Hill, NC: University of North Carolina Press.

Griffith, A. K. (2015). Expression surpassing words: Gorecki's Symphony No. 3, Op. 36 "Sorrowful Songs." *Musical Offerings, 6*(2), 85–99.

Gross, J. T. (2006). *Fear: Antisemitism in Poland after Auschwitz, an essay in historical interpretation.* New York, NY: Random House.

Hafner, J. W., Sturgell, J. L., Matlock, D. L., Bockewitz, E. G., & Barker, L. T. (2012). "Stayin' Alive": A novel mental metronome to maintain compression rates in simulated cardiac arrests. *Journal of Emergency Medicine, 43*(5), e373–e377.

Hamilton, J. (2012). *Volcano.* London, UK: Reaktion Books.

Handy, W. C. (1914). *St. Louis blues.* Memphis, TN: Pace & Handy Music.

Harney, K. (2015a). A no-nonsense introduction to the new National Core Arts Standards. *Montana Music Educators Association Cadenza, 59*(3), 38–39.

Harney, K. (2015b). Uncovering cover songs: Revealing the listening skills students already possess. *Music EdVentures, Inc. News and Notes, September,* 11–13.

Harney, K. (2017). The playlist project: Exploring the experience of pre-service elementary teachers. *Visions of Research in Music Education, 30.*

Jacobs, H. H. (1989). The growing need for interdisciplinary curriculum content. In H. H. Jacobs (Ed.), *Interdisciplinary curriculum: Design and implementation* (pp. 1–11). Alexandria, VA: Association for Supervision and Curriculum Development.

Judd, T. (2012, January 31). Hearing colors in the music of Michael Torke. Retrieved from https://thelistenersclub.com/2012/01/31/the-listeners-club-hearing-colors-in-the-music-of-michael-torke/.

Kennedy Center ArtsEdge. (n.d.). *What is arts integration?* Washington, DC: John F. Kennedy Center for the Performing Arts. Retrieved from https://artsedge.kennedy-center.org.

King, T. L. (2015). Performing Jim Crow: Blackface performance and Emancipation. *Revista de Humanidades, 23,* 75–94.

Lavery, J. (2006). *The history of Finland* (Greenwood histories of the modern nations). Westport, CN: Greenwood Press.

Lesure, F., & Howat, R. (2001). Debussy, (Achille-)Claude. *Grove Music Online.* Retrieved from https://www.oxfordmusiconline.com.

Lomax, J. A., & Lomax, A. (1934). *American ballads and folksongs.* New York, NY: Macmillan.

MacKarness, Mrs. H. (1888). *The young lady's book: A manual of amusements, exercises, studies, and pursuits.* London, UK: Routledge and Sons.

McCoy, C. W. (2000). The excitement of collaboration. *Music Educators Journal, 87*(1), 37–44.

Millay, E. S. V. (1917). Afternoon on a hill. In *Renascence and other poems,* 41. New York, NY: Mitchell Kennerly.

Moore, A. (2011). Is the unspeakable singable? The ethics of Holocaust representation and the reception of Górecki's *Symphony No. 3. Journal of Multidisciplinary International Studies, 8*(1), 1–17.

Morgan, S., Tweh, E., & Kuzzy. (2014). Ebola in town. [Digital single]. Buduburam, Ghana: Shadow Entertainment.

NASA. (2019). Climate kids [website]. National Aeronautics and Space Administration. Retrieved from http://climatekids.nasa.gov/.

National Coalition for Core Arts Standards. (2015). *National Core Arts Standards.* Dover, DE: State Education Agency Directors of Arts Education.

National Council for the Social Studies (NCSS). (2010). *National Curriculum Standards for Social Studies: A framework for teaching, learning, and assessment.* Silver Spring, MD: Author.

National Council for the Social Studies (NCSS). (2013). *The College, Career, and Civic Life (C3) Framework for Social Studies State Standards: Guidance for enhancing the rigor of K-12 civics, economics, geography, and history.* Silver Spring, MD: Author.

National Governors Association Center for Best Practices, Council of Chief State School Officers. (2010a). *Common Core State Standards: English language arts*. Washington, DC: Author.

National Governors Association Center for Best Practices, Council of Chief State School Officers. (2010b). *Common Core State Standards: Mathematics*. Washington, DC: Author.

Next Generation Science Standards Lead States. (2013). *Next Generation Science Standards: For states, by states*. Washington, DC: National Academies Press.

Oliver, P., & Kernfeld, B. (2003, January). Blues. *Grove Music Online*. Retrieved from https://www-oxfordmusiconline.

Olukoju, A. (2006). *Culture and customs of Liberia* (Culture and customs of Africa). Westport, CN: Greenwood Press.

Parmesan, C. (1996). Climate change and species' range. *Nature, 382,* 765–766.

Partnership for 21st Century Skills (P21). (2011). *P21 common core toolkit: A guide to aligning the Common Core State Standards with the Framework for 21st Century Skills*. Washington, DC: Government Printing Office.

Pasek, B., & Paul, J. (2017). Rewrite the stars. From *The Greatest Showman: Original Motion Picture Soundtrack* [Soundtrack album]. New York, NY: Atlantic Studios.

Pasler, J. (2001, January 1). Impressionism. *Grove Music Online*. Retrieved from https://www.oxfordmusiconline.com.

Pennock, M., & Wood, D. (n.d.). Exploring vertebrate classification. National Geographic Society. Retrieved from https://www.nationalgeographic.org/activity/exploring-vertebrate-classification/.

President's Committee on the Arts and the Humanities (PCAH). (2011). *Reinvesting in arts education: Winning America's future through creative schools*. Washington, DC: Author.

Public Broadcasting System. (2002). The rise and fall of Jim Crow. Educational Broadcasting Corporation. Retrieved from https://www.thirteen.org/wnet/jimcrow/.

Puffett, K. (2001). Webern, Anton. *Grove Music Online*. Retrieved from https://www.oxfordmusiconline.com.

Reimer, B. (2003). *A philosophy of music education: Advancing the vision*. Upper Saddle River, NJ: Prentice Hall.

Richards, M. H., & Langsness, A. (1984). *Music language, section two*. Portola Valley, CA: Richards Institute.

Roud, S. (Ed.). (n.d.). The rattlin' bog. In *The Roud Folksong Index,* Roud No. 129. Vaughan Williams Memorial Library. Retrieved from https://www.vwml.org/record/RoudFS/S400955.

Sherr, L. (2001). *America the beautiful: The stirring true story behind our nation's favorite song*. New York, NY: Public Affairs.

Simonis, D. (Ed.). (1999). *Lives and legacies: An encyclopedia of people who changed the world: Scientists, mathematicians, and inventors*. Phoenix, AZ: Oryx Press.

Snyder, J. A. (2018). *Making Black history the color line, culture, and race in the age of Jim Crow*. Athens, GA: University of Georgia Press.

Songs for Teaching. (n.d.). Asikatali. From *Songs for Teaching: Using Music to Promote* [Website]. Retrieved from https://www.songsforteaching.com.

Swift, T. (2008, March). Love story. On *Fearless* [Digital album]. Nashville, TN: Blackbird Studios.

Szcodronski, K. E., Debinski, D. M., & Klaver, R. W. (2018). Occupancy modeling of *Parnassius clodius* butterfly populations in Grand Teton National Park, Wyoming. *Journal of Insect Conservation, 22*(2), 267–276.

Thomas, A. (2001). Górecki, Henryk Mikołaj. *Grove Music Online*. Retrieved from https://www.oxfordmusiconline.com.

Watts, S. (1997). *The Magic Kingdom: Walt Disney and the American way of life*. Columbia, MO: First University of Missouri Press.

Wei-Hass, M. (2018). Volcanoes, explained. National Geographic Society. Retrieved from https://www.nationalgeographic.com/environment/natural-disasters/volcanoes/.

World Health Organization. (2019). Ebola virus disease. Retrieved from https://www.who.int/ebola/situation-reports/drc-2018/en/.

Subject Index

Index of Musical Examples

CPSIA information can be obtained
at www.ICGtesting.com
Printed in the USA
BVHW020219100723
666531BV00001B/2

9 780190 085599